W9-AXA-296

Critical Essays on William Golding

Critical Essays on William Golding

James R. Baker

G. K. Hall & Co. • Boston, Massachusetts

Library of Congress Cataloging in Publication Data

Baker, James R.
   Critical essays on William Golding / James R. Baker.
   p. cm. — (Critical essays on British literature)
   Includes index.
   ISBN 0-8161-8764-9
   1. Golding, William, 1911-   —Criticism and interpretation.
I. Title. II. Series.
PR6013.035Z588 1988
823'.914—dc19

                                              87-33312

                                              CIP

This publication is printed on permanent/durable acid-free paper
MANUFACTURED IN THE UNITED STATES OF AMERICA

CRITICAL ESSAYS ON BRITISH LITERATURE

The Critical Essays on British Literature series provides a variety of approaches to both the classical writers of Britain and Ireland, and the best contemporary authors. The formats of the volumes in the series vary with the thematic designs of individual editors, and with the amount and nature of existing reviews, criticism, and scholarship. In general, the series represents the best in published criticism, augmented, where appropriate, by original essays by recognized authorities. It is hoped that each volume will be unique in developing a new overall perspective on its particular subject.

James R. Baker's introduction to the present volume gives us a concise history of Golding criticism from the earlier reviewer's misinterpretations through the critical schools which have developed over more than thirty years of critical commentary on Golding's fiction. The essays, including three written specifically for this volume, represent a loose chronology of Golding criticism at the same time they provide in-depth commentary on each major Golding work.

An added dimension to the commentary is Golding's own reaction provided by a personal interview with Baker and Golding's Nobel Prize speech, both reprinted in this book. The resulting volume provides a comprehensive overview of Golding's work.

Zack Bowen, GENERAL EDITOR

University of Miami

CONTENTS

INTRODUCTION

William Golding:
Three Decades of Criticism

Although he was born in 1911, William Golding did not enter upon his literary career until after World War II. Prior to that time he had published only a small collection of poems and had experimented (unsuccessfully) with fictional styles. But the war itself and other terrible events that may be invoked by means of only a few words — Stalin, Hitler, the Holocaust, the Bomb — made up a trial of preparation in which Golding, who served in the war, came to disillusionment with his youthful humanistic beliefs. Then, in 1954, as every schoolboy now knows, *Lord of the Flies* was published, a modern "classic" was born. This first book was not immediately praised and given such status, for it appeared in an angry decade committed to political and social change, to nothing less than overthrow of "the Establishment," inspired by revival of the many hopes for the future that had been set aside during the traumatic war years. Golding, the reviewers explained, was a middle-aged schoolmaster who offered an exciting story (they would not dignify his book by calling it a novel) about little boys struggling for survival on a Pacific island during an atomic war of the future. It was only a clever addition to the popular literature of "science fiction"; or, since the author tried to show that adolescent "fun and games" were actually rites and rituals in a merciless struggle for power, it could be read as a moralistic "fable" or a pessimistic allegory on human depravity. Neither in its theme nor in its method of presentation did *Lord of the Flies* appear to be directly relevant to the important post-war problems confronted with brash courage by the "Angry Young Men" and the emerging proletarian writers. Given such a context for response, *The Inheritors* (1955), set in prehistoric time, and *Pincher Martin* (1956), the egoistic fantasy of a drowning man, did not substantially change the first evaluation of Golding's fiction.

Now, thirty years later, we may look back on that chapter in literary history and find there not only some portents of Golding's later career but also an opportunity for a little harvest of ironies. He was destined to attain greater fame than most of his contemporaries. Through the 1960s and the 1970s his readership grew enormously; he was also given more and more critical attention, becoming, as he remarked, the source of an international "academic light industry." By 1980 he was world famous, his reputation secure. In that year he was awarded in England the Booker Prize for his seventh major novel, *Rites of Passage*, and then — greatest of honors — the Nobel Prize for Literature in 1983. Nevertheless, though he has been much praised, much honored, even revered, he has remained controversial and frequently at odds with his readers, reviewers, and critics. Fellow-writers, on both sides of the Atlantic, have attacked him: John Wain, in "Lord of the Agonies," rated him only a morbid Christian moralist; Kenneth Rexroth, writing in America for the widely-circulated *Atlantic*, denounced him as a heavy-handed writer with "no style." There have been complaintants of every kind (flower children, moral guardians, churchmen, feminists, Marxists, utopians, parents, bloodthirsty humanists) down through the years. Even the awarding of the Nobel Prize was marked and marred by controversy about the scope and worth of his art. If there is any central cause for this anger and these charges, it is that at the very outset of his career Golding set himself up as antagonist to the "scientific humanism" (his term) which was, perhaps still is, the great faith of the modern age. Inevitably, the earliest reviewers and critics favored the work of the new social realists who appeared after the war, because their efforts continued the great tradition of the literature of hope; while Golding, searching in anthropology and in the mythic structures of classical Greek tragedy for some more essential truth that would explain why human hopes had been so often defeated, began with three contributions to the literature of disillusionment.

About the only contemporary, or near-contemporary, Golding could acknowledge as a spiritual cousin (and fellow fabulist) was the late George Orwell. *Animal Farm* (1945), that nearly perfect Swiftian satire, had summed up the failure of the Russian Revolution — perhaps the failure of all utopian aspiration — as a result of human inequality. On both Orwell's farm and Golding's island this natural imbalance triggers the dialectics of behavior which must end with the triumph of the strong and wily beasts. *Nineteen Eighty-Four* (1949), just like *Lord of the Flies*, projects us into a near-future to portray an apocalypse — the collapse of humanistic hopes, the defeat of man, the pyramid waiting at the end of his violent history. Orwell, apparently because of his avowed "political purpose" in writing these last classics of disillusionment, was to remain the darling of academic humanists (particularly in America), even though he shared with Golding a devastating awareness of the limitations of human nature. But time may bring them together, perhaps already it is doing so: the topical and seemingly vital literature of the angry "realists" of the 1950s now fades from view, while the great negative "fables" left by Orwell and Golding stand as dark monuments to the romantic humanism of the past.

The next decade was to be a better one for Golding. *Lord of the Flies*, a slow starter, began its rise to fame, and his fourth novel, *Free Fall* (1959), illustrated his ability to move beyond the mode of presentation common to the first three. *The Spire* (1964) was well-received and hailed by his defenders as a truly major achievement. Thus Golding himself, in the course of his evolution as a novelist, created a positive change in his first public image; but this was also the period in which serious critics and academic scholars began to examine, and to debate, the nature of his ideas and his art. It soon became clear to them that things were more complicated, much more complicated, than the newspaper reviewers had supposed, and that their simplistic frame-up of Golding as an anachronistic Christian moralist and the Prince of Pessimism would have to be modified if not abandoned altogether.

I

In spite of their debates, the first critics were in agreement on some basic matters. Golding, they recognized, was quite unique in his intentions and in the techniques he employed to carry them out: he had created an art of counterstatement which owed little or nothing to his immediate contemporaries; therefore, there would have to be a search for sources and influences; and given the nearly identical structures of the first three "fables" (followed by the bizarre and seemingly incoherent *Free Fall*) there would also have to be an investigation of his methods.

The premier study of method, John Peter's "The Fables of William Golding," appeared in the *Kenyon Review* in the autumn of 1957. It is fair to say that this admirable essay marks the real beginning (if precise dating is possible) of Golding criticism, though it is limited in scope to the three novels then in print. Every scholar has had to deal with the terminology this essay introduced and to take sides with the issues it raised. Peter distinguishes between "fiction" and "fable," acknowledges that there are novelistic elements in *Lord of the Flies* and the others, and concludes that, on balance, the three texts fall into the tradition of the art of fable. It all sounded reasonable enough, but there soon erupted a long series of arguments (sometimes heated) over the adequacy of Peter's terminology and his reading of the texts. Golding rather liked the essay but wrote to the author to complain about a misreading of an important passage in *Pincher Martin*; again, in a now famous interview published in *Books and Bookmen* under the intriguing title, "The Meaning of It All," he argued with Frank Kermode over the critical terminology and suggested that the word "myth" would better describe his intentions; and, in 1962, on tour in America, he reentered the ongoing discussion in his lecture entitled "Fable" delivered at the University of California. Yet to come was the most thorough statement on these problems — the final chapter ("Perspectives") in the book by the English critical team Mark Kinkead-Weekes and Ian Gregor, *William Golding: A Critical Study* (1967).

Another school of critics in this same period was intent upon searching out the main influences and specific literary sources that had

gone into the making of Golding's fiction. The task began in England with
a useful essay by Peter Green, "The World of William Golding," published
in the *Review of English Literature*, but his search was soon taken up and
most successfully carried out by American critics. The first was Carl
Niemeyer, who argued in an essay to be reprinted many times, "The Coral
Island Revisited," that *Lord of the Flies* was written as a modern version of
R. M. Ballantyne's Victorian novel for boys, *The Coral Island*. A far more
comprehensive attempt to explain Golding's motivation as a writer and to
explicate his texts as reactions to other writers was undertaken by Bernard
S. Oldsey and Stanley Weintraub in *The Art of William Golding* (1965).
Their strategy is made clear in the chapter on *Lord of the Flies*.

> All Golding's novels, products of his peculiar literary temperament
> and habit, are reactive experiments. The wonder is how habitual a
> process this has been. Piecemeal, several critics have nicely documented
> certain influences or stimuli affecting his work. Yet important instances
> have been left undiscovered, overlooked, underestimated. What remains
> to be said is that this reactive method of composition has become the
> *modus operandi*. It provides a key as to what Golding has derived from
> others and what he has provided that is original. Yet Golding has
> insisted, "But one book never comes out of another, and *The Coral
> Island* is not *Lord of the Flies*." And, adamantly, that *"one work does
> not come from another unless it is stillborn."* Nevertheless, with Golding
> the process may be, if he has created counter-experiments which are
> original fiction, not stillbirth but birth.

Obviously, these critics were not to be deterred by the author's objections
to their operating assumption, and in subsequent chapters they pursued
some of the "undiscovered" connections with specific works by Wells,
Shaw, Camus, Ibsen, and others—ignoring, strangely, Golding's acknowledgment of the influence of Poe and, more broadly, the influence of Greek
tragedy.

The flaw in this generic approach to literature is indicated in
Golding's protest: books do not grow out of other books alone; the genesis
of art, he implies, is far more complex than that. *The Coral Island*, for
example, serves only as a metaphor for the naive Christian humanism he
ridiculed in all his early novels, but he was obliged to repeat his
admonition in later years as still other critics were tempted to exercise
their erudition on still other analogies and parallels. It may be natural and
to some extent legitimate and useful for the scholar to pursue these literary
comparisons; after all, this kind of work contributes to our understanding
of the individual text and to the drawing of that larger picture in which
single writers and works are assigned a place in literary history. Humanistic scholarship has always rested on the assumption echoed in T. S. Eliot's
essay "Tradition and the Individual Talent"—that every new talent is
conditioned by the tradition. The danger is that the scholar who may be
intent upon the historical pattern will obscure or underestimate the

originality of the individual artist. Golding, more than any novelist of his generation, has insisted upon talking back to his critics, again and again protesting that he was being absorbed in cultural history, "mummified" in the leaves of critical papers, before he could finish his life's work.

A different conception of source and influence formed the basis for James R. Baker's *William Golding: A Critical Study* (1965). As early as 1963 this critic had argued that the paradigm for human behavior and for history in *Lord of the Flies* was modeled on the tragic drama of ancient Greece, specifically the tragic pattern found in *The Bacchae* of Euripides. Baker's book covered the first five novels and simply extended the argument that Golding's models were ancient rather than modern. In this case the scholar capitalized on the author's suggestions, for Golding had repeatedly pointed to the Greeks when asked about "influences." Some twenty years later, in an interview with Baker published in the scholarly journal, *Twentieth Century Literature*, Golding, asked to place his own art in the tradition, replied as follows:

> I suppose all I can really say is that I don't think my novels come out of novels. If they owe anything to previous work, and obviously they must, it's the theatre much more than novel writing. I think of the shape of a novel, when I do think of a novel as having a shape, as having one precisely like Greek drama. You have this rise of tension and then the sudden fall and all the rest of it. You may even find the technical Greek terms tucked away in the book, if you like, and check them off one by one. So the Greek tragedy as a form, a classical form, is very much there. The idea of the character who suffers a disastrous fall through a flaw in his character, that you find there, I think. So it does really stem as much from Greek tragedy as much as anything else. I don't think I would mark its line of descent from any novelist I can think of.

Only a few months after Baker's first essay had appeared, a second American, Bernard F. Dick, also noted the presence of Euripides in *Lord of the Flies*. He went on to offer a full-length study, *William Golding* (1967), documenting the influence of Greek tragedy in Golding's work as a whole. As a professor of classical literature, Dick was well-qualified to illustrate through textual evidence that Golding had indeed applied his knowledge of tragedy (as well as Aristotle's *Poetics*) to the art of fiction, thus adapting ancient means to modern ends. Somewhat ironically, therefore, the very critics who had intended to discover sources and influences cast real light on the structural principles that formed Golding's plots and guided the drawing of his characters.

Meanwhile, in England, the most valuable early work on Golding was accomplished by Frank Kermode. In a series of essays and interviews he did perhaps more than anyone to clarify the basic themes and aims of the fables, and when *The Spire* appeared in 1964 his review in the *New York Review of Books* proved at last that it was possible to write an intelligent review of a Golding novel. Kermode was one of the very few predecessors credited in the important critical volume by Mark Kinkead-Weekes and Ian Gregor, although by 1967 it was nearly impossible to write without reflecting one influence or another out of the growing body of critical literature. The most original contribution made in their book was to show the evolution of Golding's art from *Lord of the Flies* through *The Spire* — confirming his claim that he never wrote the same book twice or, as he was to put it many years later, that he was "a moving target" and constant challenge for his pursuers.

II

There were always critics, plenty of them, waiting for whatever came next and, in the interims and silences which must occur in the life of any writer, busy bickering among themselves or coming out with ingenious "new" approaches overlooked by their colleagues. One must not forget that Golding's own evolution unfolds in the same years that saw the great "bulge" in post-war higher education and the production of unprecedented numbers of theses, dissertations, articles, and books on every conceivable subject, examined from every conceivable point of view. These were the years in which we saw the development of a Faulkner industry and a Hemingway industry, a Joyce industry and a Lawrence industry, and, inevitably, a Golding industry — though his never rivaled the others mentioned. If Golding was indeed "a moving target," he was all the more likely to catch the eye of every hunter in the field. Such extraordinary scrutiny, initially pleasant enough and flattering, will in time become a source of irritation and then a burden for the living writer. Only fifteen years after publication of *Lord of the Flies*, so much critical commentary (and much of it repetitious) had been written that it was necessary to draw up lists and bibliographies and to gather the flying leaves into source-books, guidebooks, casebooks, and anthologies. In the 1970s, although a few useful articles and books provided something needed, Golding's critics too often repeated with minor variations what had already been said, or they lapsed into carping criticism of criticism, or they advanced zealous (often jealous) claims to heretofore unrecognized dimensions. The work of the first generation led to a battle of the paper men.

Howard S. Babb, in *The Novels of William Golding* (1970), sought through a series of "formal analyses" to improve upon our grasp of meanings and structures, yet behind the facade of objective method ran the old conviction that all of the novels (except *The Pyramid*) "comprise a sustained investigation into the nature of man from a Christian perspective." The recurring question of Golding's religious attitudes was better answered (though in truncated form) in Stephen Medcalf's 1975 booklet *William Golding*, written for the "Writers and Their Work" series. Here we read that a common concern with the principle of "darkness" links

Golding with the post-Puritan American writers, Hawthorne and Melville, among others, rather than Christian orthodoxy.

The most elaborate and successful investigation of these issues was Virginia Tiger's *William Golding: The Dark Fields of Discovery* (1974). In a striking introductory chapter, Tiger promised to do what had not been adequately done—"to discover the religious dimension toward which the technical devices of the structure, as well as other fictional features, are always directed." Her premises, based in part on promptings by Golding himself, given in correspondence or conversation, were clearly stated:

> William Golding's fiction plays with the puzzles of Proverbs xxiii. 18 that "where there is no vision, the people perish." This is, in the widest sense, a religious exploration and without stating so explicitly, all the fiction embodies this dictum for it deals in the primordial patterns of human experience. . . . In the fiction, Golding consciously tries to construct a religious mythopoeia relevant to contemporary man since he agrees generally with the anthropological notion that it is through myth that the imaginative substance of religious belief is expressed, communicated, and enhanced. As he has remarked in conversation: "Myth is a story at which we can do nothing but wonder; it involves the roots of being and reverberates there." In Golding's view, contemporary man lacks vision. How is he not to perish? In each of the novels, there is the effort of bridge-building between the physical world which contemporary man accepts and the spiritual world which he ignores. . . .

At times, these ideas were set aside for criticism (and occasionally imprecise readings) of other critics. Nevertheless, the Tiger book remains the most significant critical study of this decade, not because of the theory of "ideographic" structures it advanced but because it clarified Golding's evaluation of the modern age and modern man. It also revealed the artist for what he really was—a seeker after a vision.

A contribution of another kind was made by Jack I. Biles in his *Talk: Conversations With William Golding* (1970) — a distillation of the longest interview ever done. Biles was not only on very friendly terms with Golding, he was also an avowed humanist and well-read professor of modern British literature. These qualifications made him the perfect interrogator, friend and antagonist at the same time, and, though Golding rather severely edited the tapes, Biles was able to get useful statements on a number of points that had long vexed the critics. Like many other writers in the post-war era, Golding was to be interviewed again and again. Much of value has been revealed in these exchanges. The interview, in fact, has emerged as an important critical medium; most academicians now recognize that an informed interviewer, such as Biles or Kermode, may do more valuable work than the autonomous academician who markets his ideas in little magazines. The participation of the living author is a new thing in literary history: he is immediately drawn into the critical tasks of explication and evaluation of his own art; he is flattered, elevated to a position of authority over the treacherous ambiguities of his own imaginative world, a moment later forced into debate or a humiliating confession of his own limitations. Golding has shown a considerable ambivalence about these occasions, sometimes coming forth to correct or reprimand this critic or that critic, then retreating into silence and the supposedly perfect autonomy of the creative artist. Finally, his long concern with these problems produced a novel, *The Paper Men* (1984) — a novel that has been ill-understood and demeaned. In reality, it is a kind of "first" in the field (based on long experience and presented with admirable wit) on a truly contemporary phenomenon.

In 1978 Biles and his co-editor Robert O. Evans published the first anthology of original critical essays, *William Golding: Some Critical Considerations*. If only a few of the thirteen essays were truly new and useful, the volume, nevertheless, was made indispensable by the inclusion of Biles's exhaustive bibliography of primary and secondary sources. The long list of secondary items showed that it was high time to take stock in the Golding industry, time to count it all up, and (like any other industry) face the fact that quantity threatened quality and might lead to inimical inquiry into the whole enterprise. We had already heard one form of protest in Susan Sontag's essay *Against Interpretation*; it was not to be long before the "deconstructionists" would make their assault on the proud towers of academe. Golding, as if cognizant of some change or threat, slowed in these years. After *The Pyramid* (1967), he produced only the relatively slight trilogy, *The Scorpion God* (1971), and then came the long silence before *Darkness Visible* appeared in 1979.

III

The first critical book of the new decade, Arnold Johnston's *Of Earth and Darkness* (1980), illustrated some of the virtues of academic scholarship — the absorption and synopsis of the work of predecessors combined with careful but inventive application of this knowledge to the task of clarifying basic themes and methods from *Lord of the Flies* through *Darkness Visible*. In his opening chapter Johnston summed up the "general characteristics" of Golding's fiction:

> 1) his desire to be seen as a "maker of myths"; 2) his general reliance on simple situations and plots that either partake of or suggest mythical archetypes; 3) his concern in making his novels the concrete expressions of spiritual and moral assumptions; 4) his suggestion of an inevitability in human actions akin to the ancient concept of Fate; 5) his primary use of irony as a major narrative technique.

Missing from the list was Golding's very strong desire — evident in *The Pyramid* and *The Scorpion God* — to overcome his reputation as a "pessimist," a tragic visionary, and to emerge as a writer of comedy. This was to become a sort of project in the years ahead, and he worked at it without much success, insisting in interviews, then in his Nobel Prize speech, on the elemental optimism behind his work and on his capacity for humor. But it seems we do not want him genial or jolly. Johnston, like most of the new critics, recognized that what "pure" humor there was could be found mainly in the few short stories and not in the "black" and biting comedy that made its debut in *The Pyramid*, appeared even in *Darkness Visible*, and again (after Johnston's book) in *Rites of Passage* (1980) and *The Paper Men* (1984). This turn of events made it increasingly difficult to settle comfortably into critical generalizations and clichés. It was no longer possible to rely on the established assumptions or to trust the old critical apparatus as a means of extracting a stable, elemental Golding.

Looking back, one could see that some new entity had been born out of the moral simplicities of the early "fables." That initial certainty had given way to a sense of rich and incomprehensible ambiguity, first in *Free Fall*, then with gathering force in the conclusion of *The Spire*; the sad social comedy of *The Pyramid* and the attempt to "send up" the idea of history in *The Scorpion God*, though not entirely successful, had been steps in the evolution of a more comprehensive vision. Comedy and tragedy were now intermixed, entangled, so that one could no longer rely upon neat Aristotelian definitions of genres or prescriptions for the drawing of characters proper to those genres. Golding, rather like young Talbot awakened at the close of *Rites of Passage*, seemed overwhelmed by "too much understanding": he had crossed "the line" and now voyaged toward a new world. The classical models for this experience, this progression, are found in Dante and Milton, their modern counterpart in the rites of passage endured by Eliot.

Recognition that the new Golding presented another challenge and need for adaptation on the part of critics formed the basis for a special issue of *Twentieth Century Literature* (1982), edited by James R. Baker. At the end of a long interview, Baker attempted to sum up the central purpose of Golding's art: ". . . as I look back over all of your work, it seems that in an atheistic age you have been one who insists upon mystery, on the neglected or perhaps forgotten religious dimension of human experience. Has this been a deliberate course on your part, a sort of counteraction or corrective to our diminished sense of the numinous, the religious, the mysterious?" Golding's reply was cautious, self-effacing, as perhaps it had to be in the face of such a question: "I'd like to think it was a corrective to what you call a diminished sense of the numinous. Whether it is or not, whether that kind of Holy-Joeing may not just simply put people off, I don't know. But it seems natural in me to do it." No novelist would wish to claim such a grand strategy and lofty purpose, and, obviously, there have been interims in which Golding turned away from this high seriousness; but there is always a steady drift, some general theme, that becomes apparent in every writer's career. Golding, from the very beginning, set out to expose the limitations of "rational" man, his inability to measure and grasp the greater reality that mocks all his arrogant claims to knowledge. In the leading essay for the *Twentieth Century Literature* collection, "The Later Golding," Kinkead-Weekes and Gregor were more struck by the differences than the similarities between the late novels, *Darkness Visible* and *Rites of Passage*; yet they concede that the differences are mainly in manner and means, rather than basic purpose, affirming that both novels seek to be true to "the paradoxes of Golding's imagination" and attempt to "focus into unity." In 1984 these faithful critics revised and expanded this essay for an updated edition of their book. The effort to keep abreast of Golding's progress won no great applause from reviewers or fellow-critics, for it merely appended their essay to the text of the first edition. We still await a genuinely definitive critical study.

The most conscientious and thorough effort to understand the new Golding was Donald Crompton's *A View From the Spire: William Golding's Later Novels* (1985). Although Crompton's thesis — that *The Spire* "marked a watershed in Golding's career" and a turning point — was not original, his introductory chapter on Golding's evolution since 1964 remains the best commentary on that subject, and his essays on *The Spire*, *The Pyramid*, *Darkness Visible*, and *Rites of Passage* rank among the best explicatory and evaluative essays produced on this period of struggle and transition. Unfortunately, Don Crompton died before he was able to finish his book, but the manuscript was ably edited by Julia Briggs, who also emerged as a Golding critic in her own right with excellent chapters on *The Scorpion God* and *The Paper Men*.

IV

What has been accomplished in three decades of criticism? A general survey reveals that most of the work done has been quite specific in its aims — seeking either to explicate a single novel or to trace the development of characteristic themes and techniques through examination of two or three related novels, and sometimes the entire sequence. This narrow focus of attention may be typical of the critical literature developed on a living writer, yet it reflects also the unique complexity of Golding's art. Each new novel has been a new knot to untie; and the novelist, irritated by an academic industry that seeks to categorize him while he is still in motion, and angry over his own complicity in this paper game, has declared (half-seriously) that he makes a point of pride out of leaving behind another "critic proof" novel as he moves elusively into the landscape of his own imagination. It has been the critic, not the novelist, who has played the role of "reactive writer."

What can be done? In the deliberately unscholarly anthology edited by John Carey, *William Golding: The Man and His Books* (1986), some new directions may be found in the remarks of other living writers; in Philip Redpath's *William Golding: A Structural Reading of His Fiction* (1987) an impressive advance is made in the scholarly task. We need more work on the role of science in Golding's fiction (perhaps beginning with the impact of Poe on the formation of his attitudes), and we need to reassess Golding's accomplishment in the larger context made up of the work of his contemporaries. Through such pursuits we may build the power to generalize and to judge.

The fourteen essays collected in this volume have been chosen to present the central concerns and issues in the critical literature on Golding since the publication of *Lord of the Flies* in 1954. They are arranged in a loosely chronological order so that they represent in broad outline the history of Golding criticism produced by serious and well-informed scholars. This criterion of quality has excluded reviews, for even the few of real worth lack the depth provided in one or more of the scholarly essays available on a particular novel. In-depth commentary is provided on every novel. Thus the reader, using the introductory bibliographical essay as a guide to the main body of criticism, will find this volume a reliable point of departure for further study. Nothing is included on Golding's non-fictional writing—most of it collected in two miscellanies, *The Hot Gates* (1965) and *A Moving Target* (1982) — because no systematic evaluation has been undertaken.

Golding's Nobel Prize speech has been included on the grounds that it illustrates his long-time concern with the work of his critics and the public image they have helped to create. The speech insists that this image is somewhat inaccurate or incomplete, that it neglects his fundamental optimism and his love for humor; those who know him will support these claims.

JAMES R. BAKER

San Diego State University

Articles, Interviews, and Essays

[William Golding's *Lord of the Flies*]

Samuel Hynes*

> I am very serious. I believe that man suffers from an appalling ignorance of his own nature. I produce my own view, in the belief that it may be something like the truth. I am fully engaged to the human dilemma but see it as far more fundamental than a complex of taxes and astronomy.

William Golding wrote these words in reply to a literary magazine's questionnaire, "The Writer in His Age." The questionnaire raised the question of "engagement": should the writer concern himself with the political and social questions of his time? Golding's answer is unequivocal: the job of the writer is to show man his image *sub specie aeternitatis*. It is in this sense of engagement, not to the concerns of the moment but to what is basic in the human condition, and in the forms that this engagement has led Golding to create, that his uniqueness lies: he is *the* novelist of our time for whom the novel matters because of what it can mean, and what it can do.

In the note from which I quoted above, Golding described himself as "a citizen, a novelist and a schoolmaster." The latter term is no longer literally applicable, but there is still a good deal of both the citizen and the schoolmaster in the novelist. The citizen is concerned with "the defects of society"; the schoolmaster is concerned to correct them by proper instruction; the novelist finds the appropriate forms in which man's own nature may be embodied, that he may learn to know it. One consequence of this will-to-instruct is that Golding is an unusually disciplined, schematic writer; he thinks his novels out very slowly, and in careful detail (he wrote *Lord of the Flies*, he said, "as if tracing over words already on the page"), and he is willing, even eager, to discuss what they mean. Another consequence is his desire to have his works read with the same kind of conscious intelligence, and his distrust of irrational and intuitive views of literary creation. He clearly thinks of his novels as the expressions of

*From *William Golding*, 2d ed., Columbia Essays on Modern Writers (New York: Columbia University Press, 1968). Reprinted by permission of Columbia University Press.

conscious intentions that existed before the writing began. Indeed he has twice spelled out what those intentions were. This does not, of course, imply that they took the form of abstract moral propositions which were then clothed in plot; but it does suggest that for Golding the entire plan of the work, *and* the meaning of that plan, were worked out first — that he started with meaning rather than with character or situation. Golding's own glosses of the meanings of *Lord of the Flies* and *Pincher Martin* have not seemed satisfactory to most readers — the teller in fact supports Lawrence's view of the creative process, and not Golding's; nevertheless, the fact that Golding thinks of his books as he does tells us something useful about the forms that they have taken.

There is no adequate critical term for that form. Golding himself has called his books both *myths* and *fables*, and both terms do point to a quality in the novels that it is necessary to recognize — that they are unusually tight, conceptualized, analogical expressions of moral ideas. Still, neither term is quite satisfactory, because both imply a degree of abstraction and an element of the legendary that Golding's novels simply do not have, and it seems better to be content with calling them simply *novels*, while recognizing that they have certain formal properties that distinguish them from most current fiction.

The most striking of these properties is that Golding so patterns his narrative actions as to make them the images of ideas, the imaginative forms of generalizations; the form itself, that is to say, carries meaning apart from the meanings implied by character or those stated more or less didactically by the author. "In all my books," Golding has said, "I have suggested a shape in the universe that may, as it were, account for things." To direct the attentions of his readers to that shape, Golding has chosen situations that isolate what is basic, and avoid both the merely topical and the subjective existence of the author. All but two of his novels employ a situation that is remote in time or space, characters who are radically unlike the author, and a narrative tone that is removed, analytical, and judicial. Consequently we must look for human relevance to the patterned action itself; if we "identify," it must be with the moral — with the conception of man and the shape of the universe — and not with this character or that one.

The forms that Golding uses carry implications both for the kind of action selected and for the kind of characters involved in it. Since Golding proposes to embody general truths in his novels, he is committed, one would think, to select those human experiences that can be viewed as *exemplary*, not merely as *typical*; it is not enough to propose that a fictional event might happen. To be justifiable in a Golding novel an event must also bear its shape of the patterned meaning. Consequently the novels tend on the whole to be short and densely textured, and the characters, while they are usually convincingly three-dimensional human beings, may also function as exemplars of facets of man's nature — of common sense, or greed, or will (one of Golding's most impressive gifts is his ability to make characters exemplify abstractions without *becoming* abstractions).

What we acknowledge if we choose to call Golding a fabulist is not that the total story is reducible to a moral proposition—this is obviously not true—but rather that he writes from clear and strong moral assumptions, and that those assumptions give form and direction to his fictions. But if Aesop and La Fontaine wrote fables, we need another term for Golding. We might borrow one from scholastic aesthetics, and call them *tropological*, meaning by this that the novels individually "suggest a shape in the universe," and are constructed as models of such moral shapes. Or if tropological seems too rarefied, *moral models* will do. The point, in any case, is to suggest the patterned quality of Golding's work, and to recognize the assumptions which that quality implies. Golding accepts certain traditional ideas about man and his place in the world: that mind, by meditation and speculation, may arrive at truth; that it may find in the past, meanings which are relevant to the present, and available through memory; that it may appropriately concern itself with metaphysics and with morals. Not all of these ideas are current now, certainly not in the avant-garde, and consequently Golding's work may seem, in the context of his time, more didactic and moralizing than in fact it is. For though Golding is a moralist, he is not a moral-maker, and his novels belong, not with Aesop's fables, but with the important symbolic novels of our century—with Camus's and Kafka's.

Golding has founded *Lord of the Flies* on a number of more or less current conventions. First of all, he has used the science-fiction convention of setting his action in the future, thus substituting the eventually probable for the immediately actual, and protecting his fable from literalistic judgments of details or of credibility. A planeload of boys has been evacuated from an England engaged in some future war fought against "the reds"; after their departure an atomic bomb has fallen on England, and civilization is in ruins. The plane flies south and east, stopping at Gibraltar and Addis Ababa; still farther east—over the Indian Ocean, or perhaps the Pacific, the plane is attacked by an enemy aircraft, the "passenger tube" containing the boys is jettisoned, and the rest of the plane crashes in flames. The boys land unharmed on a desert island.

At this point, a second literary convention enters. The desert island tale shares certain literary qualities with science fiction. Both offer a "what-would-happen-if" situation, in which real experience is simplified in order that certain values and problems may be regarded in isolation. Both tend to simplify human moral issues by externalizing good and evil; both offer occasions for Utopian fantasies. Golding's most immediate source is R. M. Ballantyne's *Coral Island*, a Victorian boys' book of South Sea adventure, but Ballantyne didn't invent the island dream; that dream began when man first felt the pressures of his civilization enough to think that a life without civilization might be a life without problems.

The relation of Golding's novel to Ballantyne's is nevertheless important enough to pause over. In *Coral Island*, three English boys called Ralph, Jack, and Peterkin are shipwrecked on a tropical island, meet pirates and cannibals, and conquer all adversities with English fortitude and Christian virtue. We may say that *Coral Island* is a clumsy moral tale, in which good is defined as being English and Christian and jolly, and especially an English Christian *boy*, and in which evil is unchristian, savage, and adult. The three boys are rational, self-reliant, inventive, and virtuous—in short, they are like no boys that anyone has ever known.

Golding regards *Coral Island* morality as unrealistic, and therefore not truly moral, and he has used it ironically in his own novel, as a foil for his own version of man's moral nature. In an interview Golding described his use of Ballantyne's book in this way:

> What I'm saying to myself is "don't be such a fool, you remember when you were a boy, a small boy, how you lived on that island with Ralph and Jack and Peterkin." . . . . I said to myself finally, "Now you are grown up, you are adult; it's taken you a long time to become adult, but now you've got there you can see that people are not like that; they would not behave like that if they were God-fearing English gentlemen, and they went to an island like that." There savagery would not be found in natives on an island. As like as not they would find savages who were kindly and uncomplicated and that the devil would rise out of the intellectual complications of the three white men on the island itself.

One might say that *Lord of the Flies* is a refutation of *Coral Island*, and that Golding sets about to show us that the devil rises, not out of pirates and cannibals and such alien creatures, but out of the darkness of man's heart. The *Coral Island* attitude exists in the novel—Jack sounds very like Ballantyne's Jack when he says: "After all, we're not savages. We're English; and the English are best at everything." And the naval commander who rescues the boys at the end of the book speaks in the same vein: "I should have thought that a pack of British boys—you're all British aren't you?—would have been able to put up a better show than that—I mean—" But Jack and the commander are wrong; the pack of British boys are in fact cruel and murderous savages who reduce the island to a burning wreckage and destroy the dream of innocence.

The fable of the novel is a fairly simple one. The boys first set out to create a rational society modeled on what "grown-ups" would do. They establish a government and laws, they provide for food and shelter, and they light a signal fire. But this rational society begins to break down almost at once, under two instinctual pressures—fear and blood lust. The dark unknown that surrounds the children gradually assumes a monstrous identity, and becomes "the beast," to be feared and propitiated; and hunting for food becomes killing. The hunters break away from the society, and create their own primitive, savage, orgiastic tribal society. They kill two of the three rational boys, and are hunting down the third when the adult world intervenes.

This fable, as sketched, is susceptible of several interpretations, and Golding's critics have found it coherent on a number of levels, according to their own preoccupations. Freudians have found in the novel a conscious dramatization of psychological theory: "denied the sustaining and repressing authority of parents, church and state, [the children] form a new culture the development of which reflects that of genuine primitive society, evolving its gods and demons (its myths), its rituals and taboos (its social norms)." The political-minded have been able to read it as "the modern political nightmare," in which rational democracy is destroyed by irrational authoritarianism ("I hope," said V. S. Pritchett, "this book is being read in Germany"). The social-minded have found in it a social allegory, in which life, without civilized restraints, becomes nasty, brutish, and short. And the religious have simply said, in a complacent tone, "Original Sin, of course."

It is, of course, entirely possible that Golding has managed to construct a fable that does express all these ideas of evil, and that what we are dealing with is not alternative interpretations, but simply levels of meaning. The idea of Original Sin, for example, does have political, social, and psychological implications; if it is true that man is inherently prone to evil, then certain conclusions about the structure of his relations to other men would seem to follow. The idea of Original Sin seems, indeed, to be one of the "great commonplaces," one of those ideas which are so central to man's conception of himself that they turn up, in one form or another, in almost any systematic account of human nature. It describes one of perhaps two possible accounts of the nature of human behavior (*Coral Island* assumes the other one).

Since the novel is symbolic, the best approach would seem to be to examine first the "meaning" of each of the major characters, and then to proceed to consider the significance of their interactions. Ralph — in *Coral Island* the first-person narrator — here provides the most consistent point of view, because he most nearly speaks for us, rational, fallible humankind; Ralph is the man who accepts responsibility that he is not particularly fitted for because he sees that the alternative to responsibility is savagery and moral chaos. He tries to establish and preserve an orderly, rational society; he takes as his totem the conch, making it the symbol of rational, orderly discussion.

Ralph's antagonist is Jack, who represents "the brilliant world of hunting, tactics, fierce exhilaration, skill," as Ralph represents "the world of longing and baffled common-sense." Between them there is an "indefinable connection"; like Cain and Abel, they are antithetical, but intimately linked together — man-the-destroyer confronting man-the-preserver. Jack is the hunter, the boy who becomes a beast of prey (and who uses *kill* as an intransitive verb, an act which is for him an end in itself). He is also the dictator, the authoritarian man-of-power who enters the scene like a drill sergeant, who despises assemblies and the conch, and who becomes in the end an absolute ruler of his tribe. He devises the painted mask of the hunter, behind which a boy may hide, "liberated from shame and self-consciousness," and by painting the boys he turns them into an anonymous mob of murderous savages, "a demented but partly secure society." Jack is the first of the bigger boys to accept "the beast" as possible, and the one who offers the propitiatory sacrifice to it; he is the High Priest of Beelzebub, the Lord of the Flies.

Associated with each of these antagonists is a follower who represents in a more nearly allegorical form the principal value of his leader. Piggy, Ralph's "true, wise friend," is a scientific-minded rationalist, who models his behavior on what he thinks grownups would do, and scorns the other children for "acting like a crowd of kids." He can think better than Ralph, and in a society in which thought was enough he would be supremely valuable; but on the island he is ineffectual; he is incapable of action, and is a physical coward. His totem is his spectacles, and with them he is the fire-bringer; but when Jack first breaks one lens and then steals the other, Piggy becomes blind and helpless, a bag of fat. His trust in the power and wisdom of grownups is itself a sign of his inadequacy; for if the novel makes one point clearly, it is that adults have no special wisdom, and are engaged in a larger scale, but equally destructive, version of the savage game that the hunters play. (When Ralph wishes that the outer world might "send us something grown-up . . . a sign or something," the adult world obliges with the dead parachutist, an image of terror that destroys Ralph's rational society.)

Beside or slightly behind Jack stands Roger, around whom clings "the hangman's horror." Roger's lust is the lust for power over living things, the power to destroy life. In the beginning he is restrained by "the taboo of the old life . . . the protection of parents and school and policemen and the law." Jack and the paint of savagery liberate Roger from these taboos, and "with a sense of delirious abandonment" he rolls the rock down the cliff, killing Piggy, his opposite.

One character, the most difficult to treat, remains. Simon, the shy visionary, perceptive but inarticulate, occupies a central position in the symbolic scheme of the book. It is Simon who first stammers that perhaps the beast is "only us," who sees the beast in terms of "mankind's essential illness," and who goes alone to confront *both* beasts, the grinning pig's head and the rotting airman, because, as he says, "What else is there to do?" Golding has described Simon as a saint, "someone who voluntarily embraces this beast, goes . . . and tries to get rid of him and goes to give the good news to the ordinary bestial man on the beach, and gets killed for it." He would appear to be, then, at least in Golding's intentions, the embodiment of moral understanding. If this is so, those symbolic scenes in which he appears will be crucial to an understanding of the novel.

I have said that one distinction between Golding's novels and allegory is that the novels are meaning-in-action, general truth given narrative or dramatic form by the creative imagination. In considering the meaning of *Lord of the Flies*, one cannot therefore stop at an examination of character— meaning must emerge from character-in-action. In the narrative action certain scenes stand out as crucial, and most of these announce their importance by being overtly symbolic. There is, for example, a series of scenes in which Jack's hunters evolve a ritual dance. On the first occasion, in Chapter 4, a child *pretends* to be the pig, and the hunters *pretend* to beat him. A chapter later the dance has become crueler, "and littluns that had had enough were staggering away, howling." After the next hunt Robert, acting the pig in the dance, squeals with real pain, and the hunters cry "Kill him! Kill him!" After the dance the boys discuss ways of improving the ritual: " 'You want a real pig,' said Robert, still caressing his rump, 'because you've got to kill him.'

" 'Use a littlun,' said Jack, and everybody laughed." In the final ritual dance, the sacrificial function is acknowledged; the boys' chant is no longer "Kill the pig," but "Kill the *beast!*" and when Simon crawls from the forest, the boys fulfill their ritual sacrifice, and by killing a human being, make themselves beasts ("there were no words, and no movements but the tearing of teeth and claws"). Ironically, they have killed the one person who could have saved them from bestiality, for Simon has seen the figure on the mountaintop, and knows that the beast is "harmless and horrible."

Simon's lonely, voluntary quest for the beast is certainly the symbolic core of the book. The meaning of the book depends on the meaning of the beast, and it is that meaning that Simon sets out to determine. His first act is to withdraw to a place of contemplation, a sunlit space in the midst of the forest. It is to the same place that Jack and his hunters bring the pig's head, and leave it impaled on a stick as a sacrifice to the beast they fear. When they have gone, Simon holds hallucinatory conversation with the Lord of the Flies, Beelzebub, the Lord of Filth and Dung. The head, "with the infinite cynicism of adult life," assures Simon that "everything was a bad business," and advises him to run away, back to the other children, and to abandon his quest. "I'm part of you," it tells him (in words that echo Simon's own "maybe it's only us"), "I'm the reason why it's no go." Simon, apparently epileptic, falls in a fit. But when he wakes, he turns upward, toward the top of the mountain, where the truth lies. He finds the airman, rotting and fly-blown, and tenderly frees the figure from the wind's indignity. Then he sets off, weak and staggering, to tell the other boys that the beast is human, and is murdered by them.

How are we to interpret this sequence? We may say, first of all, that the beast symbolizes the source of evil in human life. Either it is something terrifying and external, which cannot be understood but must simply be lived with (this is Jack's version), or it is a part of man's nature, "only us," in which case it may be understood, and perhaps controlled by reason and rule. Simon understands that man must seek out the meaning of evil ("what else is there to do?"). By seeking, he comes to know it, "harmless and horrible." Thus far the moral point seems orthodox enough. But when he tries to tell his understanding to others, they take *him* for the beast, and destroy him in terror. Another common idea, though a more somber one— men fear the bearers of truth, and will destroy them. This has both political and psychological implications. A "demented but partly secure society" (read: Nazi Germany, or any authoritarian nation) will resist and attempt to destroy anyone who offers to substitute reason and responsible individual action for the irresponsible, unreasoning, *secure* action of the mass. And in psychological terms, the members of a "demented society" may create an irrational, external evil, and in its name commit deeds that as rational men they could not tolerate (the history of modern persecutions offers examples enough); such a society *has* to destroy the man who says, "The evil is in yourselves."

At this point, I should like to return to the argument that this novel is a symbolic form but not an allegory. One aspect of this distinction is that Golding has written a book that has a dense and often poetic verbal texture, in which metaphor and image work as they do in poetry, and enrich and modify the bare significances of the moral form. Golding's treatment of Simon's death is a particularly good case in point. At this instant, a storm breaks, the wind fills the parachute on the mountain, and the figure, freed by Simon, floats and falls toward the beach, scattering the boys in terror before passing out to sea. The storm ends, stars appear, the tide rises. Stars above and phosphorescent sea below fill the scene with brightness and quiet.

> Along the shoreward edge of the shallows the advancing clearness was full of strange, moonbeam-bodied creatures with fiery eyes. Here and there a larger pebble clung to its own air and was covered with a coat of pearls. The tide swelled in over the rain-pitted sand and smoothed everything with a layer of silver. Now it touched the first of the stains that seeped from the broken body and the creatures made a moving patch of light as they gathered at the edge. The water rose farther and dressed Simon's coarse hair with brightness. The line of his cheek silvered and the turn of his shoulder became sculptured marble. The strange attendant creatures, with their fiery eyes and trailing vapors, busied themselves round his head. The body lifted a fraction of an inch from the sand and a bubble of air escaped from the mouth with a wet plop. Then it turned gently in the water.
>
> Somewhere over the darkened curve of the world the sun and moon were pulling, and the film of water on the earth planet was held, bulging slightly on one side while the solid core turned. The great wave

of the tide moved farther along the island and the water lifted. Softly, surrounded by a fringe of inquisitive bright creatures, itself a silver shape beneath the steadfast constellations, Simon's dead body moved out toward the open sea.

This is Golding's rhetoric at its richest, but it works. The imagery of light and value — *moonbeam, pearls, silver, brightness, marble* — effect a transfiguration, by which the dead child is made worthy, his death an elevation. In terms of allegory, this sort of metaphorical weighting would perhaps be imprecise and deceptive; in terms of a symbolic novel, it seems to me a legitimate application of a skillful writer's art.

In discussing the actions of *Lord of the Flies* I have again and again slipped from talking about boys to describing the characters as men, or simply as human beings. It is true that as the action rises to its crises — to the *agon* of Chapter 5, Simon's confrontation with the beast, the murders, the final hunt — we cease to respond to the story as a story about children, and see them simply as *people*, engaged in desperate, destructive actions. Consequently, Golding can achieve a highly dramatic effect at the end of the book by bringing our eyes down, with Ralph's, to a beach-level view of an adult, and then swinging round, to show us Ralph from the adult's point of view. The result is an irony that makes two points. First, we see with sudden clarity that these murderous savages were civilized children; the point is not, I take it, that children are more horrid than we thought (though they are), but rather that the human propensity for evil knows no limits, not even limits of age, and that there is no Age of Innocence (Ralph weeps for the end of innocence, but when did it exist, except as an illusion made of his own ignorance?). Second, there is the adult, large, efficient, confident — the "grown-up" that the children have wished for all along. But his words show at once that he is a large, stupid *Coral Island* mentality in a peaked cap, entirely blind to the moral realities of the situation. He may save Ralph's life, but he will not understand. And once he has gathered up the castaways, he will return to his ship, and the grown-up business of hunting men (just as the boys have been hunting Ralph). "And who," asks Golding, "will rescue the adult and his cruiser?"

To return briefly to the question of levels of interpretation: it seems clear that *Lord of the Flies* should be read as a moral novel embodying a conception of human depravity which is compatible with, but not limited to, the Christian doctrine of Original Sin. To call the novel religious is to suggest that its values are more developed, and more affirmative, than in fact they are; Golding makes no reference to Grace, or to Divinity, but only to the darkness of men's hearts, and to the God of Dung and Filth who rules there. Simon is perhaps a saint, and sainthood is a valuable human condition, but there is no sign in the novel that Simon's sainthood has touched any soul but his own. The novel tells us a good deal about evil; but about salvation it is silent.

Why It's No Go
James R. Baker*

Lord of the Flies offers a variation upon the ever-popular tale of island adventure, and it holds all of the excitements common to that long tradition. Golding's castaways are faced with the usual struggle for survival, the terrors of isolation, and a desperate but finally successful effort to signal a passing ship which will return them to the civilized world they have lost. This time, however, the story is told against the background of atomic war. A plane carrying some English boys away from the center of conflict is shot down by the enemy and the youths are left without adult company on an unpopulated Pacific island. The environment in which they find themselves actually presents no serious challenge: the island is a paradise of flowers and fruit, fresh water flows from the mountain, and the climate is gentle. In spite of these unusual natural advantages, the children fail miserably, and the adventure ends in a reversal of their (and the reader's) expectations. Within a short time the rule of reason is overthrown and the survivors regress to savagery.

During the first days on the island there is little forewarning of this eventual collapse of order. The boys (aged six to twelve) are delighted with the prospect of some real fun before the adults come to fetch them. With innocent enthusiasm they recall the storybook romances they have read and now expect to experience in reality. Among these is *The Coral Island*, Robert Michael Ballantyne's heavily moralistic idyl of castaway boys, written in 1857, yet still, in our atomic age, a popular adolescent classic in England. In Ballantyne's story everything comes off in exemplary style. For Ralph, Jack, and Peterkin (his charming young imperialists) mastery of the natural environment is an elementary exercise in Anglo-Saxon ingenuity. The fierce pirates who invade the island are defeated by sheer moral force, and the tribe of cannibalistic savages is easily converted and reformed by the example of Christian conduct afforded them. *The Coral Island* is again mentioned by the naval officer who comes to rescue Golding's boys from the nightmare island they have created, and so the adventure of these modern *enfants terribles* is ironically juxtaposed with the spectacular success of the Victorian darlings.[1]

The effect is to hold before us two radically different pictures of human nature and society. Ballantyne, no less than Golding, is a fabulist[2] who asks us to believe that the evolution of affairs on his coral island models or reflects the adult world — a world in which men are unfailingly reasonable, cooperative, loving and lovable. We are hardly prepared to accept such optimistic exaggerations, but Ballantyne's tale suggests essentially the same flattering image of civilized man found in so many familiar

---

*This essay first appeared in *Arizona Quarterly* 19 (Winter 1963) and is reprinted here with the permission of the author. © 1986 by James R. Baker.

island fables. In choosing to parody and invert this romantic image, Golding posits a reality the literary tradition has generally denied.

The character of this reality is to be seen in the final episode of *Lord of the Flies*. When the British cruiser appears offshore, the boy Ralph is the one remaining advocate of reason; but he has no more status than the wild pigs of the forest and is being hunted down for the kill. Shocked by their filth, their disorder, and the revelation that there have been real casualties, the officer, with appropriate fatherly indignation, expresses his disappointment in this "pack of British boys." There is no real basis for his surprise, for life on the island has only imitated the larger tragedy in which the adults of the outside world attempted to govern themselves reasonably but ended in the same game of hunt and kill. Thus, according to Golding, the aim of his narrative is "to trace the defects of society back to the defects of human nature"; the moral illustrated is that "the shape of society must depend on the ethical nature of the individual and not on any political system however apparently logical or respectable."[3] And, since the lost children are the inheritors of the same defects of nature which doomed their fathers, the tragedy on the island is bound to repeat the actual pattern of human history.

The central fact in that pattern is one which we, like the fatuous naval officer, are virtually incapable of perceiving: first, because it is one that constitutes an affront to our ego; second, because it controverts the carefully and elaborately rationalized record of history which sustains the pride of "rational" man. The reality is that regardless of the intelligence we possess — an intelligence which drives us in a tireless effort to impose an order upon our affairs — we are defeated with monotonous regularity by our own irrationality. "History," said Joyce's Dedalus, "is a nightmare from which I am trying to awake."[4] But we do not awake. Though we constantly make a heroic attempt to rise to a level ethically superior to nature, and to our own nature, again and again we suffer a fall, brought low by some outburst of madness because of the limiting defects inherent in our species.

If there is any literary precedent for the image of man contained in Golding's fable, it is obviously not to be discovered within the framework of a tradition that embraces *Robinson Crusoe* and *Swiss Family Robinson*[5] and that includes also the island episodes in Conrad's novels where we see the self-defeating skepticism of a Heyst or a Decoud serving only to demonstrate the value of illusions.[6] All of these novels offer some version of the rationalist orthodoxy we so readily accept, even though the text may not be so boldly simple as Ballantyne's fable for innocent Victorians.

Quite removed from this tradition (which Golding mocks in nearly everything he has written) is the directly acknowledged influence of classical Greek literature. Within this designation, though Golding's critics have ignored it, is the acknowledged admiration for Euripides.[7] Among the plays of Euripides it is *The Bacchae* that Golding, like his

Mamillius of *The Brass Butterfly*, obviously knows by heart. The tragedy is a bitter allegory on the degeneration of society, and it contains a basic parable which informs much of Golding's work. It is clearly pertinent in *Lord of the Flies*, for here the point of view is similar to that of Euripides after he was driven into exile from Athens. Before his departure the tragedian brought down upon himself the mockery and disfavor of a mediocre regime like the one which later condemned Socrates. *The Bacchae*, however, is more than an expression of disillusionment with a failing democracy. Its aim is precisely what Golding has declared to be his own: "to trace the defects of society back to the defects of human nature," and so to account for the failure of rational man who invariably undertakes the blind ritual-hunt in which he seeks to kill the threatening "beast" within his own being.

The *Bacchae* is based on a legend of Dionysus wherein the god (a son of Zeus and the mortal Semele, daughter of Cadmus) descends upon Thebes in great wrath, determined to take revenge upon the young king, Pentheus, who has denied him recognition and prohibited his worship. Dionysus wins the daughters of Cadmus as his devotees; and, through his power of enchantment, he decrees that Agave, mother of Pentheus, shall lead the group in frenzied celebrations. Pentheus bluntly opposes the god and tries by every means to preserve order against the rising tide of madness in his kingdom. The folly of his proud resistance is shown in the total defeat of all his efforts: the bacchantes trample on his rules and edicts; in wild marches through the land they wreck everything in their path. Thus prepared for his vengeance, Dionysus casts a spell over Pentheus. With his judgment weakened and his identity obscured by dressing as a woman, the humiliated prince sets out to spy upon the orgies. In the excitement of their rituals the bacchantes live in a world of illusion, and all that falls within their sight undergoes a metamorphosis which brings it into accord with the natural images of their worship. When Pentheus is seen, he is taken for a lion.[8] Led by Agave, the blind victims of the god tear the king limb from limb. The final punishment of those who denied the god of nature is to render them conscious of their awful crimes and to cast them out from their homeland as guilt-stricken exiles and wanderers upon the earth.

For most modern readers the chief obstacle in the way of proper understanding of *The Bacchae*, and therefore of Golding's use of it, is the popular notion that Dionysus is nothing more than a charming god of wine. This image descends from "the Alexandrines, and above all the Romans — with their tidy functionalism and their cheerful obtuseness in all matters of the spirit — who departmentalized Dionysus as 'jolly Bacchus' . . . with his riotous crew of nymphs and satyrs. As such he was taken over from the Romans by Renaissance painters and poets; and it was they in turn who shaped the image in which the modern world pictures him." In reality the god was more important and "much more dangerous":

he was "the principle of animal life . . . the hunted and the hunter—the unrestrained potency which man envies in the beasts and seeks to assimilate." Thus the intention and chief effect of the bacchanal is "to liberate the instinctive life in man from the bondage imposed upon it by reason and social custom. . . ." In his tragedy Euripides also suggests "a further effect, a merging of the individual consciousness in a group consciousness" so that the participant is "at one not only with the Master of Life but his fellow-worshippers . . . and with the life of the earth.[9]

Dionysus was worshiped in various animal incarnations (snake, bull, lion, boar), whatever form was appropriate to place; and all of these incarnations were symbolic of the impulses he evoked in his worshipers. In *The Bacchae* a leader of the bacchanal summons him with the incantation, "O God, Beast, Mystery, come!"[10] Agave's attack upon the "lion" (her own son) conforms to the codes of Dionysic ritual; like other gods, this one is slain and devoured, his devotees sustained by his flesh and blood. The terrible error of the bacchantes is a punishment brought upon the proud Greeks by the lord of beasts: "To resist Dionysus is to repress the elemental in one's own nature; the punishment is the sudden collapse of the inward dykes when the elemental breaks through perforce and civilization vanishes."[11]

This same lesson in humility is meted out to the schoolboys of *Lord of the Flies*. In their innocent pride they attempt to impose a rational order or pattern upon the vital chaos of their own nature, and so they commit the error and "sin" of Pentheus, the "man of many sorrows." The penalties (as in the play) are bloodshed, guilt, utter defeat of reason. Finally, they stand before the officer, "A semicircle of little boys, their bodies streaked with colored clay, sharp sticks in their hands . . ." (pp. 240–41). Facing that purblind commander (with his revolver and peaked cap), Ralph cries "for the end of innocence, the darkness of man's heart" (p. 242); and the tribe of vicious hunters joins him in spontaneous choral lament. But even Ralph could not trace the arc of their descent, could not explain why it's no go, why things are as they are. For in the course of events he was at times among the hunters, one of them; and he grieves in part for the appalling ambiguities he has discovered in his own being. In this moment of "tragic knowledge" he remembers those strange interims of blindness and despair when a "shutter" clicked down over his mind and left him at the mercy of his own dark heart. In Ralph's experience, then, the essence of the fable is spelled out: he suffers the dialectic we must all endure, and his failure to resolve it as we would wish demonstrates the limitations which have always plagued our species.

In the first hours on the island Ralph sports untroubled in the twilight of childhood and innocence, but after he sounds the conch he must confront the forces he has summoned to the granite platform beside the sunny lagoon. During that first assembly he seems to arbitrate with the grace of a young god (his natural bearing is dignified, princely); and, for the time being, a balance is maintained. The difficulties begin with the dream revelation of the child distinguished by the birthmark. The boy tells of a snakelike monster prowling the woods by night, and at this moment the seed of fear is planted. Out of it will grow the mythic beast destined to become lord of the island. There is a plague of haunting dreams, and these constitute the first symptoms of the irrational fear which is "mankind's essential illness."

In the chapter entitled "Beast from Water" the parliamentary debate becomes a blatant allegory in which each spokesman caricatures the position he defends. Piggy (the voice of reason) leads with the statement that "life is scientific," and adds the usual utopian promises ("when the war's over they'll be traveling to Mars and back"); and his assurance that such things will come to pass if only we control the senseless conflicts which impede our progress. He is met with laughter and jeers (the crude multitude), and at this juncture a little one interrupts to declare that the beast (ubiquitous evil) comes out of the sea. Maurice interjects to voice the doubt which curses them all: "I don't believe in the beast of course. As Piggy says, life's scientific, but we don't know, do we? Not certainly . . ." (p. 102). Then Simon (the inarticulate seer) rises to utter the truth in garbled, ineffective phrases: there is a beast, but "it's only us." As always, his saving words are misunderstood, and the prophet shrinks away in confusion. Amid the speculation that Simon means some kind of ghost, there is a silent show of hands for ghosts as Piggy breaks in with angry rhetorical questions: "What are we? Humans? Or animals? Or Savages?" (p. 105). Taking his cue, Jack (savagery in excelsis) leaps to his feet and leads all but the "three blind mice" (Ralph, Piggy, and Simon) into a mad jig of release down the darkening beach. The parliamentarians naïvely contrast their failure with the supposed efficiency of adults; and Ralph, in despair, asks for a sign from that ruined world.

In "Beast from Air" the sign, a dead man in a parachute, is sent down from the grownups, and the collapse of order foreshadowed in the allegorical parliament comes on with surprising speed. Ralph himself looks into the face of the enthroned tyrant on the mountain, and from that moment his young intelligence is crippled by fear. He confirms the reality of the beast, insuring Jack's spectacular rise to absolute power. Yet the ease with which Jack establishes his Dionysian regime is hardly unaccountable. From its very first appearance, the black-caped choir, vaguely evil in its military esprit, emerged ominously from a mirage and marched down upon the minority forces assembled on the platform. Except for Simon, pressed into service and out of step with the common rhythm, the choir is composed of servitors bound by the rituals and the mysteries of group consciousness. They share in that communion, and there is no real "conversion" or transfer of allegiance from good to evil when the chorus, ostensibly Christian, becomes the tribe of hunters. The god they serve inhabits their own being. If they turn with relief from the burdens and responsibilities of the platform, it is because they cannot transcend the limitations of their own nature. Even the parliamentary pool of intelligence must fail in the attempt to explain all that manifests itself in our turbulent hearts, and the assertion that life is ordered, "scientific," often appears mere bravado. It embodies the sin of pride and, inevitably, it evokes the great god which the rational man would like to deny.

It is Simon who witnesses his coming and hears his words of wrath. In the thick undergrowth of the forest the boy discovers a refuge from the war of words. His shelter of leaves is a place of contemplation, a sequestered temple scented and lighted by the white flowers of the night-blooming candle-nut tree. There, in secret, he meditates on the lucid but somehow oversimple logic of Piggy and Ralph and on the venal emotion of Jack's challenges to their authority. There, in the infernal glare of the afternoon sun, he sees the killing of the sow by the hunters and the erection of the pig's head on the sharpened stick. These acts signify not only the final release from the blood taboo but also obeisance to the mystery and god who has come to be lord of the island world. In the hours of one powerfully symbolic afternoon, Simon sees the perennial fall which is the central reality of our history: the defeat of reason and the release of Dionysian madness in souls wounded by fear.

Awed by the hideousness of the dripping head—an image of the hunters' own nature—the apprentice bacchantes suddenly run away; but Simon's gaze is "held by that ancient, inescapable recognition" (p. 165)— an incarnation of the beast or devil born again and again out of the human heart. Before he loses consciousness, the epileptic visionary "hears" the truth which is inaccessible to the illusion-bound rationalist and to the unconscious or irrational man alike. " 'Fancy thinking the Beast was something you could hunt and kill!' said the head. For a moment or two the forest and all the other dimly appreciated places echoed with the parody of laughter. 'You knew, didn't you? I'm part of you? Close, close, close! I'm the reason why it's no go? Why things are as they are?' " (p. 172). When Simon recovers from this trauma of revelation, he finds on the mountaintop that the "beast" is only a man. Like the pig itself, the dead man in the chute is fly-blown, corrupt; he is an obscene image of the evil that has triumphed in the adult world as well. Tenderly the boy releases the lines so that the body can descend to earth, but the fallen man does not descend. After Simon's death, when the truth is once more lost, the figure rises, moves over the terrified tribe on the beach, and finally out to sea—a tyrannous ghost (history itself) which haunts and curses every social order.

In his martyrdom Simon meets the fate of all saints. The truth he brings would set us free from the repetitious nightmare of history, but we are, by nature, incapable of perceiving the truth. Demented by fears our intelligence cannot control, we are "at once heroic and sick" (p. 121), ingenious and ingenuous at the same time. Inevitably we gather in tribal union and communion to hunt the molesting "beast," and always the intolerable frustration of the hunt ends as it must: within the enchanted circle formed by the searchers the beast materializes in the only form he can possibly assume, the very image of his creator. And once he is visible, projected (once the hunted has become the hunter), the circle closes in an agony of relief. Simon, the saintly one, is blessed and cursed by those unique intuitions which threaten the ritual of the tribe. In whatever culture he appears, the saint is doomed by his insights. There is a vital, if obvious, irony to be observed in the fact that the lost children of Golding's fable are of Christian heritage; but, when they blindly kill their savior, they reenact not only an ancient tragedy but a universal one because it has its true source in the defects of the species.

The beast, too, is as old as his maker and has assumed many names, though of course his character must remain quite consistent. The particular beast who speaks to Simon is much like his namesake, Beelzebub. A prince of demons of Assyrian or Hebrew descent, but later appropriated by Christians, he is a lord of flies, an idol for unclean beings. He is what all devils are: merely an embodiment of the lusts and cruelties which possess his worshipers and of peculiar power among the Philistines, the unenlightened, fearful herd. He shares some kinship with Dionysus, for his powers and effects are much the same. In *The Baccahe* Dionysus is shown "as the source of ecstasies and disasters, as the enemy of intellect and the defense of man against his isolation, as a power that can make him feel like a god while acting like a beast. . . ." As such, he is "a god whom all can recognize."[12]

Nor is it difficult to recognize the island on which Golding's innocents are set down as a natural paradise, an uncorrupted Eden offering all the lush abundance of the primal earth. But it is lost with the first rumors of the "snake-thing," because he is the ancient, inescapable presence who insures a repetition of the fall. If this fall from grace is indeed the "perennial myth" that Golding explores in all his work,[13] it does not seem that he has found in Genesis a metaphor capable of illuminating the full range of his theme. In *The Bacchae* Golding the classicist found another version of the fall of man, and it is clearly more useful to him than its Biblical counterpart. For one thing, it makes it possible to avoid the comparatively narrow moral implications most of us are inclined to read into the warfare between Satan (unqualifiedly evil) and God (unqualifiedly good). Satan is a fallen angel seeking vengeance on the godhead, and we therefore think of him as an autonomous entity, as a force in his own right and as prince of his own domain. Dionysus, on the other hand, is a son of God (Zeus) and thus a manifestation of one aspect of the godhead or mystery with whom man seeks communion or, perverse in his rational pride, denies at his own peril. To resist Dionysus is to resist nature itself, and this attempt to transcend the laws of creation brings down upon us the punishment of the god. Further, the ritual hunt of *The Bacchae* provides something else not found in the Biblical account of the fall. The hunt on Golding's island emerges spontaneously out of childish play, but it comes to serve as a key to the psychology underlying adult conflicts and, of course, as an effective symbol for the bloody game we have played throughout our history. This is not to say that Biblical metaphor is unimportant in *Lord of the Flies*, or in the later works, but that it forms only a part of the larger mythic frame in which Golding sees the nature and destiny of man.

Unfortunately, the critics have concentrated all too much on Golding's debts to Christian sources, with the result that he is now popularly regarded as a rigid Christian moralist. This is a false image. The emphasis of the critics has obscured Golding's fundamental realism and made it difficult to recognize that he satirizes both the Christian and the rationalist point of view. In *Lord of the Flies*, for example, the much discussed last chapter offers none of the traditional comforts of Christian orthodoxy. A fable, by virtue of its far-reaching suggestions, touches upon a dimension that most fiction does not — the dimension of prophecy. With the appearance of the naval officer, it is no longer possible to accept the evolution of the island society as an isolated failure. The events we have witnessed constitute a picture of realities which obtain in the world at large. There, too, a legendary beast has emerged from the dark wood, come from the sea, or fallen from the sky; and men have gathered for the communion of the hunt.

In retrospect, the entire fable suggests a grim parallel with the prophecies of the Biblical Apocalypse. According to that vision, the weary repetition of human failure is assured by the birth of new devils for each generation of men. The first demon, who fathers all the others, falls from the heavens; the second is summoned from the sea to make war upon the saints and overcome them; the third, emerging from the earth itself, induces man to make and worship an image of the beast. It also ordains that this image shall speak and cause those who do not worship the beast to be killed. Each devil in turn lords over the earth for an era, and then the long nightmare of history is broken by the second coming and the divine millennium. In *Lord of the Flies* (note some of the chapter titles) we see much the same sequence, but it occurs in a highly accelerated evolution. The parallel ends, however, with the irony of Golding's climactic revelation. The childish hope of rescue perishes as the beast-man comes to the shore, for he bears in his nature the bitter promise that things will remain as they are — and as they have been since his first appearance ages and ages ago.

The rebirth of evil is made certain by the fatal defects inherent in human nature, and the haunted island we occupy must always be a fortress on which enchanted hunters pursue the beast. There is no rescue. The making of history and the making of myth are finally the selfsame process — an old one in which the soul makes its own place, its own reality.

In spite of its rich and varied metaphor *Lord of the Flies* is not a bookish fable, and Golding has warned that he will concede little or nothing to *The Golden Bough*.[14] There are grave dangers in ignoring this disclaimer. To do so is to ignore the experiential sources of Golding's art and to obscure its contemporary relevance. During the period of World War II, he witnessed at firsthand the expenditure of human ingenuity in the old ritual of war. As the illusions of his earlier rationalism and humanism fell away, new images emerged; and, as for Simon, a picture of "a human at once heroic and sick" formed in his mind. When the war ended, Golding was ready to write (as he had not been before), and it was only natural to find in the tradition he knew the metaphors which could define the continuity of the soul's ancient flaws. In one sense, the "fable" was already written. Golding had but to trace over the words upon the scroll[15] and so collaborate with history.

Notes

1. A longer discussion of Golding's use of Ballantyne appears in Carl Niemeyer's "The Coral Island Revisited," *College English*, XXII (January, 1961), pp. 241–45.

2. See John Peter, "The Fables of William Golding." Peter distinguishes fiction from fable and classifies *Lord of the Flies*, *The Inheritors*, and *Pincher Martin* as "fables." Golding suggested that the term "myth" might be even better but he liked the essay and most critics are heavily indebted to it. A less simplistic view of Golding's structures is offered by Ian Gregor and Mark Kinkead-Weekes in their introductory remarks for Faber's "School Edition" of *Lord of the Flies* (London, 1962). *Lord of the Flies*, they argue, evidences as many of the characteristics of fiction as it does of fable.

3. Quoted by E. L. Epstein, "Notes on *Lord of the Flies*," in *Lord of the Flies* (New York, 1959), p. 250.

4. *Ulysses* (New York, 1961), p. 34.

5. Golding comments on these novels and on *Treasure Island* in his review called "Islands," *Spectator*, CCIV (June 10, 1960), pp. 844–46.

6. Most of the attempts to compare Golding with Conrad have been unsuccessful, but continued effort might bear some small fruit. At Purdue, Golding was asked by James Keating whether he had read Hughes's *High Wind in Jamaica* before writing *Lord of the Flies*: "No," he replied, "and if you're going to come around to Conrad's *Heart of Darkness*, I might as well confess that I've never read that."

7. On every possible occasion Golding has noted his reading in Greek literature and history during the last twenty years. He reads in the original.

8. In Ovid's version (*Metamorphoses*, III), the bacchantes see Pentheus in the form of a boar.

9. E. R. Dodds, *Euripides Bacchae*, Second Edition (Oxford, 1960), p. xii and p. xx. Dodds also finds evidence that some Dionysian rites involved human sacrifice.

10. From the verse translation by Gilbert Murray.

11. Dodds, p. xvi.

12. R. P. Winnington-Ingram, *Euripides and Dionysus: An Interpretation of the Bacchae* (Cambridge, England; 1948); pp. 9–10.

13. See Ian Gregor and Mark Kinkead-Weekes, "The Strange Case of Mr. Golding and His Critics," *Twentieth-Century*, CLXVIII (February, 1960), p. 118.

14. See Golding's reply to Professor Kermode in "The Meaning of it All," *Books and Bookmen*, V (October, 1959), p. 9.

15. In a letter to me (September, 1962) Professor Kermode cites Golding's remark to the effect that he was "tracing words already on the paper" during the writing of *Lord of the Flies*.

"Dogs Would Find an Arid Space round My Feet": A Humanist Reading of *The Inheritors*

Philip Redpath*

> We look daily at the appalling mystery of plain stuff. We stand where any upright food-gatherer has stood, on the edge of our own unconscious, and hope, perhaps, for the terror and excitement of the print of a single foot.[1]

> The hair of outside-Lok rose at the touch of the cold stuff round his thighs and the gripping of the unseen mud sucking at his feet.[2]

I've been thinking about the gaps in *The Inheritors*, about those breaks in the narrative when point of view shifts from one perspective into another. There are two such gaps in the novel: one when point of view moves from the Neanderthal Lok to that of a third-person narrator, and the other when narrative perspective shifts from the third-person narrator to that of Tuami, one of the homo sapiens or "new people." My mind keeps returning to the five-and-a-half pages of third-person narrative which is surely the most effective shift in point of view in any Golding novel. In this essay I wish to work out some of the implications of this narratorial shift and relate it to point of view in the rest of the novel. My reason for doing this is to analyze reader response to the novel and, hopefully, overturn a few hardened critical opinions.

Very briefly and schematically, the narrative structure of *The Inheritors* is:

1. Neanderthal point of view (pp. 11–216)
2. Third-person point of view (pp. 216–222)
3. Homo sapiens point of view (pp. 223–333).

As can be seen, a good ninety percent of the novel is taken up with presenting the world from the Neanderthal point of view. This has one

*This essay was written specifically for this volume and is published here for the first time by permission of the author.

important effect — it creates a great deal of pity and sympathy for the Neanderthals. Let me quote a few critics to show the general attitude of readers towards Lok and his tribe. Howard S. Babb observes that "No doubt Golding engages our emotions chiefly through associating us, via the story's point of view, with a group of fundamentally innocent and good-hearted Neanderthal people . . . whose fate is to be destroyed (or captured), one after another, by a tribe of new men, by Homo Sapiens."[3] Craig Raine points out that "In *The Inheritors*, he [Golding] takes a family of savages and shows that they are more truly civilised than homo sapiens,"[4] whilst Barbara Everett notes: " 'The People,' represented here by Lok's little family-community, have been hunted down by the arriving New Men."[5] Finally, Philippa Tristram feels that "the total reliance upon the senses, which makes Lok's people brutes, implies an attitude towards life which is the antithesis of brutality. It is Tuami's people, not Lok's who are bestial. Because they respond to immediate demands of the senses, Lok's people inhabit a world free from notions of past and future and innocent of apprehension or possession."[6] Clearly, these readers' sympathies lie with the innocent and harmless Neanderthals. This is hardly surprising considering that so much of the novel is presented from their point of view. We grow close to Lok, begin to understand him, and pity his helplessness when confronted by the homo sapiens whom he cannot understand. But then, we even sympathize with the morally repellent Christopher Martin in *Pincher Martin* or the physically repulsive Matty in *Darkness Visible* because so much of these novels are written from their individual perspectives.

Yet let me quote two other critics who arrive at the opposite conclusion. Ted E. Boyle writes that "It is difficult to sympathise, however, with Mal, Ha, Fa, Nil, Lok, Liku, and the 'old woman,' for their plight is not ours and their pictures are irrelevant. Golding's primitives are gentle; we are not. They abhor killing; we do not. They live in the present with little conception of past or future; we are different."[7] Gabriel Josipovici argues from a similar stance: "we rest easily inside Lok's sensibility till the last pages show him to us as we would normally see him: an unalterably alien creature, loping away into the forest."[8] There is obviously a wide gulf here between those critics who sympathize with the Neanderthals and those who regard them as alien and unhuman. This gulf is the product of point of view in the novel: critics who sympathize focus their attention on the narrative presented from Lok's point of view, whilst those who do not sympathize turn their attention to the perspective of the new men who are human beings like ourselves. My sympathies and allegiances lie, *must* lie, with the latter argument, and this is a product of that third-person account on pages 216–22, and not with the presentation of the narrative from Tuami's point of view.

The Inheritors presents us with only one authorial third-person view of Lok, worth quoting in full because it serves to illustrate my argument:

It was a strange creature, smallish, and bowed. The legs and thighs were
bent and there was a whole thatch of curls on the outside of the legs and
the arms. The back was high, and covered over the shoulders with curly
hair. Its feet and hands were broad, and flat, the great toe projecting
inwards to grip. The square hands swung down to the knees. The head
was set slightly forward on the strong neck that seemed to lead straight
on to the row of curls under the lip. The mouth was wide and soft and
above the curls of the upper lip the great nostrils flared like wings. There
was no bridge to the nose and the moon-shadow of the jutting brow lay
just above the tip. The shadows lay most darkly in the caverns above its
cheeks and the eyes were invisible in them. Above this again, the brow
was a straight line fledged with hair; and above that there was nothing.
(pp. 218–19)

Obviously this isn't a human being. "It" is a "strange creature." Lok may
be like a man in a few respects, but it is the difference between Lok and
"like" which the word "Lok" so nearly is that defines the gap between
homo sapiens and "it." The passage above, and the whole third-person
section of narrative, serves to emphasize what an alien creature Lok is.
This difference is a problem the Neanderthals experience when they
become aware that new people are on the island. Fa is the first to come to
terms with the situation and tries to explain it: "Here is a picture. Someone
is—other. Not one of the people" (p. 71). Through his acute senses Lok
manages to achieve a form of negative capability and puts himself in the
place of the "other." He peers down into the firelit overhang where the old
woman is moving about: "All at once Lok was frightened because she had
not seen him. The old woman knew so much; yet she had not seen him. He
was cut off and no longer one of the people; as though his communion
with the other had changed him he was different from them and they
could not see him. He had no words to formulate these thoughts but he felt
his difference and invisibility as a cold wind that blew on his skin" (p. 78).
Here Lok becomes aware, without being able to explain the fact, of the
difference between Neanderthal and homo sapiens, what the meaning of
"otherness" is. It is when the narrative shifts to the third-person account
that we become aware of the implications of "otherness," that is, aware of
the gap between ourselves and "it." What differentiates these two moments
of awareness of "other" is that we can formulate the fact and work out its
ramifications. Lok cannot. We do this through the language of *The
Inheritors* because language is our primary medium of rational concep-
tualization. It is this language that helps to define us as homo sapiens. We
may feel sympathy for this creature with its "queer loping run that made
the head bob up and down and the forearms alternate like the legs of a
horse" (p. 217), but it is not the sympathy of one human being for another,
it's human sympathy for the suffering of an animal. A misplaced sympathy
for the Neanderthals over human beings leads finally to the inhumanity of
Miss Dawlish in *The Pyramid*: "If I could save a child or a budgie from a

burning house, I'd save the budgie."[9] Golding remarked on this in a recent interview that "her humanity was gone. . . . I do think of it . . . as about the ultimate."[10]

What the third-person narrative is doing, therefore, is emphasizing the fact that the Neanderthals are not human and that we are mistaken if we sympathize and pity them as one human being for another. Golding has indicated that in his view animals (is it pure chance that "Ha" and "Nil" and "Mal" sounds very close to "animal"?) belong to their own non-human realm: "I would preserve a dinosaur in my ark if I could, but not out of affection. . . . Animals are capital, but they are not ours. . . . So the positive *love* of animals has always amazed me. I had told myself that these lovers must be persons of superabundant affections, who, having exhausted the possibilities of loving their own species, have enough left for the brute creation. . . . Dogs would find an arid space round my feet."[11] The new peoples' attitude towards the Neanderthal baby they take away with them supports Golding's view. They do not love the creature, but they don't hate it either. Their feelings are "love and fear" (p. 231); they are attracted and repelled and regard the baby as other than themselves.

When we see from the Neanderthal point of view Golding attempts to capture the world as seen through innocent eyes, but we should be aware of exactly what is going on. We might take almost any description that is presented from Lok's perspective as an example of the narrative technique of the first part of the novel: "He remembered the hyenas and padded along the terrace until he could look down the slope to the forest. Miles of darkness and sooty blots stretched away to the grey bar that was the sea; nearer, the river shone dispersedly in swamps and meanders. He looked up at the sky and saw it was clear except where layers of fleecy cloud lay above the sea" (p. 40). This is effective writing which presents the physical immediacy of the world. It represents the Neanderthal perception and is mimetic of their conscious awareness. But it only represents and mimes, it is *not* a presentation of their perception or consciousness. In other words, it is not the Neanderthal point of view but an approach to *their* perspective represented in *our* language. This is the language of the third-person narrative which emphasized the difference between Neanderthal and human. It is for this reason that *The Inheritors* is a third-person narrative with its first and third sections presented from Lok's and Tuami's point of view. As human beings neither Golding nor ourselves can enter a non-human consciousness when the only medium we possess through which to do so is language—our human medium of consciousness. Thus the extract above is seen through the eyes of Lok but is translated and conceptualized and then presented from our human point of view in our language. We cannot get out of our language any more than Lok can break into our consciousness. Our language defines our world, not Lok's. Wittgenstein, in the *Tractatus*, made a related point: "We cannot think what we cannot think: so what we cannot think we cannot say either. . . . The world is my world: this is manifest in the fact that the limits of language (of that language which alone I understand) means the limits of my world."[12] It is my world, your world, not Lok's world that is recorded in *The Inheritors*.

This is significant. We, like the new people, are homo sapiens, and that Lok's world is described through the language of homo sapiens is an indication of the displacement that has taken place. If our world is defined and understood through our language, then Lok's world is unknown and unknowable to us. Also, our point of view of the world has displaced his as the Neanderthal world is linguistically supplanted by that of homo sapiens. Point of view in the novel mimes the actions that the novel recounts. The shift into a third-person perspective moves us from Lok to Lok from a homo sapiens point of view. He becomes a "creature," "it," and then ultimately a "red devil" as point of view shifts again to Tuami's perspective. The language of the novel deprives Lok of his world as effectively as the new people wrench his world from him physically. Indeed, the novel presents us only with the language of the homo sapiens, not the language of the Neanderthals. The latter would have been "unalterably alien" to us and therefore so would the world presented through it.

This brings me to the subject of H. G. Wells who has received a mauling at the hands of Golding scholars. It is a commonplace that *The Inheritors* is an inversion of Wells's description of Neanderthal man in the *Outline of History*. Golding himself said a long time ago:

> Wells' *Outline of History* is the rationalist gospel, in excelsis I should think. I got this from my father, and by and by it seemed to me not to be large enough. It seemed to me to be too neat and too slick. And when I read it as an adult I came across his picture of Neanderthal man, our immediate predecessors, as being these gross brutal creatures who were possibly the basis of the mythological bad man, whatever he may be, the ogre. I thought to myself that this is just absurd. What we're doing is externalising our own inside. We're saying: "Well he must have been like that, because I don't want to be like it, although I know I am like it."[13]

Some important points emerge from this statement. First of all, Wells and the homo sapiens are on the side of rationalism; second, the Neanderthals constitute the basis of the ogre; and third, this situation arose from our externalizing our own inner darkness and projecting it onto the Neanderthals. But the evidence from the novel should qualify a too-glib acceptance of this view.

Wells pictured Neanderthal man as a cannibal, a fact Golding uses in his epigraph to the novel. But if he intends to invert Wells's view and show that man was the cannibal by having his famished homo sapiens eat Liku, the young Neanderthal female, his inversion is easy to pick holes in. Liku is not a human being, she is, as the third-person section of the novel makes clear, a "creature" that has as much relation to homo sapiens as a cow or a sheep. The new people do not eat their own kind, they eat "other," something that is unhuman in a similar kind of way to that in which the Neanderthals unthinkingly devour grubs. On the contrary, it is the Neanderthals whose practice is cannibalistic and necrophagous. They eat the brains and marrow of their dead companions. The ailing Mal warns them "Do not open my head and my bones. You would only taste weakness" (p. 87). As he is digging Mal's grave Lok unearths "the crushed and open bones of a head" (p. 89). The homo sapiens are hunters of meat whilst the Neanderthals revere all life (except grubs apparently) which they believe comes from Oa, their earth-deity. But the way in which they fall upon and tear apart the carcass of a deer is savagely unpleasant:

> Lok found a boulder which he could use hammer-wise. He began to pound at the body, breaking out the joints. Fa was grunting with excitement. Lok talked as his great hands tore and twisted and snapped the sinews. . . . The doe was wrecked and scattered. Fa split open her belly, slit the complicated stomach and split the sour cropped grass and broken shoots on the earth. Lok beat in the skull to get at the brain and levered open the mouth to wrench away the tongue. . . . The air between the rocks was forbidding with violence and sweat, with the rich smell of meat and wickedness.
>
> (pp. 53–54)

Lok feels guilty over this "wickedness" and tries to excuse himself: "This is bad. But a cat killed you so there is no blame" (p. 54) and " 'The meat is for Mal who is sick' " (p. 56). This is worryingly reminiscent of Piggy in *Lord of the Flies* trying to wriggle out of responsibility for his part in the murder of Simon: "It was an accident. . . . Coming in the dark—he had no business crawling like that out of the dark. He was batty. He asked for it."[14] Perhaps it is significant that Piggy is the most rational boy on the island, and here is Lok, a non-reasoning creature, trying to justify himself in similar terms. Given the circumstances of their worlds, both are helpless and we feel sympathy with neither at this point.

   The Inheritors is also an inversion of Wells's short story "The Grisly Folk." In this story the ferocious Neanderthals battle with men who are following the receding ice cap in search of food. Golding reverses this plot and has his homo sapiens take away a Neanderthal child and not vice-versa as in Wells's story. But *The Inheritors* cannot be a total inversion; indeed, at many points it coincides with "The Grisly Folk." Wells wrote that "the grisly folk we cannot begin to understand. We cannot conceive in our different minds the strange ideas that chased one another through those queerly shaped brains. As well might we try to dream and feel as a gorilla dreams and feels."[15] As we've already seen, Golding cannot show us what or how the Neanderthals think (if they do). He can only present them to us in our language, and to that extent he has to humanize them and in effect deny their unique existence as Neanderthals.

A much-quoted example of the working of the Neanderthal mind occurs in the novel when one of the new men fires an arrow at Lok:

> The man turned sideways in the bushes and looked at Lok along his shoulder. A stick rose upright and there was a lump of bone in the middle. . . . Suddenly Lok understood that the man was holding the stick out to him but neither he nor Lok could reach across the river. . . . The stick began to grow shorter at both ends. Then it shot out to full length again.
> The dead tree by Lok's ear acquired a voice.
> "Clop!"
> His ears twitched and he turned to the tree. By his face there had grown a twig. . . . The twig had a white bone at the end.
>
> (p. 106)

There is a great deal of irony in the phrase "Lok understood"—he doesn't understand. If he did he would be human. We follow his perception of what is happening from a purely physical point of view. The rational understanding is totally lacking. Let me quote a similar example from Conrad's *Heart of Darkness* in which the rationalization is made and understanding achieved:

> I was looking down at the sounding-pole, and feeling much annoyed to see at each try a little more of it stick out of the river, when I saw my poleman give up the business suddenly, and stretch himself flat on the deck. . . . At the same time the fireman . . . sat down abruptly before his furnace and ducked his head. I was amazed. . . . Sticks, little sticks, were flying about—thick: they were whizzing before my nose, dropping below me, striking behind me against my pilot-house. . . . We cleared the snag clumsily. Arrows, by Jove! We were being shot at![16]

As with Lok, we follow Marlow's perception of physical detail, but unlike Lok we also follow the thread of his reasoning towards a rational conclusion. The difference between the two is an indication of the gap between Neanderthal and homo sapiens. It should also be stressed here that when we read from Lok's point of view he does not understand but we do. We deduce that someone is shooting an arrow at him and therefore we are closer to the new man shooting the arrow and to Marlow than to Lok—although we're reading from his point of view.

A great deal of the reader's sympathy for the Neanderthals arises from the fact that they appear to be innocent creatures. Many critics offer a religious interpretation of *The Inheritors* and regard the Neanderthals as unfallen man. Samuel Hynes claimed that the novel "offers an anthropological analogue of the Fall, which distinguishes between prelapsarian and postlapsarian man in terms of knowledge of evil and capacity for thought."[17] Paul Elman remarks of the Neanderthals that "They are without sin, like animals and flowers,"[18] and Arnold Johnston points out that "if *The Inheritors* is an ironic revelation of man's fallen state, it also demonstrates that there seems no alternative to that state, no hope of a return to innocence. In Golding's world the meek cannot inherit the earth."[19] The problem with this type of argument is that it assumes that the Neanderthals are human beings and that they are innocent whereas the new people are guilty and cannot return to an unfallen state. There is no evidence of a fall in the novel, and if homo sapiens are fallen creatures it seems that they have always been so and have never been innocent. To be totally innocent would be to be a Neanderthal, not a human being. "Not to know evil is, in a sense, to know nothing," Frank Kermode points out.[20] And to know nothing is not to know what you are; to have no self-consciousness of existence; and again, therefore, not to be human.

We should also question whether non-understanding is the same as innocence. If it is, then any rational action or thought is evidence of guilt and we would all be better off as non-thinking animals. But Golding would be the last man to support this view. He does not compound progress and greater understanding with sin and despair. He begins an essay on Copernicus by asserting that "The sky is the roof of human life and has been since man first lifted himself off his knuckles. He has always had ideas about that roof, and they have become more marvelous rather than less. This should confound those who believe that Change and Hopelessness go hand in hand."[21] In the introduction to his play *The Brass Butterfly* he wrote that "We must invent and change, we must control and let loose; if we stop, we shall die out like the dinosaurs."[22] Or like Neanderthal man. It is this human capacity to invent and change that the Neanderthals lack. Their view that "To-day is like yesterday and tomorrow" (p. 46) is a static philosophy in a changing world and leads to their extinction. The indications of change are littered throughout the book: "this was only another complication in a day of total newness" (p. 114), "Already the familiar had altered" (p. 140). Golding has an extended metaphor for the life of any living thing which emphasizes the need to change: "Consider a man riding a bicycle. Whoever he is we can say three things about him. We know he got on the bicycle and started to move. We know that at some point he will stop and get off. Most important of all, we know that if at any point between the beginning and end of his journey he stops moving and does not get off the bicycle he will fall off it."[23] Man must keep moving, progressing, and changing. To become static is to invite destruction.

A simplistic dichotomy such as "knowledge = guilt/non-knowledge = innocence" would be a misreading of Golding's intentions in this novel. To be innocent one must be morally aware of the possibility of being guilty; one must be aware of the existence of the choice between guilt and innocence. This is a question Golding has explored in *Darkness Visible*, *Rites of Passage*, and *The Paper Men*. The Neanderthalers do not have the choice and therefore cannot be innocent in human terms. They are not guilty either. They are simply "other." The very terms "innocence" and "guilt" are, after all, human moral/value judgements. Anthony Burgess, a writer who is as concerned as Golding is with good and evil, deals with the subject of moral choice in *A Clockwork Orange*. Alex recognizes that the state, the "not-self," attempts to impose goodness from without, thus denying man his own moral choice: "But the not-self cannot have the bad, meaning they of the government and the judges and the schools cannot allow the bad because they cannot allow the self."[24] When Alex chooses to let the state condition him to act only in a good way he is asked by the prison chaplain: "What does God want? Does God want goodness or the choice of goodness? Is a man who chooses the bad perhaps in some way better than a man who has the good imposed on him?"[25] The Neanderthals have no choice, are not aware of good and evil existing as a dichotomy (that is a human rationalization) and cannot therefore be defined as innocent. *The Inheritors* raises far more complex moral issues than easy categorizations will allow.

We do not condone the new people killing the Neanderthals, but when we see how they appear to the new people we can understand their actions — and this understanding is a possession the Neanderthals do not have. In a desperate attempt at exorcism Tuami draws a representation of the Neanderthals: "This figure was red, with enormous spreading arms and legs and the face glared up at him for the eyes were white pebbles. The hair stood out round the head as though the figure were in the act of some frantic cruelty" (p. 199). The picture is frightening and reveals that the new people act as they do from blind terror. There is no malevolence behind their actions, only fear. One of the new people tries to describe the Neanderthals to his friends: "He crawled like a snake, he went to the wreck of the caves; he stood; he came back to the fire snapping like a wolf so that the people shrank from him. He pointed; he created a running, crouching thing, his arms flapped like the wings of a bird" (p. 187). This mime bears a striking resemblance to Wells's description of Neanderthal man: "It was running across an open space, running almost on all fours, in joltering leaps. It was hunchbacked and very big and low, a grey hairy wolf-like monster. At times its long arms nearly touched the ground."[26] The move into the third-person narrative serves to support the homo sapiens's view of the Neanderthals. Golding's claim that man was simply externalizing his own darkness does not seem particularly valid here. The new people are not frightened of nothing — that is Fa's terrible misunderstanding: "They are frightened of the air where there is nothing" (p. 206). The new people are frightened of the red creatures in the shadows of the forest. They do not need to externalize their fear: the Neanderthals are there for them to be afraid of. When we move into the point of view of the new people we see that the red creature is regarded as a red devil driving man away from the security of the island to the wilds of the plains. If we sympathize, it must be with the terrified human beings rather than with the non-human red creatures. After all, homo sapiens are the inheritors referred to in the title of the book, and our last glimpse of the new people is of their sailing away into modernity. *The Inheritors* is about man and not about Neanderthals.

We could claim that in *The Inheritors* Golding is deliberately making us read from the wrong point of view, from the non-human perspective, for most of the novel. We need only consider how different a book it would be if everything was presented from Tuami's point of view. And yet Tuami's point of view must be our point of view. Golding presents two hundred and sixteen pages of the novel from the Neanderthal perspective in order to explain Tuami's perspective in the final chapter. Without those two hundred-odd pages we couldn't adequately understand why he and the homo sapiens act and think as they do. Only by seeing ourselves through other eyes — the eyes of Lok with his vision translated into human language — can we understand ourselves. And we do understand Tuami's point of view while Lok is still uncomprehending when he lays down to die. *The Inheritors* sets out to make us understand the human point of view and it achieves its aim perfectly through some craftsman-like handling of narrative perspective.

The third-person narrator coincides with the reader in that he, too, is the inheritor of the situation the novel depicts. After Tuami and Marlan, we are the inheritors of the world, trapped within our language perhaps, but capable of rationalizing and of making moral choices. And, as Golding has said, it's this that makes us human: "Our humanity rests in the capacity to make value judgements . . . the power to decide that this is right, that wrong, this ugly, that beautiful, this just, that unjust."[27] We inherit the new peoples' point of view, and to that extent the book is also about us — the inheritors of their world, not Lok's world. Whatever his world was, it was other than ours. Our humanity is founded upon this point of view, and it is our humanity that *The Inheritors* helps us to understand.

Notes

1. William Golding, "In My Ark," *The Hot Gates* (London: Faber and Faber, 1965), 103.

2. William Golding, *The Inheritors* (London: Faber and Faber, 1955), 196; hereafter cited in the text.

3. Howard S. Babb, *The Novels of William Golding* (Columbus: Ohio State University Press, 1970), 37.

4. Craig Raine, "Belly without Blemish: Golding's Sources," in *William Golding: The Man and his Books*, ed. John Carey (London: Faber and Faber, 1986), 108.

5. Barbara Everett, "Golding's Pity," in *William Golding: The Man and his Books*, 115.

6. Philippa Tristram, "Golding and the Language of Caliban," in *William Golding: Some Critical Considerations*, ed. Jack I. Biles and Robert O. Evans (Lexington: University of Kentucky Press, 1978), 42.

7. Ted E. Boyle, "Golding's Existential Vision," in *William Golding: Some Critical Considerations*, 25.

8. Gabriel Josipovici, *The World and the Book*, 2d ed. (London: Macmillan, 1979), 252.

9. William Golding, *The Pyramid* (London: Faber and Faber, 1967), 212.

10. Golding to John Carey, "William Golding talks to John Carey," in *William Golding: The Man and his Books*, 173.

11. Golding, "In My Ark," 103.

12. Ludwig Wittgenstein, *Tractatus Logico-Philosophicus*, trans. D. F. Pears and B. F. McGuinness (1921; London: Routledge and Kegan Paul, 1978), 57.

13. Golding to Frank Kermode, "The Meaning of it All," *Books and Bookmen* (October 1959): 10.

14. William Golding, *Lord of the Flies* (London: Faber and Faber, 1954), 173.

15. H. G. Wells, "The Grisly Folk," *Selected Short Stories* (Harmondsworth: Penguin, 1981), 289.

16. Joseph Conrad, *Heart of Darkness* (1902; Harmondsworth: Penguin, 1977), 64.

17. Samuel Hynes, *William Golding* (London: Columbia University Press, 1964), 22.

18. Paul Elman, *William Golding: A Critical Essay* (Michigan: William B. Eerdmans, 1967), 24.

19. Arnold Johnston, *Of Earth and Darkness: The Novels of William Golding* (London: University of Missouri Press, 1980), 28.

20. Frank Kermode, "William Golding," *Puzzles and Epiphanies* (London: Routledge and Kegan Paul, 1962), 206.

21. Golding, "Copernicus," *The Hot Gates*, 31.

22. William Golding, Introduction to *The Brass Butterfly*, quoted in Leighton Hodson, *William Golding* (Edinburgh: Oliver and Boyd, 1969), 102.

23. William Golding, "Utopias and Antiutopias," *A Moving Target* (London: Faber and Faber, 1982), 178.

24. Anthony Burgess, *A Clockwork Orange* (1962; Harmondsworth: Penguin, 1984), 34.

25. Ibid., 76.

26. Wells, "The Grisly Folk," 292.

27. Golding, "On the Crest of the Wave," *The Hot Gates*, 130.

The Moment out of Time: Golding's *Pincher Martin*

Lee M. Whitehead*

In *Pincher Martin* William Golding employed a kind of "phenomenological reduction" or "bracketing," a technique that focuses attention upon some entity in order to understand it without inquiring at every point: "But is this real?" It puts "vulgar conceptions" about the reality of the world in "brackets," as in mathematics one might put a quantity in

*This essay first appeared in *Contemporary Literature* 12 (Winter 1971) and is reprinted with the permission of the University of Wisconsin Press.

parenthesis which for the moment it would be distracting to pursue. With an imaginary object, such as a poem, it is very like Coleridge's "suspension of disbelief." When trying to understand what a poet has done we do not ask ourselves whether we believe in the reality (or relevance) of what he has made, although these are not unimportant questions in themselves and clearly belong to the equation. If we let questions of this nature intrude prior to *having seen the poem* we are apt not to see it at all; as soon as we let questions of reality or belief enter, we are flooded with a multitude of stereotypes and prejudices that intrude upon and usurp our perception.

By having his protagonist die on the first page, Golding brackets the "vulgar conception of time." Christopher Hadley Martin's body is left to drift on the waves towards its disturbing rendezvous with Mr. Campbell and Davidson on a lonely island presumably in the Hebrides while a quite different world from the one he had lived in unfolds, questions about the "reality" of which are irrelevant. The reader, however, does not know that the world of the dead body and Mr. Campbell and Davidson has been bracketed until the last sentence of the novel; thus his imaginative sympathies and repugnances are brought into play and are themselves an object of attention when the reader is suddenly forced by the last sentence to look back with new eyes at the imaginative experience that has engaged him.

What this other world is I hesitate to say. The terms "soul" or "spirit" would be appropriate, but they bring too much baggage with them and might tempt us to see the novel as a Christian allegory of some kind. On the other hand, it is not simply the world of subjectivity as opposed to the objective world, although again such a distinction, as that between spirit and body, would at least be generally accurate. "Mind" or "psyche" as opposed to body again are not quite sufficient. The distinction that seems appropriate to my mind is the one that the phenomenologists make between the intending consciousness and the intended world, or the kindred distinction of the existentialists between the "nothingness" that is the human consciousness and the "things" of the world which it constitutes in imaginative acts. I suggest this, knowing that Golding has rejected the imputation that he has been influenced by existentialism.

Golding's peculiar method focuses for our attention the "intending" power of a human consciousness, the nature of which can be more clearly seen since we do not have to bother ourselves about difficult epistemological and metaphysical questions such as whether or not the world so intended is an illusion. I am confident that for Golding the "real world" is as much a matter of measurable time and space, of "hard facts" such as war and rape and love and the reality of others, as it is for any of his readers, but the "other world" in *Pincher Martin* is a world in which space can collapse and blow away like a dead leaf and in which what seems like several days of agony occur in the dimensionless instant of death, a world where hard facts go limp — such as the fact that rocky islands do not move, that guano is insoluble, or that lobsters are not red until they are prepared for eating.

Golding's name for whatever it is that creates this world in the instant of death, rather than spirit, or soul, or subjectivity, is simply "the centre," a neutral word that parallels in spatial terms the temporal instant of death; the center of, say, a wheel, is a dimensionless point, a mathematical limit like the notion of infinity. From this point without dimension at this moment without dimension, a second life and a second death for Christopher Hadley Martin are created, and the shape they take reveals the gross shape that the center had created for itself in order to live in the world of space and time that it has just lost. It is as if, to use Golding's metaphor, it had created an armored shape like a lobster's shell of time and space in order to resist the crushing pressure of infinity and eternity, but the armor is stripped away at the moment of death; the full crushing weight of all it had resisted bears inexorably down upon it and will, in its "compassion . . . without mercy,"[1] at some timeless, dimensionless point, utterly absorb it.

The world thus bracketed, questions of fact, time, and space thus irrelevant, the novel can focus upon "the centre," and since all human perception is in terms of contrast, what is revealed about the center lies in the contrast between the world it creates and the "thing that created it." It is tempting to use the term "God" for the latter, but "God" raises theological questions that are possibly misleading. Golding does not call it God; he describes it, however, as the "black lightning" — a term I will use to avoid unnecessary confusion. We can see what the center *is* by seeing what it *does* against the background of the black lightning. Simply to see it *doing* sets off the contrast, for the black lightning does nothing; it is absolute, without limits, infinite, and, finally, ineluctable. It has simply to wait, for which it has an infinite capacity; the center must busily *do* in order to maintain a precarious identity. The black lightning, "the ultimate truth of things," is a "positive, unquestionable nothingness" (p. 91). All the doing of the center is assertion, creation, which, by the inner logic of its mode of being, leads inevitably to its own negation.

The primary metaphor for the activity of the center is "eating." Christopher Hadley Martin — nicknamed "Pincher" Martin by the men below decks — is the identity that the center seeks to maintain. He must eat to live, and we find him accordingly forcing down by an act of will the unpalatable anemones and mussels he finds on his rock. Even he comes to see this as the paradigm of the way he had lived in the world: "The whole business of eating was peculiarly significant. . . . And of course eating with the mouth was only the gross expression of what was a universal process. You could eat with your cock or with your fists, or with your voice. You could eat with hobnailed boots or buying and selling or marrying and begetting or cuckolding . . ." (p. 88).

He was led to this insight by the following associations, which I will trace backwards: eating — toothbrush — bathroom — the sluggishness of his bowels, which he had forgotten — an imagined injunction to his men to "remember . . ." — the pride of being a "Brass Hat" in the British navy (p. 88). Eating is thus associated with pride and domination over others (as well as with defecation). Elsewhere we find him thinking of the others in his life as people he has used as he used the limpets to climb up Safety Rock — things to be used in one's climb to the top. The lobster claws that his hands become are an extension of this phenomenon. The struggle of life is epitomized by the maggots in the chinese box which, having eaten the fish, eat one another until there is only one large maggot left. But life as a process of eating and using others carries with it the possibility of being eaten and used by others; at several points Christopher's realization that he has been used by others is underlined by his exclamation, "Eaten!"

Appropriately, the island which suggests the secure rock of his identity appears to him as an immense tooth: "A single point of rock, peak of a mountain range, one tooth set in the ancient jaw of a sunken world . . ." (p. 30), and, towards the end, as the center begins to realize how insecure this self-created identity is, he discovers that the tooth upon which he rests is a projection of his own lost tooth: "His tongue felt along the barrier of his teeth — round to the side where the big ones were and the gap. . . . His tongue was remembering. It pried into the gap between the teeth and re-created the old, aching shape. It touched the rough edge of the cliff, traced the slope down, trench after aching trench, down towards the smooth surface where the Red Lion was, just above the gum — understood what was so hauntingly familiar and painful about an isolated and decaying rock in the middle of the sea" (p. 174). This passage suggests that Christopher has completed his life of eating by eating himself; i.e., the mode by which he creates and maintains his identity ends by negating itself. The grasping, clutching claws remain at the end clutching nothing but themselves. It will be noted also that the island was created out of the memory of a missing tooth; in other words, this island out of time and space was created by the center from a gap, an absence. Furthermore, it was created from a memory of pain, as if pain were somehow necessarily and essentially a quality of the world conjured up by the center.

The self-negating movement of his other ways of asserting his existence runs parallel to the way in which the eater ends by eating himself. Education and intelligence, Martin feels, are the unique human qualities that will aid him in his struggle for survival and, remembering that "speech was proof of identity" ("so long as I can tell myself that I am alone on a rock in the middle of the Atlantic and that I have to fight to survive — then I can manage," p. 84), he tries to appropriate and fix his identity by tying down the rock with names: "I am busy surviving. I am netting down this rock with names and taming it. . . . What is given a name is given a seal, a chain. . . . I will impose my routine on it, my geography" (pp. 86–87). The net suggests the pattern which begins to emerge as his education (he has learned, for example, that guano is insoluble) and intelligence makes him more and more aware of the unreality of the island he has created: the rock is harder than it should be, the rainwater in the guano-filled trench could not have stung his eye because guano does not dissolve; he could not have seen a red lobster in the real world because lobsters do not turn red until cooked.

The center tries desperately to reject or ignore its knowledge of the emerging pattern and, finally, attempts to abandon intelligence by pretending that it has gone mad. But it is not mad and its intelligence cannot be abandoned. It realizes that "there is no centre of sanity in madness. Nothing like this 'I' sitting in here, staving off the time that must come. The last repeat of the pattern. Then the black lightning" (p. 181). The pattern emerging is the full realization of what he is; the realization of the pattern brings with it the realization that the black lightning will destroy and absorb it. "Because of what I did," the center continues, thinking, "I am an outsider and alone."

"Because of what I did" refers specifically to particular acts he has remembered of using others — forcing his sexual advance upon Mary, seducing the Producer's wife in order to get the roles he wanted, attempting to murder Nathaniel to have Mary to himself, etc. — but it refers also to all the acts of "doing" by which the center had created the identity of Christopher Hadley Martin. Appropriately Christopher was an actor in civilian life — and an author, a manipulator of words. But he was not just an actor by profession; he "put on an act" in all of his relationships as a means of manipulating others. He pretends that he will kill them both if Mary will not yield to his advances; he pretends passion for Helen when he wants her to persuade her husband to keep him out of the military service; he pretends he had not "zigged" the ship at the proper moment because he was trying to avoid floating debris when the truth was that in his concentration of hatred upon Nathaniel he had simply forgotten his duty. Even his last act aboard ship is the culmination of an elaborate drama by which he intended to throw Nathaniel off his precarious perch to drown in the sea. Ironically, his unscheduled order to "zag" the ship was the right order in more ways than one; his last act in the real world brings him face to face with himself upon his self-created island. The last act of the center there is its pretense of madness. Having seen itself in the tragic roles of Hamlet and Ajax and Prometheus, it now tries "poor Tom" and mad Lear upon the heath. But the act collapses, as we have seen, when the center realizes that all its acting and doing can provide no armor against the weight of the heavens and he is brought face to face with the black lightning.

The cuckolded director had seen how much of Christopher's identity was bound up in the masks he put on before others. Trying to select a mask for Christopher to use in a morality play, the director asks a friend, "What about Pride, George? He could play that without a mask and just stylized make-up, couldn't he?" (p. 119). But he settles on Greed and introduces Christopher to the mask: "Let me make you two better acquainted. This painted bastard here takes anything he can lay his hands on. Not food, Chris, that's far too simple. He takes the best part, the best seat, the most money, the best notice, the best woman. He was born with his mouth and his flies open and both hands out to grab." Then, with a thrust home, he addresses the mask: "Think you can play Martin, Greed?" (p. 120). It is as if he had waved aside Christopher Hadley Martin to address the center, and this suggests the way in which its acting will lead finally to the stripping away of all masks.

Before the black lightning finally strikes, however, the center has begun to recognize in itself something beyond the greed, something enduring, timeless, and solid, something that does not negate itself and stands out in contrast to the eating, using, and acting by which the center attempted to assert an identity. Intimations of this come like a flood upon Christopher when he remembers the Captain's reaction to his lie about the supposed wreckage that prevented his scheduled "zig." The Captain's face "changed, not dramatically, not registering, not making obvious, but changing like a Nat-face, from within" (p. 102). The Captain does not pretend; the contempt and disbelief on his face are a direct expression of the center within. Immediately afterwards, as Christopher looks upside down under his arm at Nathaniel, the center has a further illumination: "The centre, looking in this reversed world over the binnacle, found itself beset by a storm of emotions, acid and inky and cruel. There was a desperate amazement that anyone so good as Nat, so unwillingly loved for the face that was always rearranged from within, for the serious attention, for love given without thought, should also be so quiveringly hated as though he were the only enemy. There was amazement that to love and to hate were now one thing and one emotion" (p. 103). It is indeed a reversed world from the one Christopher has been living in, a reversal that portends the absorption of that world by the black lightning. For the unwilling love that is the reverse side of the hate he feels for Nat is a crack in his carefully made identity. The hate itself is a tie that links them and thus demonstrates that Christopher's world is not wholly self-contained. Christopher's obsession for Mary is similar: "Ever since I met her and she interrupted the pattern coming at random, obeying no law of life, facing me with the insoluble, unbearable problem of her existence the acid's been chewing my guts. I can't even kill her because that would be final victory over me. Yet as long as she lives the acid will eat. She's there. In the flesh. In the not even lovely flesh. In the cheap mind. Obsession. Not love. Or if love, insanely compounded of this jealousy of her very being. *Odi et amo*" (pp. 103–104).

For Mary, unlike the Captain or Nathaniel, it is her eyes rather than her face that are the windows to her center. Christopher had managed finally to excite her sexual passion, which is evident to him by the flush on her cheekbones, "but the eyes—they had nothing in common with the mask of flesh that nature had fixed on what must surely be a real and invisible face" (p. 148). It is her eyes, rather than her excited body, that make her for Christopher "a madness, not so much in the loins as in the pride" (p. 148). He must humble her, engorge her defiant otherness, because her very existence as something unattainable to him threatens his identity. But even though he might touch and excite her body, her center, her otherness has not been touched: "Then the summer lightning over a white face with, staring eyes only a few inches away two eyes of the artificial woman, confounded in her pretences and evasion, forced to admit her own crude, human body—eyes staring now in deep and implacable hate" (p. 152). Rather than his possessing her, Christopher finds that even though "the only real feeling [he has] for her is hate," she holds "the centre of [his] darkness" (p. 149). He is eaten, rather than eating. And Nathaniel shares with her, as Christopher discovers, "the lighted centre of [his] darkness" (p. 158).

He finds himself alone not because he is alone but because the acts by which he has asserted his identity have thrown up a net or a screen between his identity and his real center—which is, willy-nilly, populated by others. They are there by virtue of the otherness that negates the pretenses of his "I" to be absolute. He will not accept the need to be eaten as the necessary fulfillment and culmination of the need to eat.

Mary's surname, Lovell, had threatened Christopher; it "forced him to a reference book lest it should wind back to some distinction that would set her even more firmly at the centre than she was" (p. 149). By discovering an etymology, a past, for her name, Christopher hopes to objectify it and thus remove the latent danger of its symbolic and timeless meaning to his identity. It stands by the association of sounds at the opposite pole from the island the center has created in the image of its mode of living. That the island that Christopher thinks he is isolated upon is Rockall, the remote and lonely rock belonging to England in the North Atlantic, is, I think, clear from the passage in which Christopher remembers its name on the chart, but the Captain's unexpressed name for it, for which "Rockall" is a "near miss," is more appropriately expressive for the island the center has created:

> That name was written on the chart, well out in the Atlantic, eccentrically isolated so that seamen who could to a certain extent laugh at wind and weather had made a joke of the rock. . . . The captain spoke with his clipped Dartmouth accent—spoke and laughed.
> "I call that name a near miss." (p. 31)

What "Rockall" just misses being is "Fuckall," an emphatic term used by seamen and others to mean "nothing at all."

Lovell—love all—versus Fuckall, a plentitude versus a total nothingness, the genuine article versus its obscene reduction, are the two poles that meet at the center. Christopher's mode of life has been an obscenity; his death is its purge. If the primary metaphor of his mode of life is eating, the primary metaphor for "the technique of dying," as Nathaniel calls it, from Christopher's world is elimination. Eating and defecating, as we saw earlier, are associated in Christopher's mind with pride and survival. He tries to blame the discrepancies he has begun to see in his world upon sickness; it is because of something he has eaten and he is all "bound" up — he has not had a "crap" since coming to the island. "I am poisoned. I am in servitude to a coiled tube the length of a cricket pitch. All the terrors of hell can come down to nothing more than a stoppage. Why drag in good and evil when the serpent lies coiled in my own body?" (p. 163). He acts — with "intelligence and education" — to defeat this serpent, thinking that if he can eliminate the poison he will be able to maintain his identity, but, again, his action brings its own negation. In a pool of water that, in an effort to establish his identity, he had used as a mirror (where his face should have been he saw "nothing but a patch of darkness with the wild outline of hair round the edge" [p. 133]; that is, the darkness of his true identity although he does not see it at this point), there is a tiny fish. Later, when he fills his life belt with water from the pool preparatory to using it for an enema, the tiny fish is left high and dry and dies (pp. 164–165). This fish that had inhabited Christopher's mirror symbolizes the way of purgation, although the center, which has created the symbol, does not choose to recognize its meaning. The fish, thrust out of its proper element (as Christopher had been by being blasted into the sea), died — and is fed by Christopher to an anemone — because its water has been used for purgative purposes. Death is the purgation of the obscenity that life has been. The last act of the body at death, I believe, is the voiding of the bowels — which is, in effect, a purging from the body of the things it has eaten. In this light the last act of the center, hurling an obscenity at the heaven of the black lightning — "I shit on your heaven!" — can be seen as both a final assertion of identity in opposition to the compassionate promise of nonidentity and as a self-purifying act in preparation for his spiritual death. And we are justified in believing that, although the center may desperately maintain its claws clenched into each other for an eternity as its final assertion of self against the black lightning, the black lightning, which endures for an eternity of eternities, will outlast it. The center both is damned to an eternal hell of its own making and will at some timeless moment be saved by the "compassion that was timeless and without mercy" (p. 201).

The burning desire for life signified by eating is also purged by the renunciation of desire signified by a willingness to be eaten. Although it had earlier thought of fishing for food as a change from the bilious diet of anemones and mussels, the center did not recognize the little fish as food; its death is a promise of peace beyond the living process of eating and being eaten.

I have not emphasized the overtones of Christian symbolism in the novel, which are many and profound (e.g., Christopher is the "Christ-bearer," his fall into the destroying water is both a baptism and a "fortunate fall," his island-mountain is a self-created mount purgatory, the fish that swims in the dark center's mirrored identity carries overtones of the ancient life-symbol appropriated by the early Christians as their own symbol, etc.), partly because they are relatively obvious, partly because these have been dealt with at length by others, but primarily because I want to avoid the overemphasis of them that would in my view cloud perception of the novel.

I do not know what Golding's "official beliefs" are and I do not feel any need to know. Mr. Campbell's comment, as he asks Davidson, who has come to collect Christopher's still seabooted body from the lonely island in the Hebrides whether he would say there was any "surviving," effectively disconnects the relevance of Golding's official beliefs: "You know nothing of my — shall I say — official beliefs, Mr. Davidson"; "we are the type of human intercourse" (pp. 208, 207). The type of human intercourse is not that among people who share systems of meaning completely; rather, it is the chance and unpredictable encounter between strangers who attempt to communicate across the gap of otherness. Thus the beliefs that each has do not themselves matter; what matters is the attempt at communication. We do not communicate with those we reject as fitting some convenient pigeonhole because of their beliefs.

When Davidson replies to Campbell's question it is with a question of his own: "If you're worried about Martin — whether he suffered or not — ." After a long pause Mr. Campbell sighed, " 'Aye,' he said, 'I meant just that' " (p. 208). It is not exactly what he meant. His question was more metaphysical; he was profoundly troubled by the question of whether there was something that inhabited the body as a man inhabits a dwelling place ("Broken, defiled. Returning to the earth, the rafters rotted, the roof fallen in — a wreck. Would you believe that anything ever lived there?" — p. 207), or as the soft body of the lobster inhabits its armor against the pressure of existence. Davidson's question, on the other hand, is rational, empirical. Did he suffer? Both are profoundly disturbed by the decaying body but for quite different reasons. Campbell's soul is tormented, but Davidson's flesh is made to crawl by his imaginative sympathy with the drowning man. Yet in spite of the gap between them, they have communicated something important — not concern for themselves, although that is certainly there, but fellow-feeling, sympathy, an awareness of shared life beyond the bounds of the individual self. The lifeless body is the symbol — even the host — by which they communicate.

Even though the metaphor I just used suggests a Christian interpretation of the novel, I do not, nevertheless, think its vision is essentially or peculiarly Christian. For instance, in *The Masks of God*, Joseph Campbell draws a number of interesting distinctions between the Indian and the

Judaeo-Christian religions which suggest that *Pincher Martin* might be interpreted in quite other terms. In the Indian version of creation,

> it is the god himself that divides and becomes not man alone but all creation. . . ; whereas in the Bible, God and man, from the beginning, are distinct. . . . Moreover, according to the biblical version of this myth, it was only after creation that man fell, whereas in the Indian example creation itself was a fall—the fragmentation of a god. . . . The fall of Adam and Eve was an event within the already created frame of time and space, an accident that should not have taken place. The myth of the Self in the form of a man, on the other hand, who looked around and saw nothing but himself, said "I," felt fear, and then desired to be two, tells of an intrinsic, not errant, factor in the manifold of being, the correction or undoing of which would not improve, but dissolve, creation.[2]

In *Pincher Martin* the center, having been created by a separation from the "positive nothingness" in its image, creates the manifold world of space and time which dissolves when it is "undone" and returns to that from which it separated. Although it tried to continue to assert an independent identity, when it comes to the point of dying it "began to know itself as other" (p. 194)—as other than the world of time and space within which its identity had been created. It suddenly confronts the god of its own making ("there was awe in the trench"—p. 194); it is the dead body of Christopher Hadley Martin with its seaboots still on. Deluded still, however, the center quacks: "On the sixth day he created God. . . . In his own image created he Him." But at this point Christopher's body begins to merge with the stormy sky portending lightning behind him—his bloodshot eye "and the sunset merge" (p. 196)—and the truth of the center's claim to have created on this sixth day of his imaginary island God in his own image becomes apparent. He has reversed the process of genesis and is creating God in his own image truly, for as was intimated when he tried to find his own image in the pool of water, his true image is nothingness. It is to be hoped that he will be able to rest from his labors on the seventh day. The god he creates is the god who created him—the black lightning, the positive nothingness. When the process is completed, when the black lightning finds the moment outside of time at which it can pierce the center, creation will be dissolved.

The black lightning which divided to create the unexamined center might well have sung this early Vedic-Upanishadic hymn:

> Oh, wonderful! Oh, wonderful! Oh, wonderful!
> I am food! I am food! I am food!
> I am a food-eater! I am a food-eater! I am a food-eater!
> I am a fame-maker! I am a fame-maker! I am a fame-maker!
> I am the first-born of the world-order,
> Antecedent to the gods, in the navel of immortality!
> Who gives me away, he indeed had aided me!

I, who am food, eat the eater of food!
I have overcome the whole world![3]

I do not offer this as an Indian interpretation of *Pincher Martin*; I offer it only to show similarities of conception. The Judaeo-Christian conceptions outlined by Campbell of the relation of God to man and the Fall could be justified as well by the language of the novel. It is not a case of either/or.

James R. Baker, in his study of Golding, appears to agree with this opinion when, after having shown that "the basic and structural metaphor in *Pincher Martin* depends upon the account of the Creation in the Book of Genesis," he says that nevertheless "there is no risk in asserting that Golding's beleaguered castaways suffer and die in a universe which is more pagan than Christian" and points out that Golding draws upon both traditions "in an effort to define the realities of his cosmos."[4] Earlier, in a footnote he suggested that comparison by critics of Golding to existentialists and to Conrad "are not very convincing. Further scholarly effort is needed, but it is likely to end by tracing the relationships between Greek tragedy and modern existentialism."[5] I agree wholeheartedly with this view (but I might add that I think that Golding is closer to Conrad than to any other English novelist and that I think is a profound relation between Conrad's fiction and both Greek tragedy and existentialism). I am not going to offer in full the "further scholarly effort" Baker asked for, but I will offer a few suggestions that I think are relevant about the relation of *Pincher Martin* to the Greek tragic sense of life and to the existentialism of Jean-Paul Sartre.

In the first place the Greek notion of the relation of the individual soul to the universe (or to God, or Being) that underlies tragedy is closer in some ways to that of Hinduism than it is to that of the Book of Genesis. (Indeed, objections to the notion that tragedy is possible in Christian terms are usually based upon variations of the view that the fate of man as the creation of a transcendent being is not truly tragic.) F. M. Cornford, in fact, points out exact parallels between Greek and Indian conceptions of the relations between the individual one to the universal One: "The case of the Indian âtman appears to be exactly parallel to that of *physis* and the individual soul in Greece. The oldest Upanishads recognize only one soul: "It is thy soul, which is within all. . . . This âtman who alone exists in the knowing subject in us . . . and with knowledge of the âtman, therefore, all is known. . . . The âtman created the universe and then entered into it as soul. . . ."[6]

Such a view is not in itself tragic, however. In the Indian conception, the uniqueness of the particular existence of an individual life is not important because the individual self undergoes continual transmigration from one existence to another. But when the uniqueness of the existence of the individual is itself valued as it was by the Greeks and yet at the same time felt to be integrally part of the all, whose perceptible form as the *physis* was the eternally returning cyclic order of nature, its fate becomes tragic. The tragic nature of the fate of the individual man as these Greeks felt it is indicated by the images Cornford uses to describe the notions of two pre-Socratic philosophers about the condition of the individual soul in relation to the *physis*: first, Heraclitus, who, as Cornford says, "goes back to the older notion of the one continuous and homogeneous Soul, or Life, in all things—a perennial stream, *on whose surface individual forms are mere momentary bubbles*, bursting and leaving no trace of their transient existence" (italics mine);[7] the second, Anaximander: "Onwards from Anaximander, who declares that all that comes into being *must pay the penalty of injustice by perishing again, according to the order of time . . .* and the ordinance of destiny, Greek philosophers are haunted by the idea of the periodic growth, culmination, and destruction of the world and all that it contains" (italics before the comma mine).[8]

The life of the individual soul (or consciousness, or "center") by coming into existence creates a gap in the order of things. The image is that of a crime against the One, the *physis*, for which the penalty is death. In relation to all that is, consciousness is nothing, an emptiness, a negation—like a bubble (here one could begin to draw parallels with Sartre's existentialism; Sartre's metaphor for consciousness is that "it is like a hole of being at the heart of Being"). It is "other than" the plenum of being, and by willing to remain an emptiness in the face of being, which it does as long as it wills to live, it commits the sin of pride, or *hubris*. Individual existence for these Greeks, as it was for the Indian, is a fall, but for the Greeks a tragic fall. Existence as a willing individual soul is predicated upon the crime of eating,[9] but as one who is also "eaten" one "pays the penalty" for the crime of existence. "Justice is not the separation of opposites, but their meeting in attunement or 'harmony.' "[10]

According to Susanne Langer's analysis in *Feeling and Form* of the comic and the tragic rhythm, our sense of participation in the process of life that transcends the individual—as the life of the species transcends the life of individual members of the species—underlies the comic rhythm. Our sense of our own unique individual life within the bubble that must burst underlies the tragic: "[Tragedy] reveals the patterns of possible sentience, vitality, and mentality, objectifying our subjective being—the most intimate "Reality" that we know. . . . the big unfolding of feeling in the organic, personal pattern of a human life, rising, growing, accomplishing destiny and meeting doom—that is tragedy."[11] The "harvest of tragedy," according to Alfred North Whitehead in *Adventures of Ideas*, is that "the suffering attains its end in a Harmony of Harmonies," the immediate experience of which is "the sense of Peace."[12]

There is much in this, I believe, that illuminates Golding's *Pincher Martin*. One of the achievements of this book is its relation of Christian symbols of man's fate to a vision similar to that of Greek tragedy. Christopher's body, the lobster's armor, and the ruined and empty structure of man's habitation, the hut, are symbols equivalent to Heraclitus' bubble. What dwelt within them had been separated from Being, but, when they burst, is reunited. Its very suffering, the acid of its existence within which it seemed to float, leads first to the creation of a world, but, as we have seen, it leads then in time to its own dissolution; outside the bubble lies the compassionate justice of the black lightning.

The center's choice of pain, its choice to create its own hell, gives it a tragic dimension that is linked, as Oldsey and Weintraub have pointed out,[13] to Satan's assertion in *Paradise Lost* that "The mind is its own place, and in itself / Can make a Heaven of Hell, a Hell of Heaven." Their book is devoted primarily to tracing some of the rich texture of allusion or analogue in Golding's work, but while much is useful they have in the case of *Pincher Martin* at least missed a number of relevant allusions,[14] and even what they do point out is not satisfactorily explained; little is done to show the way in which the allusions or analogues work in the novels. Something very important might have been made, for instance, of the way in which Golding treats not Milton's Satan but the Romantic attitude towards his stance. The Romantic affirmation of the will that could see in Satan's attitude toward God promethean qualities (we think of Shelley and Blake) is neatly, even hilariously, qualified by the Romantic music that accompanies Christopher's purging enema:

> "I am Atlas. I am Prometheus."
> He felt himself loom, gigantic on the rock. His jaws clenched, his chin sank. He became a hero for whom the impossible was an achievement. . . . He crawled on down towards the Red Lion and now there was background music, snatches of Tchaikovsky, Wagner, Holst. It was not really necessary to crawl but the background music underlined the heroism of a slow, undefeated advance against odds.

Administering the cleansing waters, he

> crept carefully to the edge of the rock while the orchestra thundered to a pause.
> And the cadenza was coming—did come. It performed with explosive and triumphant completeness of technique into the sea. It was like the bursting of a dam, the smashing of all hindrance. Spasm after spasm with massive chords and sparkling arpeggios, the cadenza *took of his strength* till he lay straining and empty on the rock and the orchestra had gone. (pp. 164–165; my italics)

At this moment, when the strength of will that had possessed him is purged, he sees that the little fish is dead.

The Romantic will with its accompanying embodiment in the music of Tchaikovsky, Wagner, and Holst, reaches its apotheosis in an act of defecation. Melville's Ahab or Byron himself might well have shouted, "I shit on your heaven!" Implicit in the Romantic assertion of the will is its own purgation.

There are other echoes. The Romantic assertion is a choice of pain and suffering as an alternative to nothingness. We might be reminded of Conrad's "excessively romantic" dreamer, Jim, who as a boy, his untested imagination stimulated by a diet of "light holiday literature," dreamed of heroic existence "as a lonely castaway, barefooted and half naked, walking on uncovered reefs in search of shellfish to stave off starvation. . . ."[15] Golding testified to a similar gusto for the extreme when as a boy he had read the novels of Jules Verne: "They held me rapt, I dived with the *Nautilus*, was shot round the moon, crossed Darkest Africa in a balloon, descended to the centre of the earth, drifted in the South Atlantic, dying of thirst, and tasted — oh rapture!"[16] But such reactions "require an innocence of approach which, while it is natural enough to a child, would be a mark of puerility in an adult." What the child misses "is the fact that Verne was a heavy-handed satirist." This is perhaps true enough and there is certainly an element of satire in Golding's treatment of the Romantic desire for extremity, but his evocation of this childhood dream in *Pincher Martin* is not simply satirical. It is also a revelation of the nature of the imagination that creates such visions. Like Christopher Martin, Lord Jim discovered an isolated place where, by "the pure exercise of the imagination," he too could create his own *purgatorio*. The imagination and the will are intimately related for the Romantic; by its assertion in acts of the imagination the will enjoys the pain that makes it know its existence. ("What is it," Stein asks Captain Marlow in *Lord Jim* when he defines Jim's romanticism, "that by inward pain makes him know himself? What is it that for you and me makes him — exist?")[17] The Romantic dream of extremity (which often assumed the shape of isolation upon a desolate island) is thus symbolic of the will's desire to know itself and its relation to all that lies beyond its extremities. It felt that by thrusting itself against the painful barriers of the human condition it might get some glimpse of what lies beyond, an imagination of the unimaginable.

The point will be perhaps clearer if we look for a moment at a Romantic novel that inspired Jules Verne to write a sequel to it, Edgar Allan Poe's *The Narrative of Arthur Gordon Pym*.[18] Young Pym was a boy much as Conrad's Jim and Golding himself had been: regaled by an older seaman with tales of life at sea, Pym narrates: "he most strangely enlisted my feeling in behalf of the life of a seaman, when he depicted his more terrible moments of suffering and despair. For the bright side of the painting I had a limited sympathy. My visions were of shipwreck and famine; of death or captivity among barbarian hordes; of a lifetime dragged out in sorrow and tears, upon some gray and desolate rock, in an ocean unapproachable and unknown."[19]

Pym and his symbolically dark companion, Peters, a kind of alter ego, are marooned upon a black island near the South Pole after a long and terrible journey through and beyond the world of normal expectations as it is shared by others, past islands upon which the precisely geometrical arrangements of birds' nests seem a parody of the rational powers of man.

The black island upon which they are marooned is totally symbolic; in its features Pym's terrors, perverse desires, and perplexities about existence take shape. The black natives — black even to their teeth and eyes — cannot be communicated with; Pym and Peters are buried alive; Pym yields to his perverse yearning to fall, but is saved by Peters and feels "a new being," as if he had been reborn.[20] The enigma of existence is reflected in enigmatic engravings upon the surface of the island (Christopher finds enigmatic engravings upon the rocks of his island that are strangely reminiscent of Pym's). Some of these engravings, as a note by Pym's editor suggests, seem to indicate that the way out of the blackness (and the mystery and terror of the world as it is created by the imagination) lies towards the South. This is the direction Pym and his companion unwittingly take in their escape from the island, and it is at the South Pole where, having penetrated the envelope of the world, as they are about to fall into its interior and mysterious whiteness, they are confronted by "a shrouded human figure, very far larger in its proportions than any dweller among men," whose skin "was one of the perfect whiteness of snow."[21] Upon this note the narrative itself ends, but this fall, too, seems to have portended rebirth, for, as the note explains, Pym and his companions returned to tell their story, although they again mysteriously disappear before they could tell what lay beyond the veil of whiteness at the world's end.

Poe's use of this dream of extremity had its roots in the aspiration for the sublime; here, as in stories like "The Fall of the House of Usher" — in which he is fascinated by the possibility of knowing "the glories beyond the grave" — he is impelled by "an immortal instinct," "a sense of the Beautiful," to try to reach beyond the fabrications of time: "Inspired by an ecstatic prescience of the glories beyond the grave, we struggle, by multiform combinations among the things and thoughts of Time, to attain a portion of that loveliness whose very elements, perhaps, appertain to eternity alone."[22]

Perhaps Pym's glimpse of the white interior of things was lovely and beautiful, for, as Golding's Nathaniel would have it, we invent our own heaven (p. 183). But in *Pincher Martin* the center's glimpse beyond the veil reveals a heaven quite different, because its imagination is of a radically different kind from Pym's. For the Romantic Poe the sense of beauty was the expression of the powers of the imagination, and the timeless world beyond the grave that it conjures up is white and inhabited by immense human figures; this kind of transcendentalism is not possible for the center; the heaven created by its imagination is "sheer negation. Without form and void. . . . A sort of black lightning, destroying everything we call life —" (p. 183) because its imagination was itself a negation, a consuming and destroying. Along with all its other reversals of past attitudes embodied in literature, *Pincher Martin* reverses the Romantic conceptions of will and imagination.

The imagination of the center in Golding's novel is similar in conception to the imagination as it is described by Jean-Paul Sartre in *The Psychology of the Imagination*. Earlier I suggested a similarity between the image Heraclitus found to describe the human condition, a bubble in the stream of being, and Sartre's image in *Being and Nothingness* for the same thing: "The For-itself [human consciousness], in fact, is nothing but the pure nihilation of the In-itself [Being]; it is like a hole of being at the heart of Being."[23] By drawing the parallel I intended to suggest that their conception of individual existence is similarly tragic. This hole at the "heart of Being" is consciousness, according to Sartre, for which the imagination, rather than being simply an element, is its condition, or "constitutive structure." (I refer the interested reader who would like to follow Sartre's logic to the first part, "Consciousness and Imagination," of the "Conclusion" to *The Psychology of the Imagination*.)[24] The imagination of nonexistent things is necessary, Sartre argues, for us to be able to grasp the real things of the world: "Thus the imaginative act is at once *constituting, isolating and annihilating*."[25] But any attempt (such as Poe's, we might interject) to "directly conceive death or the nothingness of experience is by nature bound to fail,"[26] for these are beyond the capacity of intuition to grasp. Yet the very nature and activity of the "nothingness" of the imagination and thus of consciousness can be grasped by an imaginative comprehension of the pattern of mortality and emergence: "The gliding of the world into the bosom of nothingness and the emergence of human reality in this very nothingness can happen only through the position of *something* which is nothingness in relation to the world and in relation to which the world is nothing. By this we evidently define the structure of the imagination. . . . soon as [one] apprehends in one way or another . . . the whole as a *situation* ["an immediate way of apprehending the real as a world"[27]], he retreats from it towards that in relation to which he is *a lack, an empty space*. . . ."[28] (italics Sartre's).

This is, I suggest, the pattern that Christopher's center on his rock begins to see emerge, "the personal pattern," as Susanne Langer said, "of a human life, rising, growing, accomplishing destiny and meeting doom." Against its will the center has begun to recognize the approaching end of its life, the price it must pay for existing, its doom; in the premonition that the pattern of its life will be swallowed up by the black lightning, it begins to be aware of itself as "an empty space," as a "nothingness in relation to the world" in which its pattern, its situation, is real.

In this revelation to the center of its imaginative constitution, Golding has turned our attention to "the inexplicable mysteries of conscious existence" that so trouble Conrad's Chief Inspector Heat, and we can see the nature of the imagination itself. Sartre describes two complementary negations by which the imagination creates a world: "the totality of the real, so long as it is grasped by consciousness as a synthetic *situation* for that consciousness, is the world. There is then a two-fold requisite if consciousness is to imagine: it must be able to posit the world in its synthetic totality, and it must be able to posit the imagined object as being out of reach of this synthetic totality, that is, posit the world as a nothingness in relation to the image."[29] By having Christopher die on the first page, Golding "brackets" the first requisite — sets it for the moment out of consideration — in order to concentrate upon the way in which the consciousness reveals its nature in fulfillment of the second requisite.

One of the most important things revealed about the consciousness when it is seen as essentially imagination is that it is free: "The conception of an imagination enmired in the world [i.e., one that cannot perform the second requirement, see itself as free of its imagined objects] is not unknown to us since it is precisely that of psychological determinism. . . . For a consciousness to be able to imagine it must be able to escape from the world by its very nature, it must be able by its own efforts to withdraw from the world. In a word it must be free.[30] "The imagination," Sartre concludes, "is the whole of consciousness as it realizes its freedom."[31] Sartre's has been called a "tragic philosophy" and I think we can begin to see why. The free acts of the consciousness constitute the world of space and time by which it can share in and communicate with other consciousnesses, the "real world" in which we are all "in situation," but that world, being in time, grows, flourishes, and, by the logic of its creation, declines; that which has emerged from nothingness glides back into "the bosom of nothingness."

Thus it is, it seems to me, with the "unexamined centre" which created the identity of Christopher Hadley Martin. Whether Golding was "influenced" by Sartre or other existentialists — or phenomenologists for that matter — I do not know. Perhaps that again is a question of his "official beliefs." But whether we call it a "phenomenological reduction," a "bracketing," or not, Golding's unusual technique is employed in the way this philosophical technique is employed, to set aside hindering preconceptions in order for us clearly to "see" — in Golding's case to see the nature of the timeless center as it reveals itself in its moment out of time.

We can now meet what is perhaps the most prevalent criticism of *Pincher Martin*, the feeling many readers have had that the concluding chapter is a "trick" ending, something worthy of O. Henry but not of Golding. It is a necessary aspect of the "bracketing" technique Golding employs and as such might be defended as a kind of necessary *peripeteia* and *anagnorisis*, a reversal and recognition, for the spectator of Christopher's drama, so that he can clearly see what has been bracketed and why. As Christopher goes down for the third time on the first page of the novel (another convention Golding uses, like his use of the convention that at the moment of death one's past life flashes before one), he tries to call out "Mother!" but succeeds only in "Moth-." He has died in the interval between the two syllables. It is relevant, incidentally, that he calls upon his mother at the moment of his extremity, for she is associated with the old woman on the rock and in the cellar and through these and the literal fact that she bore him with the black lightning. Here his body has retraced its steps backward and downward to the source of its being. It is interesting too that for a seaman who can remember "Rockall" as "Fuckall," "Mother" is also an obscene term and anticipates here from Christopher's mouth the mouthless obscenity of the center: "I shit on your heaven!" The confusion of sacred and profane in such obscene punning is of course germane to the harmony of opposites of the novel.

Christopher dies on the first page, but the reader does not know it. He perhaps suspects it, but his suspicions are soon lulled by the factuality of the account of existence on the rock. Accordingly, the "vulgar conceptions" that he has about the existence or nonexistence of something inhabiting the body as a lobster its armor—e.g., that man has an immortal soul, or that mind is merely an illusion, an epiphenomenon of brain processes—are held in abeyance and the full range of his human responses is allowed sway. These responses are, I suggest, very mixed and contradictory. As some critics give evidence, there is a great deal of sympathy for the existential plight of man alone, fighting for identity and survival in an alien universe, but this is mixed, I think, with growing repugnance for the moral shape that slowly emerges. With the repugnance, nevertheless (and to this extent Golding is certainly a moralist), there is also a growing empathy, an identification with the protagonist which stems partly from our own dream of heroic endurance but increasingly from a recognition in ourselves of the slimy greed and egotism in Pincher.

Pincher thus does to an extent become a kind of everyman, but only insofar as he is an extreme case that has, as it were, probed the limits of the human situation. He has tried to deny all of what is shared or "other" in his identity, but we find that in his denial—even because of it—he is linked to others and to the Other beyond him. Despite his attempts to engorge Nathaniel and Mary, these two remain obstinately "other," and yet, as he discovers, stand together in his very center. He cannot grasp them and thus they lead back to his own center and the black lightning. We are not all Pincher Martins, but we all have a Pincher Martin potential in us. We all do not live at such limits—certainly neither Nathaniel nor Mary does—but they are nevertheless there in the nature of our imagination and in the conditions of existence. Pincher has, however, uncovered other limits of a more positive nature than greed and pride—love, connection, sharing—for islands, in the world whose reality of time and space we share with others, are the solid tops of mountains. "The rock is solid," Christopher thinks. "It goes down and joins the floor of the sea and that is joined to other floors I have known, to the coasts and cities" (p. 163). His lonely island outside of time and thus outside the shared world, however, is not solid. The rock moves and dissolves into the black lightning.

The reader's response upon emerging from the purgatory created by the center depends, it seems to me, very much upon how he regarded that world. If he regarded it as having some duration in time — even a few prolonged seconds — then there is no reason for him to suspend any belief he might have in mechanistic or physiological theories of consciousness. And in this event he would not be afflicted by imaginations of the suffering in the eternal hell the center creates for itself, nor would he see the essential and tragic freedom of the center. He would be in the position of Davidson, perhaps, who thinks that since Christopher Martin had not had time to take off his seaboots his suffering, physically terrible to be sure, must shortly have ended. One who believes in an eternal soul enduring after death, on the other hand, might well credit the timelessness of the moment of Christopher's death but have difficulty seeing any possible cessation of the eternal hell awaiting such a monstrous soul and thus again deny its essential freedom.

But the novel concludes on a note of questioning; the discovery that Christopher died at the moment he tried to call on his mother forces the reader to reflect back upon the nature of the experience that the novel has evoked in his imagination. If Pincher died on the first page, the rest of the novel must have taken place out of time and, if this is the case, the "inexplicable mysteries of conscious existence" cannot be explained by "vulgar conceptions" of time. What then is the status of the responses brought to bear upon Christopher Martin's story? Hopefully, some kind of catharsis or purgation has taken place. We had identified ourselves with Pincher, now perhaps we can identify ourselves with Christopher, the Christ-bearer, and through this have some premonition of our own freedom found in this glimpse of "the gliding of the world into the bosom of nothingness." The "trick" conclusion, in other words, is employed to shatter the hard armor of our preconceptions about identity so that we might rise like Chief Inspector Heat above our "vulgar conceptions" of time "by the force of sympathy, which is a form of fear" and, thus naked at the center, confront with our own darkness the darkness of the nothingness from which we sprang and into which we return.

Notes

1. William Golding, *Pincher Martin* (London: Faber and Faber, 1956), p. 201. Further references to this edition will be made in the text.

2. Joseph Campbell, *The Masks of God*, II (*Oriental Mythology*) (London: 1962), 10–11.

3. *Ibid.*, p. 210.

4. James R. Baker, *William Golding* (New York, 1965), pp. 44–45.

5. *Ibid.*, p. 40n.

6. F. M. Cornford, *From Religion to Philosophy* (New York, 1957), p. 130n.

7. *Ibid.*, pp. 183–184.

8. *Ibid.*, pp. 176–177.

9. *Ibid.*, p. 182.

10. *Ibid.*, p. 190.

11. Susanne Langer, *Feeling and Form* (New York, 1953), p. 366.

12. Alfred North Whitehead, *Adventures of Ideas* (New York, 1956), pp. 294–295.

13. Bernard S. Oldsey and Stanley Weintraub, *The Art of William Golding* (Bloomington, Ind., 1965), p. 95.

14. They make hardly anything at all, for instance, of the relationship of *Pincher Martin* to *Robinson Crusoe*, although the allusions to Defoe's novel are very clear and the implications very important. The passage in which Christopher, discovering coins in his pocket, makes as if to throw them back into the sea but, upon reflection ("That would be too cracker-motto. Too ham" — i.e., on the one hand he refuses to "play the game" at this point, with both a rationalization for his greed and another indication of the direction in which his salvation lies; on the other hand, this might also be a reflection upon Crusoe's "cracker-motto" morality which has so little to do with his behavior), keeps them, is surely more than a merely fortuitous echo of Crusoe's discovery of the gold coins in the wreck which occasions an apostrophe upon the vanity of money, although Crusoe nevertheless packs them up and takes them with him. Moreover, like Christopher, Crusoe soon sets about "netting" his island down with names, making it his own as an assertion of his identity. Golding's treatment of the Robinson Crusoe theme is, to anticipate the distinction I quote later from Golding's comment upon Jules Verne's novels, the difference between the adult's vision and the child's. Crusoe's radical and voracious egotism is clear to the attentive eye (although I doubt that Defoe in this novel, as Golding suggests about Verne, was a satirist; i.e., I doubt that he was conscious of the ugliness Crusoe's behavior reveals): e.g., he sells back into slavery the fellow slave who helped him escape from the Moroccan pirates; he forces the luckless Spaniards, whom he had earlier promised to help escape, to become his "stewards" on the island which, like a deity, he wholly owns and controls, etc. Crusoe, for all his lip service to conventional morality, is utterly incapable of treating other human beings as anything but things, tools for his use.

15. Joseph Conrad, *Lord Jim* (New York, 1931), p. 6.

16. William Golding, "Astronaut by Gaslight," in *The Hot Gates and Other Occasional Pieces* (New York, 1966), pp. 111–115.

17. *Lord Jim*, p. 216.

18. See Harry Levin, *The Power of Blackness* (New York, 1958), p. 117. Verne, according to Levin, wrote *The Sphinx of Ice* to provide "a naturalistic sequel, where the enigma is solved by magnetism."

19. Edgar Allan Poe, "The Narrative of Arthur Gordon Pym," in *Selected Writings of Edgar Allan Poe*, ed. Edward H. Davidson (Boston, 1956), p. 257.

20. *Ibid.*, p. 397.

21. *Ibid.*, p. 405.

22. "The Poetic Principle," *ibid.*, pp. 469–470.

23. Jean-Paul Sartre, *Being and Nothingness*, trans. Hazel E. Barnes (New York, 1956), p. 617.

24. Sartre, "Conclusions," *The Psychology of the Imagination*, trans. Bernard Frechtman (New York, 1965), pp. 233–246.

25. *Ibid.*, p. 236.

26. *Ibid.*, p. 244.

27. *Ibid.*, p. 241.

28. *Ibid.*, p. 244.

29. *Ibid.*, pp. 239–240.

30. *Ibid.*, p. 240.

31. *Ibid.*, p. 243.

Golding's First Argument:
Theme and Structure in *Free Fall*   B. R. Johnson*

For over thirty years, since the publication of the famed *Lord of the Flies*, many critics have considered William Golding a writer of simplistic fables, an author spinning tales to illustrate a preconceived thesis. This reputation served to "formulate" Golding so that he was left, like Eliot's Prufrock, "pinned and wriggling on the wall." With the publication of *Free Fall* in 1959, however, such a facile conception no longer served as a clarifying interpretive device but rather became a barrier to a full understanding of the fiction. Golding himself was the first to argue with his reputation as a fabulist when, in a 1962 interview, he explained that "after the first three [novels], I found myself . . . in some danger of being "sage"-ified—one of the worst things that can happen to a writer. . . . So I wrote my fourth book to prove that I didn't know anything—a conclusion that most of its reviewers thought was just about right."[1] Beneath Golding's droll humor lies the complaint of an author who has continued, in his personal remarks as well as in his fiction, to voice dissatisfaction with the reputation created by his early reviewers and critics. Though *The Paper Men* (1984) is Golding's most recent and vituperative reaction to his critics, he has for many years expressed the ideas of one who is anything but a teller of fables. In 1965, in correspondence, Golding wrote: "I *am* obscure because I don't know what I am talking about, or only vaguely, and translate obscurity into—modified—obscurity";[2] in 1970, he spoke candidly to an interviewer: "don't credit me, the way people do all the time, with solutions. I haven't *got* them. You see, *ever*";[3] and again, in 1980, Golding wrote a correspondent: "I value inconsistency today more than I have ever done since it's the only stance or stances in a shifting, incomprehensible, ambiguous, sliding-away-from-me totality."[4] Finally, in *A Moving Target* (1982), Golding noted that throughout his career he has switched his "aim from target to target," that he himself is a "moving target" who has eluded the "critical shotgun": "The books that have been written about my books have made a statue of me, fixed in one not very decorative gesticulation, a po-faced image too earnest to live with."[5]

But old notions, like old soldiers, die hard. Neither Golding's distinctly non-fabulist fiction, beginning with *Free Fall*, nor his remarks that insist on his lack of a preconceived thesis seemed to dent his iron-clad reputation. Only recently has there been a show of dissent. Commented James R. Baker in 1982: "But critics learn, however slowly, and I think the best of them now realize the impossibility of reducing even early Golding to conveniently elemental phrases. This happy evolution is epitomized in a certain shift in our vocabulary: we no longer use the descriptive term

*This essay was written specifically for this volume and is published here for the first time by permission of the author.

'fable,' with its implications of rigid preconception and moralistic formula, but prefer instead the word 'mythic.' "[6] This statement, coupled with Golding's 1983 award of the Nobel Prize for Literature, seemed to indicate that at long last his work was not only receiving the recognition it deserved but stood on the threshold of a thorough re-evaluation by scholars who recognized the inadequacy of the fabulist approach. Yet such critical work has been slow in appearing, readers as perceptive as Robert M. Adams continuing, even in 1984, to toss all of Golding's novels into one generic basket, referring to them as "religious parables" whose "recurrent theme is the innate depravity of man."[7] Observations of this sort, all too frequent throughout Golding criticism, need careful reconsideration: that Golding is a "religious" writer, the author himself contests, though he will accept the term "spiritual";[8] that the novels, with the possible exception of *Lord of the Flies*, cannot rightly be called pessimistic "parables" or "fables" showing man's "innate depravity" is evident when the novels are reread with attention to the relationship between the themes and the varying structures of each work. *Free Fall*, the first novel in which Golding deliberately avoided the so-called "reversal ending" of the earlier fiction, demonstrates his abiding concern with structure as a tool that, if considered as an extension of theme, functions subtly to provide a key to the narrative's ideological dualism.

Lord of the Flies (1954), *The Inheritors* (1955), and *Pincher Martin* (1956) appeared so quickly at the beginning of Golding's career, though the author was forty-three when his first novel was published, that they seemed — in theme and structure — to have been written in one surge of creative energy, to have derived from the same impulse of the imagination. Not only did each conclude with a dramatic shift in perspective, but clearly present was a dualism which guided the development of the plot, a rational element in conflict with an irrational element, what Golding has over the years described as the rational and the spiritual worlds in which all of us live. Thus, both the "reversal" endings and themes of the first three novels were unmistakably similar: the irrational Jack versus the logical Piggy; the pre-rational Neanderthals set against the rational *homo sapiens*; the spiritual subconscious of Pincher Martin in conflict with his rational consciousness. In *Free Fall*, Golding continued his exploration of the duality, using various characters in the life of the protagonist, Sammy Mountjoy, as the primary mode of dramatization, though the two forces of the duality come to merge with one another so that to distinguish between the two becomes a quest relying on a twentieth century provisional exercise to capture a "shifting, incomprehensible, ambiguous" reality. This duality, as in the earlier novels, served not primarily as a vehicle of conflict, nor rigidly to delineate two antipathetic worlds (revealing Golding, a world-weary pessimist), but more importantly served as a tool to explore the possibility of finding a bridge between the two, if not reconciling them to one another then at least establishing lines of communication between them. Golding, then, in *Free Fall*, dramatizes a complex interrelationship between the two forces, tracing the duality from its most simplistic (as Sammy perceives it in his childhood) to an increasingly complex rendering as the narrator explores his past and those who have most influenced him — all brought to bear on his quest for redemption and freedom.

Critics have often enough pointed out the dualism in *Free Fall* — the juxtaposition of characters such as the intuitive Johnny and the Machiavellian Philip, friends of the young Sammy who each appeal to correlative portions of Sammy's consciousness; later, the dualism reappears in the guise of Rowena Pringle who teaches the scripture class and Nick Shales who teaches science. But the critical commentary generally overlooks the fact that this dualism is not a mere static rendering of conflicting forces but a progressive complication of them as Sammy's simplistic childhood perception gives way to a reality that is challenged, reconsidered, even obfuscated by contradicting realities. Human consciousness, caught in the free fall of its own subjectivity, confronts a complexity so nefarious that incomprehension seems to be Sammy Mountjoy's final stance at the novel's end, and it is just this exploration of the duality, not its either-or nature, which lies at the heart of Golding's fourth novel.

Consider, for example, the elegant simplicity of the dualism as Sammy perceives it during his early childhood, there expressed by the free-spirited Johnny and the pragmatic Philip. Compare this to a later evolution of the dualism as Sammy reaches adolescence and ponders again two figures who likewise represent this conflict between opposing realities. Nick Shales, for all his apparent adulation of scientific rationalism, is an unwitting spiritualist filled with "a love of people, a selflessness," not full of science "but poetry";[9] Rowena Pringle, dedicated as she seems to the spiritual, is nevertheless a die-hard rationalist who explains the miracle of the Red Sea by tersely noting that it could be "parted — the waters driven back — by wind" (198). Golding's dualism as apparent in characterization is most surely not to be understood so simplistically as a rigid presentation of heroes and villains, of simplistic perceptions endemic of early childhood. On the contrary, in presenting an increasingly complex portrait of each force, Golding questions the nature of phenomenological reality, seeming to wonder whether appearance and language may not conceal rather than reveal. Might not appearances lull us into a rational somnambulism so that, like Sammy, we are tricked into mistaking Nick Shales's wonder of the universe as a mechanistic theosophy that transforms the well-meaning teacher to a Mephistopholes whose ill-timed advice results in Sammy's decision to ravage, betray, and ultimately destroy Beatrice Ifor? In equating Nick and his philosophy, Sammy mistakes love for his teacher as love for rationalism, a mistake derived from a confusion between emotion and intellect. Sammy's book, impelled by this one moment of having made a wrong choice in full freedom, traces the sacrifice of freedom even while acknowledging that freedom itself is the means of its own destruction.

But Golding goes beyond a nominal deconstruction of the dualism. All along, he has portrayed Sammy Mountjoy as a character driven more than anything by a recognition of the two competing natures present within his one consciousness. Had he, like Johnny or Philip, been less human and fully at home in one sphere or the other, his inner conflict would have gone no further than a rather uninspired portrait of saint or villain. Carrying the dualism to its more realistic applications, Golding extends the conflict, and further complicates it, by creating Dr. Halde, the Nazi psychologist who is in some sense the ultimate rationalist, a character illustrating that the intellect — even at its most highly developed — cannot reliably serve as the sole means of analysis.

Dr. Halde is an incisive portrait of twentieth-century man whose villainy derives not from some innate absence of spiritual compassion (as Philip) nor from a misunderstanding of his own inner nature (as Nick Shales), but rather from his deliberate choice to sacrifice his spiritual capacity and to serve only his reasoning faculty. As Golding's most complex characterization (excepting Sammy) of the spiritual/rational dichotomy in *Free Fall*, Halde has an awareness of both; recognizing this affinity, Sammy and Halde feel a magnetic attraction toward one another. Says Sammy as he walks into the interrogation room, "I liked him, was drawn to him" (134). Halde, too, finds a likeness: " 'We are neither of us ordinary men. . . . There is already a certain indefinable sympathy between us' " (1937). Further, Halde knows Sammy from the inside out, understands his weaknesses by empathetically "becoming" Sammy: " 'I've been studying you. Putting myself in your place' " (141). Both Sammy and Halde, sharing a predilection for rationality yet keenly aware of their forfeited spiritual natures, are introspective explorers of the human psyche. In many ways, Halde is an emblematic reflection of the Sammy who has chosen rationality, yet two crucial differences separate these men.

First, Halde has made a resolute decision to relinquish his university position and serve the Nazi regime with much more awareness than Sammy of the "sacrifices" required of rationality. Sammy chose with the wild blood of youth pounding in his ears, desiring Beatrice so intensely that he neglected to consider what exactly he was giving up, what door would close behind him; Halde, on the other hand, chose in the brilliant light of rational understanding which dictated that the greatest good for the greatest number was impeccable logic, that his sacrifice would (as Nick Shales before him also believed) help create a world "logical and kind and of astonishing beauty" (213). Halde says to his prisoner: " 'One must be for or against. I made my choice with much difficulty but I have made it' " (140). But Sammy's Faustian bargain with rationalism is less firmly grounded than Halde's. The commandant, too, is aware of his prisoner's uneasy position between the two worlds: " 'And between the poles of belief, I mean the belief in material things and the belief in a world made and supported by a supreme being, you oscillate jerkily from day to day, from hour to hour' " (144).

It is this initial difference in commitment which leads to the second and most telling of the differences between Halde and Sammy, one that does not go unmarked by the commandant: "But there is a mystery in you which is opaque to both of us" (145). This "mystery" is Sammy's unremitting attraction to the spiritual domain, his refusal to accept that the door which his bargain with rationalism closed might not somehow be reopened. Such is the impulse which compels Sammy, after all, to write a story that traces his guilt while searching relentlessly for freedom, for a means to reopen the door to the spiritual world. If Halde forces the dualism into the near nether reaches of "truth being nothing but an infinite regression, a shifting island in the middle of chaos" (151), then Sammy is also a creation caught in the "free fall" of twentieth-century rationalism: "I could see this war as the ghastly and ferocious play of children who having made a wrong choice or a whole series of them were now helplessly tormenting each other because a wrong use of freedom had lost them their freedom. Everything was relative, nothing absolute" (150). Golding employs the individual psyche as the grounds for universal conflicts: inner is outer, mind and universe equated. Halde's inability to plumb the darkness in Sammy reflects the inability of rationalism to penetrate the recesses of a repressed yet still living spirituality. And when he orders Sammy to be imprisoned for a few hours in a harmless dark closet, he ironically — in spite of his formidable intellectual capacities — puts Sammy into contact with that world of spirit, a world cast into an extended eclipse yet waiting for the moment of renewed brightness.

This antipathy between the rational and the spiritual worlds comprises the dualism dominating the theme of all Golding's novels. In *Free Fall*, however, Golding projects the two forces interacting closely with one another, thus complicating the dualism thematically in a way that the earlier novels had not. If, as I contend, Golding deliberately set out in his fourth novel to counteract the critics' assessment of his fiction as simplistic parables demonstrating man's inherent (and irredeemable) evil, to argue conversely that he "didn't know anything," then the dualism is indeed successful in its convolutions and its suggestion of contradictory realities: caught in the sensation of indigenous meaninglessness, the helpless Sammy concludes near the novel's end, after visiting Nick Shales and Miss Pringle, that "Her world was real, both worlds are real. There is no bridge" (253). This statement ends Sammy's quest, his pursuit of freedom which is predicated on finding a bridge in order to re-open the door to the spiritual world, to find redemption for his past sins.

But the novel does not end here. While Golding's use of characterization does clearly reflect his concern with the complexity of everyday living, with the apparent difficulty of reconciling the rational and spiritual forces, Sammy's conclusion precedes the final enigmatic ending: the cell door opens to release him from his prison, back into the physical world where the old commandant's observation that Halde "does not know about peoples" (253) thoroughly mystifies the uncomprehending Sammy. This ending (and endings are always crucial when interpreting a Golding novel) has caused readers, like the protagonist, to puzzle at its significance, to wonder whether Golding may not have been willfully obscure here. I suggest that this is not the case. To the contrary, the ending, if taken as an integral part of the novel's structure, elaborates and ultimately clarifies the quest dramatized at the thematic level. Indeed, this closing scene is so structurally crucial that any interpretation of *Free Fall* which fails somehow to explicate its significance cannot but be an incomplete discussion of the novel as a whole.

In approaching this structural level, it is important to bear in mind the thematic dualism, the rational and spiritual modes of perception existing simultaneously within the consciousness of Halde, Sammy, and — by inference — the reader. Doubtless, it was these two modes that Golding referred to when, in 1970, he remarked: "it seems to me that we do live in two worlds. There is this physical one, which is coherent, and there is the spiritual one. To the average man — with his flashes of religious experience, if you like to call them that — that world is very often incoherent. But nevertheless, as a matter of experience, for *me* and I suspect for millions of other people, this experience of having two worlds to live in all the time — or not all the time, occasionally — is a vital one and is what living is like."[10] And it is these two ways of perceiving reality that bring Sammy to preface his story by commenting, "Time is two modes. The one is an effortless perception native to us as water to the mackerel. The other is a memory, a sense of shuffle fold and coil, of that day nearer than that because more important, of that event mirroring this, or those three set apart, exceptional and out of the straight line altogether" (6). Golding's comments about the "two worlds" of physical and spiritual experience and Sammy's observation of the "two modes" of perception suggest that Sammy is in many ways the author's spokesman and that Golding did, as he commented in his 1983 Nobel Lecture, write *Free Fall* as an argument against his reputation, attempting to qualify his acclaim as a pessimistic fabulist and "to reverse the process by explaining myself."[11]

But the "argument" is also a novel, a fiction like Golding's others that relies on a carefully structured narrative to elaborate further the issues broached at the thematic level. This underlying structure raises the fourth novel above the level of a thinly disguised treatise and brings it into the realm of art, the structure calling into question Sammy's failure on the last page and completing Golding's argument commenced at the thematic level. For the dualism apparent in the characterization is also reflected in the two types of narrative Golding uses to dramatize his understanding of the "two worlds" and the protagonist's "two modes": one portion of the narrative is cast according to the "effortless perception" endemic of the physical world, juxtaposed against the "shuffle fold and coil" narrative expressive of the spiritual world — these two antithetical, yet nevertheless simultaneously present.

Cast in the rational mode, chapters one through nine follow a linear recollection of events as Sammy relates his childhood in Rotten Row, his youthful friendships with Johnny and Philip, his adolescence under the guardianship of Father Watts-Watt, his pursuit and betrayal of Beatrice, his marriage to Taffy, his prisoner-of-war experiences when interrogated by Halde, and his subsequent imprisonment in the dark closet. But the last few lines of chapter nine announce the beginning of the new "shuffle fold and coil" narrative that follows; in its terror of darkness, Sammy's mind "struck with full force backward into *time past* . . . turned therefore and lunged, uncoiled, struck at the *future*. . . . And burst that door" (185; my emphases). As though following this itinerary of how Sammy's mind will jump erratically between past and future, chapters ten through fourteen are certainly "out of the straight line altogether," recalling Sammy's mocking admonition that the "straight line from the first hiccup to the last gasp is a dead thing" (6). "For time," remarks Sammy, "is not to be laid out endlessly like a row of bricks" (6). These last chapters, combined, represent one expanded moment of time during which Sammy experiences not only memories of the past but also visionary flashes of a future he has yet to live: his upcoming release into the prisoner of war camp, his past in the classrooms of Pringle and Shales, and his future post-war attempts to approach Beatrice and his two former teachers to receive or extend forgiveness.

While the linear chapters, demonstrating the rational time mode, have presented few problems for most readers, the fractured time of chapters ten through fourteen has perhaps been the source of so many critics' dissatisfaction with *Free Fall* — a dissatisfaction that Golding's fictive narrator anticipates near the beginning of his story as he speaks directly to his reader: "Do I exasperate you by translating incoherence into incoherence?" (8). Yet these last chapters have their own rationale. If taken as an expression of the spiritual mode of perceiving reality, their leaps into past and future meld into one comprehensive moment of experience which is juxtaposed against Sammy's prior rational attempt in the earlier chapters to discover the one moment in time where he has lost his freedom. Without the epiphany of chapter ten when Sammy re-enters the prison yard, the moral center of the novel, Sammy would never have been propelled to write his book that is inspired by the "loathsome substances . . . inhabiting the centre of [his] own awareness" (190) and the contingent revelation of the "live morality" (189) imbuing the natural universe: "Those crowded shapes extending up into the air and down into the rich earth, those deeds of far space and deep earth were aflame at the surface and daunting by right of their own natures though a day before I should have disguised them as trees" (186). Thus, the following leaps backward and forward in time derive from this spiritual insight: in the time past of chapter eleven, Sammy re-examines the dualism presented in the classrooms of Pringle and Shales, and in chapter twelve he discovers the precise moment when his rational bargain had cost him his freedom; in the time future of chapters thirteen and fourteen, after failing to receive forgiveness from Beatrice or to extend forgiveness to his former teachers, he can only surmise that the redemption of the spiritual world is forever denied him, that he is stranded in the rational world where "All day the trains run on rails. Eclipses are predictable" (252), where "the spirit breathes through the universe but does not touch it" (253).

Yet several aspects of the novel lead me to wonder whether Golding might have been relying on his reader to make a connection that his protagonist does not. A master of manipulating the limited point of view, Golding has specialized in creating narrative consciousnesses which are notoriously unreliable, and I suspect that in *Free Fall*, too, his narrator spoke for him only up to a point. That point ends, it seems to me, in the several blank spaces on the novel's last page, between Sammy's observation that no bridge exists and the "bright line" announcing the opening door. Here, I believe, the novel comes into its own as a fiction rather than as a philosophical narrative. In these spaces, as the "shuffle fold and coil" narrative concludes, Golding returns to the cockpit of his fiction, shoving Sammy out of the way and taking over the controls so that the reader must dive head-on into the real world where the dualism between rationalism and spiritualism is not so much an abstracted concept as a perplexing experiential reality. On the last page of *Free Fall*, the reader can no longer rely on Sammy to interpret the significance of his experience.

Taking the novel, then, as another in which Golding demonstrates his penchant for creating a mind which, however perceptive in Sammy's case, may not be unequivocally reliable, the reader must decipher this closing scene that remains incomprehensible to Sammy. Yet Golding has sprinkled clues enough throughout the preceding narrative that, when considered together, they seem to refute Sammy's observation that there is no bridge. The door motif is perhaps the most significant of these, recurring as it does at both the structural and thematic levels. In the former instance, the placement of the two doors, the "burst" door of chapter nine's last sentence and the door which opens on the last page, actually serves to emphasize the two narrative modes, operating as "brackets" so that the "shuffle fold and coil" of the spiritual narrative is veritably "suspended" within the "physical world" of the rational narrative. Golding himself has commented on the importance of the doors when one critic questioned him about the cryptic ending of *Free Fall*, noting that the opening door was like a "handprint on the canvas that changed the whole thing . . . [The] *key to it was that the door of the cell opened. I suddenly saw that, and it became the first genuine passion I felt about the book*".[12] If we take the doors as brackets, accentuating the novel's two narrative modes, the structure of the novel reflects the dualism between the rational and spiritual worlds evident in the theme, the reality of both affirmed by their respective presences in the novel even while each remains structurally isolated from the other. Read in this way, *Free Fall* assumes a quite definite shape, less the pariah novel of the Golding canon, a shapeless philosophical treatise, than a carefully wrought fiction that vies to take its rightful place on a shelf alongside the author's other novels.

The doors also serve a thematic function, expanding the novel's primary motif — Sammy's quest to discover a means of re-entry into the world of spirit. Thus, his frequent references to "a shut door" (184) combine into a familiar refrain, an image recalling "a shut sky" (184) and his imprisonment in the rational world. At the close of chapter eleven, after thinking back upon Pringle and Shales, his "spiritual parents" (194), Sammy turns to his science teacher: "I ran towards my friend. In that moment a door closed behind me. I slammed it shut on Moses and Jehovah. I was not to knock on that door again, until in a Nazi prison camp I lay huddled against it" (217). As the "shut door" comes to represent imprisonment in the rational world, so does its opening by contrast imply a liberation from that confinement. For between those two bracketing doors, within the "shuffle fold and coil" narrative, Sammy has discovered that moment when he has made his rational bargain, fallen from innocence, and sacrificed "Everything" (236) — a discovery which had eluded him in the "effortless perception" of the rational narrative mode. And it is also between the two opening doors that, in chapter ten, he has most intensely experienced the "complete and luminous sanity" (187) of the spiritual world, an ordeal so vividly memorable that it is the impelling source driving Sammy to write his book. How, then, possessing these vestiges of his spiritual moment, can Sammy be right when he says that "the spirit breathes through the universe and does not touch it" (253)? For, whether Sammy is aware of it or not, he has unquestionably been touched by this world of the spirit.

As well as reverberating backward through the novel, the opening door on the last page also accentuates the importance of what follows as Sammy re-enters the physical world where "Living is like nothing because it is everything — is too subtle and copious for unassisted thought" (7). For on the last page Golding has indeed been subtle, inserting dialogue which further undermines Sammy's statement of despair. If he is surprised by the opening door, he is doubly astounded by the old commandant's greeting: " 'I am sorry' " (253). Yet these words recall the immediately preceding narrative of chapters thirteen and fourteen wherein Sammy has attempted to receive or extend forgiveness: with Beatrice he failed because the "lines at that particular exchange are dead" (9); with Shales and Pringle he failed because both in their own worlds are unable to receive the forgiveness Sammy longs to offer. The commandant's apology, stressing the theme of forgiveness and redemption that is a central motif throughout *Free Fall*, also recalls the scar/star metaphor which implies sin and redemption. In chapter three, after the verger has given the young Sammy a harsh blow to the ear, the man attempts to apologize: " 'I'm sorry, lad, sorrier than I can say' " (74). Yet, at this point, in his innocence, Sammy (like Beatrice later) cannot offer the man forgiveness. Remarks the elder Sammy: "Something to forgive is a purer joy than geometry. . . . It is a positive act of healing, a burst of light . . . crystalline and strong. . . . But innocence does not recognize an injury. . . . And injury to the innocent cannot be forgiven because the innocent cannot forgive what they do not understand as an injury. . . . the nature of our universe is such that the strong and crystalline adult action heals a wound and takes away a scar not out of today but out of the future" (74–75). As a sign of guilt emanating from sin, the "scar" can be removed only by an act of forgiveness which is a "star," a "burst of light," a means of redemption which lies at the heart of Sammy's quest. Thus, having at the end of chapter twelve discovered the precise moment of this sin, he searches in the last two chapters for the "star" of forgiveness and redemption, a search which indeed has preoccupied him from the opening paragraph: "I have understood how the scar becomes a star, I have felt the flake of fire fall, miraculous and pentecostal" (5). Sammy's quest in *Free Fall* is two-fold: it is not only a perhaps cathartic confession of his fall from innocence and freedom by means of an oppressive rationalism but also an attempt to find forgiveness. The scar/star metaphor further elaborates this dualism between rationalism and spiritualism, the latter particularly visible in chapter ten where, on entering the prison yard, Sammy is "visited by a flake of fire, miraculous and pentecostal; and fire transmuted me, once and forever" (188). It is this "flake of fire," this "positive act of healing" synonymous with "something to forgive," that glows subtly in the commandant's apology, in his words which extend to Sammy the opportunity of "a purer joy" than his preceding rational pessimism could have divined.

Along with bestowing Sammy with the apology he has sought, the crucial last page ends with the commandant's words concerning Halde: " 'The Herr Doctor does not know about peoples' " (253). Though Sammy is completely mystified by these words, they recall the thematic dualism between the rational and spiritual modes of perception, casting doubt on the intellect as the solitary means of knowledge as well as hinting at Golding's own view that differs from Sammy's pessimism. As this closing line recalls Dr. Halde, it likewise challenges Sammy's veneration of him as an intellectual who possesses a near omniscient understanding of the human mind, one of those "psychologists of suffering" (173) who "know about people." Thus, the commandant's words question Sammy's reverence of the intellect, ironically echoing Sammy's youthful attitude toward the Machiavellian rationalist Philip who also "knew about people" (49). Yet this reliance on the intellect, even as demonstrated by the cerebral

Halde, has its inherent shortcomings. The Herr Doctor cannot, we recall, see into the "mystery" in Sammy, that spiritual portion of his consciousness which still lives although it is, as Halde comments, "opaque to both of us" (145). Further, by the old commandant's use of the doggerel "peoples," we should understand that he, unlike Halde who speaks an "assured and superior English" (136), is not a man of overwhelming intellect, but that he is nevertheless a man of compassion who "knows about people." This type of knowledge, as Golding has described it, does not emanate from the intellect, but rather from what he has termed "passionate insight" — a trait possessed by young Simon in *Lord of the Flies* and by such historical figures as Jean Vianney. Says Golding of the latter: "*He knew about people*, not in the way of the trappings and exterior appearances — even the exterior actions — but in the nature of their very vital processes and movements, the beating of their spiritual hearts."[13] It is such a passionate insight and spiritual heart that both Philip and Halde, in their pervasive rationalism, lack. Though Sammy will "puzzle over [the commandant's words] as though they were the Sphinx's riddle" (253), this final incomprehension of the narrator is not, I think, one which Golding invites his reader to share.

It is at this point that Golding's characteristic use of a stringently limited point of view becomes crucial to a full interpretation of *Free Fall*, for in creating a literature of consciousness, he has never allowed his protagonists a comprehensive view of the world in which they live, and though Sammy does often seem to speak for Golding during the narrative, on the last page the creator and his created have parted company. Without a doubt, this type of literature places considerable burdens on the reader who must, perhaps, interpret the narrative by an act of "passionate insight." Yet, in spite of this difficulty, these narratives spun from the minds of unreliable narrators reveal Golding as an author who is not so much a didactic fabulist casting words of wisdom against the winds of twentieth-century rationalism as one who writes in a quite different vein, what Northrop Frye has called the "ironic mode" wherein the central figure of the fiction "achieves no quest" yet a quest does seem to have been achieved. Remarks Frye: "Eventually it dawns on us that it is the *reader* who achieves the quest."[14] This, I think, is the key to interpreting each of Golding's novels, and the fourth is no exception. Rather than Sammy and Golding speaking with the same voice, as they do when pursuing the problem of man caught in the "free fall" of rationalism, Golding goes further as he dramatizes Sammy freed, Sammy confronting the apology which he has sought during his spiritual moment. We might recall Sammy's observation near the beginning of his book when he comments, "As for communication, to understand all they say is to pardon all" (9). Sammy, of course, does not "understand all," yet if *Free Fall* has communicated to its reader, if we understand more than Sammy the significance of the old commandant's observation about Halde, then clearly Sammy's failure to understand, along with his possible failure to "pardon all" and thus forgive, need not necessarily mean that the reader has failed. For, as so often in Golding's novels of consciousness, the reader will experience an understanding which the narrator has not, thus achieving Sammy's quest by *understanding* and then possibly forgiving him, in this way enacting our own redemption, turning one's own "scar" into a "star."

While I am by no means arguing that Golding is a starry-eyed optimist, neither am I convinced that his novels, after the first, are so pessimistic as generally supposed. Sammy, at the end of his story, evidences what Doris Lessing once termed a "failure in intelligence"; at the moment Sammy rationally deduces that there is no bridge, the door to his mental prison opens and the commandant offers the apology which the protagonist has long sought. Read in this light, *Free Fall* is not only Golding's first fictive argument against his reputation as a fabulist, but a fictive rendering of a protagonist who succeeds most when his rationality fails.

Notes

1. Maurice Dolbier, "Running J. D. Salinger a Close Second: An Interview with William Golding," *New York Herald Tribune Book Week*, 20 May 1962, 15.

2. James R. Baker, "Preface," *Twentieth Century Literature* 28 (1982):v.

3. Jack I. Biles, *Talk: Conversations with William Golding* (New York: Harcourt, 1970), 104.

4. Baker, "Preface," v–vi.

5. William Golding, *A Moving Target*, 2d ed. rev. (New York: Farrar, 1986), 167, 170, 169.

6. Baker, "Preface," vi.

7. Robert M. Adams, "Partners in Damnation," *New York Times Book Review*, 1 April 1984:3.

8. Julian Barnes, "The Spire," *New Statesman*, 21 November 1980, 25.

9. William Golding, *Free Fall* (London: Faber and Faber, 1959), 213, 212; hereafter cited in the text.

10. Biles, *Talk*, 79.

11. Golding, *Moving Target*, 203.

12. Virginia Tiger, *William Golding: The Dark Fields of Discovery* (London: Calder & Boyars, 1974), 160; my emphasis.

13. Golding, *Moving Target*, 143; my emphasis.

14. Northrop Frye, *Anatomy of Criticism: Four Essays* (Princeton: Princeton University Press, 1957), 324.

The Unsearchable Dispose

Bernard F. Dick*

A Modern Classicism

It was inevitable that the blueprint for tragedy that Golding had been tracing in his first four novels would culminate in a work that was thoroughly informed by the tragic spirit; a work that charted the rise and fall of a protagonist cast between the extremes of virtue and vice but who pursues one goal exclusively. The protagonist of *The Spire* (1964) is Jocelin, Dean of the Cathedral of the Virgin Mary, who is obsessed with the goal of capping his church with a spire. Although his master builder warns him that the foundations cannot support the weight, Jocelin pays no heed and proceeds with a plan that brings death, madness, but ultimately triumph: as Jocelin lies dying, the spire still stands.

The Spire is not only as close a reproduction of classical tragedy as a contemporary author is likely to achieve; it is also as clear an example of mythmaking as students of literature are likely to find. Golding's classical allegiance makes his art difficult to define because, like that of the Greek tragedians, it achieves an artistic balance between opposites. Golding's case is complicated by the fact that the opposites not only include the primitive and the modern but also the pagan and the Christian. Even so, Golding is still very close to the Greek playwrights who worked with myths reflecting a barbarous past; myths of blood guilt, cannibalism, infanticide, parricide, matricide. The Greeks imposed artistic form on myth so that it became drama. Art tempered myth; it did not destroy it. The violence is still there, but it has been purified by poetry.

Sophocles' *Oedipus the King* is probably the best example of the transformation of myth into art. In its original, unpoetic state, the myth of Oedipus, involving as it does parricide and incest, would have seemed crude to Sophocles' fifth century B.C. audience. Likewise, Sophocles' irony, particularly such devices as the violent punning of *oida* ("I know") with the hero's name, would have been alien, if not unintelligible, to Greeks of an earlier period. The process, then, required the assimilation of myth into dramatic form, just as later *fabliau* was transformed into tale and chronicle into tragedy. The myth supplied the plot; the form purged the myth of those elements (inconsistency, lack of causality) that would otherwise anchor it to dream-narrative.

Although mythmakers are dependent on the past, that dependence does not make them unoriginal. Golding's novels are indeed derivative in the sense that they are parodies (in the author's special use of the word) of other works and myths. Nevertheless, drawing on the past is really a classical (or traditional, to T. S. Eliot's way of thinking) tendency. The

*From *William Golding*, rev. ed. (Boston: Twayne Publishers, 1987). © 1987. Reprinted with the permission of Twayne Publishers, a division of G. K. Hall & Co., Boston.

classical artist was expected to conform to tradition. One way of conforming is to adhere to the boundaries staked out by one's predecessors — in itself, a form of acknowledgment. Another, better way to show one's gratitude to past authors is through allusions, reworked lines, and echoes. The ultimate goal is the assimilation of the past into the present.

In *Free Fall*, the assimilation is incomplete because the Dantean elements are primarily decorative. In *The Spire*, however, the assimilation is total; Golding works as a historical novelist would, transmuting sources into narrative so that the reader is completely unaware of the research. *The Spire* is, among other things, a historical novel; Golding is drawing on early English history — the construction of the spire of the Salisbury Cathedral in the fourteenth century.

In the Shadow of the Spire

Golding has spent most of his life in and around Salisbury, the site of the Cathedral Church of the Blessed Virgin Mary, whose great spire is visible from every point in the city as it pinions the sky in an act of self-transcendence. Ten miles to the north is Stonehenge, sown with relics of the past including a temple dating from around 1800 B.C.; thirty-five miles away is Avebury and a much larger ancient sanctuary. Wiltshire and the district around Salisbury, an area Golding knows intimately and loves passionately, illustrate the coalescence of paganism and Christianity but not the absorption of the former by the latter. There is tension in the landscape. Although Christianity triumphed, it could no more tame the wild and windswept plains of Salisbury than the Greek dramatists could purge myth of its violent passions. Despite the prominence of the cathedral, there is still something defiantly unbaptized about the hills around Salisbury.

Like its setting, *The Spire* is filled with a tension between the primitive past and the supposedly redeemed present. Even the workmen reflect that tension; they commit murder within the cathedral whose spire they are erecting. Christianity has failed to satisfy their darker needs; hence they still celebrate Midsummer's Eve and offer a human sacrifice to the gods of the foundations.

"There is no innocent work," Golding insists in the novel. Constructing a spire in the Middle Ages involved death and violence. Golding is not arguing that the end justifies the means, but rather that the means must be known if the end is to be understood. Thus Golding, moralist and mythmaker, historian and novelist, supports his thesis with facts. Certainly much of what is described in the novel can be corroborated. Jocelin's spire was to have a height of four hundred feet, approximately that of Salisbury's. Both spires are octagonal in shape; neither was constructed without rebellion, dissension, and a general indifference to liturgical forms — how else could construction progress unless services were curtailed or suspended? In 1762, when the capstone of the spire was undergoing repair, a small leaden box containing a relic of the Virgin Mary was discovered in a cavity.[1] In *The Spire*, Jocelin performs one last desperate act of faith by driving a Holy Nail, which has come from Rome, into the very point of the spire.

In an essay Golding retells the legend of the cathedral:

> Round about the year 1200, Bishop Poore was standing on a hill overlooking the confluence of the local rivers, according to legend, when the mother of Jesus appeared to him, told him to shoot an arrow and build her a church where the arrow fell. The arrow . . . fell in the middle of a swamp. There, with complete indifference to such things as health, foundations, access and general practicability, the cathedral was built. Eighty years later . . . the builders erected the highest spire in the country on top of it, thousands of tons of lead and iron and wood and stone. Yet the whole building still stands. It totters. It bends. But it still stands.[2]

Just as Bishop Poore's instructions came from an apparition, Jocelin's inspiration comes from a vision. Furthermore, both Richard Fairleigh, the actual architect of the Salisbury spire, and Roger Mason, the master builder of the novel, went ahead with the construction even though they doubted the foundations would hold. Since Salisbury itself is built on marsh land, the Salisbury spire is said to have been "built on faith." In this instance, nature cooperated with faith; as it turned out, below the marsh was a stratum that was able to bear the load. Still, in the thirteenth century, erecting such a spire would have been an act of folly. Thus Jocelin, whose name in Anglo-Saxon means "fool," is indeed a fool — if not for Christ's sake, then for God's.

Here the parallels end. A mythic or a historical novel can accommodate only so much background; then the writer's imagination comes into play. It is evident that the spire in Golding's novel is the Salisbury spire; however, the events leading to its construction and their configuration (or what Aristotle would call the *mythos*) are Golding's. The author who lived and even taught in its shadow saw the spire not as an architectural fact but as a symbol of faith, proceeding from an uncertain foundation but finally rising heavenward. Yet the erection of the spire poses some difficult questions: Does it warrant the sacrifice of four people? Is Jocelin right in ignoring murder and depravity in his cathedral so that his dream can be achieved? How can something be designed for God's glory when it threatens human life? The germs of tragedy latent in the story of the Salisbury spire might have eluded the literal eye of a chronicler, but they captured the imagination of Golding. The events obviously never happened as Golding describes them; but in art things happen as they *should* happen. As Aristotle noted in the *Poetics*, history depicts the particular; tragedy, the universal.

The Spire as Greek Tragedy

At the heart of the tragic process is a tension between two forces: the primitive and the civilized, the irrational and the rational. The same tension is inherent in myth itself, as Lillian Feder has argued with uncommon clarity in her definition of myth: "Myth is a narrative structure of two basic areas of unconscious experience which are, of course, related. First it expresses instinctual drives and the repressed wishes, fears, and conflicts that they motivate. These appear in the themes of myth. Second, myth also conveys the remnants within the individual consciousness of the early stage of phylogenetic development in which myths were created. This characteristic is evident mainly in its plots."[3]

The myths on which the Greeks based their dramas illustrate the tension between racial memory and liberated consciousness — a tension that, when dramatized, becomes a perennial conflict of opposites: the rationalism of Oedipus pitted against the mysticism of Teiresias, Medea's barbarism clashing with Jason's sophistry, Antigone's moral law challenged by Creon's man-made edict, the repressed Pentheus confronting the emancipated Bacchants. As the spiritual heir of the Greeks, Golding has inherited their traditions and their tensions.

The Spire works very much like a Greek tragedy in the sense that the tension or polarity determines the structure. The central conflict — Jocelin's supposedly noble vision to glorify the cathedral despite the dark forces within him that seek expression in the erection of the spire — is the axis on which the narrative rotates. That the construction will involve glory, suffering, and sacrifice is implicit in the opening paragraph: "He was laughing, chin up, and shaking his head. God the Father was exploding in his face with a glory of sunlight through painted glass, a glory that moved with his movements to consume and exalt Abraham and Isaac and then God again. The tears of laughter in his eyes made additional spokes and wheels and rainbows."[4]

Someone will have to be sacrificed for this vision; someone — or several persons, as it happens — will play Isaac to Jocelin's Abraham. Nor will God intervene to save the victim. There will be no confusion of heaven, hell, and purgatory as there was at the beginning of *Free Fall*. Back in a universe that he understands, Golding is able to generate ideas from images; in this case, three ideas derive from a single image of the sacrifice of Isaac on a stained glass window that is illuminated with sunlight as if the sacrifice had divine approval.

Glory and sacrifice are not mutually exclusive. Immediately after this explosion of light, the shafts of sun prove deceptive: they are not pure gold. The light is speckled with dust from the construction. Jocelin's motives, then, are not pure. But nothing is: "*There is no innocent work.*" The spire is as much a reflection of Jocelin as it is a glorification of God.

Golding originally planned to call the novel *An Erection in Barcester*;

fortunately, discretion prevailed. That the spire is Jocelin's dream erection is not only obvious; it also restricts the metaphor to one of sexual frustration, which is only one of several interrelated themes. The spire may be phallic, but there is something more unsettling about it. Jocelin pictures his church as a man lying on his back—arms outstretched in a Christus pose, with the spire projecting from his heart: "The model was like a man lying on his back. The nave was his legs placed together, the transepts on either side were his arms outspread. The choir was his body; and the Lady Chapel . . . was his head. And now also, springing, projecting, bursting, erupting from the heart of the building, there was its crown and majesty, the new spire" (4).

The disproportion in the model points to an imbalance in the maker. The spire should exist as the crowning glory of a cathedral; instead, in Jocelin's vision it is the part that overshadows the whole. Jocelin is guilty of excess, always the contributing factor in the tragic hero's downfall. But before Golding relegates Jocelin to the charnel house of tragedy, he forces the reader to reconsider Jocelin's model. Architecturally, the model lacks proportion, yet conceptually it is valid. The cathedral, both in the novel and at Salisbury, is cruciform. Whether one compares it to a cross or to a crucified man is irrelevant. The "body" of the cathedral extends length-wise from the west door to the Lady Chapel; the "arms," from the north to the south transepts with four pillars supporting the roof at the crossways.

The image, then, is one of concentric crucifixion—a crossway within a cross. Golding rarely works with a monovalent image; this one bur-geons like the apple tree in Jocelin's vision. If the interior of the cathedral is cruciform, crucifixion is inevitable—but with a twist: just as the hunter was the hunted in *Lord of the Flies*, the crucifier is the crucified in *The Spire*. Jocelin, who subordinates everyone to the spire, measuring their worth by what they can contribute to it, becomes the crucifier of two couples symbolized by the four pillars.

The Marriage of Hell and Heaven

The first couple is the verger Pangall and his wife Goody, whose baptismal name is never given; she is just a "Mrs.," unworthy of a given name because Jocelin does not think of her as a total person, but as a shock of red hair. The second couple is the master builder, Roger Mason, and his wife Rachel. Of the two couples, only Roger and Rachel are alive at the end. Actually Roger is more dead than alive; an unsuccessful suicide attempt has left him mad. Jocelin fares no better; the crucifier is now the crucified. His spine wasted away by tuberculosis, Jocelin dies in the same supine position as his model.

Just as there is no innocent work, there is no one interpretation of *The Spire*. Golding's meanings are multilayered; his polyvalence is especially evident in his handling of the marriage theme. Since Jocelin's vocation precludes his marrying, he finds an outlet in the spire, "so that now there was a kind of necessary marriage: Jocelin and the spire" (88). But the spire is only a means of diverting his sexual energy (of which there seems to be an abundance) for something — or someone — else, namely, Goody Pangall, who continually excites him. Her red hair activates his satanic side — red being the satanic color. Although Jocelin is Goody's confessor and would like to consider her his daughter in God, the pull of the flesh is too strong.

Golding, the consummate ironist, does not leave it at that. Goody shares Jocelin's frustration; just as Jocelin's vows prevent him from consummating his love for her, Pangall's impotence prevents the consummation of their marriage. When Goody finds herself in the presence of a virile male like Roger, Jocelin, unable to possess Goody himself, begins to envision her and Roger as a couple, separated from the rest of the cathedral by wood and canvas. What Jocelin cannot have with Goody, Roger can — and with Jocelin's blessing. Although Jocelin is initially appalled at Roger's growing attraction to Goody, he knows the practical function she will serve: "She will keep him here" (59); and that, at a time when qualified masons are rare, is not to be dismissed.

As Jocelin's marriage to the spire becomes indissoluble, he changes markedly. First he is transfigured with joy, God the Father exploding in his face. But the euphoria does not last. Although he insists "the spire isn't everything," it becomes clear that it is. The vision swells into an obsession, altering everything that comes within its orbit. For construction to take place, religious services are suspended, and the high altar is barricaded. Devotion is impossible in the midst of scaffolds and in the presence of workmen later revealed to be little more than degenerates. When Pangall tells Jocelin there has been a murder, Jocelin's dispassionate reply is "I know"; when Pangall complains of being mistreated, Jocelin's answer is "You're too thin-skinned, man" (15). Jocelin has no more intention of alienating the workers than he does of losing Roger's services. Jocelin is quite capable of averting his gaze, even to the point of ignoring the workers' paganism, which Christianity has been unable to change. In some ways, Jocelin's behavior recalls Piggy's. After Simon's murder, Piggy insists it was an accident rather than admit the truth. Jocelin does virtually the same when the workers kill Pangall, who, like Simon, is a sacrifice to the dark gods — specifically, to the cthonic deities in the foundations they believe might be appeased by a human offering.

In Golding, just as one meaning spawns another, one paradox generates a series. A helllike pit gapes at the crossways; while the pit is necessary for construction, the workers use it as the equivalent of the ancient cornfields where the Year Kings were buried in the expectation that their corpses would fertilize the soil. From another point of view, the pit is hell-on-earth, located in the least infernal of places, in a cathedral.

The spire must go down as far as it goes up. Descent, then, is the prerequisite for ascent; in mythic terms, descending to the underworld is

preliminary to assuming a role in revitalizing society or, in the case of
Aeneas, to founding a city. In *The Spire*, the characters must go through
hell before they can be judged worthy of heaven, or at least of salvation.
Once their ordeal is over, once the spire has been raised, the pit will cease
to exist. But until then, the old order prevails; the end—the glory of
God—justifies the means, the inglorious manipulation of humankind: "If
they are part of the cost, why so be it" (95). Thus Jocelin deceives a
competitor, causing Roger to lose a better offer. People are reduced to
physical features or to subservient forms of life. Just as Goody becomes an
erotic object, synecdochally reduced to her blazing hair, Roger becomes a
prey, an animal in Jocelin's "open trap," a "prisoner for this duty," a "slave
for the work." And Jocelin becomes God's hunter as well as His fool.

Classical/Christian, Conscious/Unconscious

Since *The Spire* is an alloy of the classical and the Christian, Golding
shifts back and forth between them, using motifs first of one and then of
the other. Jocelin has his own pagan substratum, his Dionysian cellarage,
on which he has built his priesthood. Thus he sometimes behaves like a
classical protagonist, so obsessed with his vision that he refuses to heed the
warnings of nature. He ignores a series of prodigies—the inexplicable
crying of children, the eerie singing of the cathedral pillars, a plague
rumor, an earth tremor, and a raven that flies past him on three separate
occasions. The final proof that the spire has become a personal undertak-
ing occurs when Jocelin affixes his own seal to a document approving
additional building costs.

There are times when Jocelin behaves like a myth-haunted figure,
able to see the world only through the gauze of the collective unconscious.
Then the action grows ambiguous, and the narrative halting; yet Golding
never loses control. *The Spire* is a perfect example of what Wayne Booth
calls a third-person narrator-agent novel; that is, a third-person novel
whose central character exerts such an influence on the action that he or
she seems to be telling the story. *The Spire* has the air of a confession, with
the central consciousness split into psyche and ego, each recording and
reacting in its own way. When situations arise that are too painful for
Jocelin or that are at variance with his priesthood, he responds like a
dreamer who is aware that there is such a thing as the waking state but is
unwilling to accept it. Thus incidents such as the budding romance
between Goody and Roger, Goody's pregnancy, and Rachel's description
of her husband's suicide attempt have a suppressed, sublimated quality, as
if they have been understood only on an unconscious level. Like everything
in the novel, Jocelin is divided; part of him seeks self-transcendence
through an act of faith; part yields to a sensuous reverie from the sight of
red hair or the phallic model of a spire.

Jocelin is so neurotically circumspect about sex that whenever he feels the slightest physical urge, his unconscious takes over the narration, presenting the action metaphorically and imagistically, as if it were loath to be direct. At the end of chapter 6, Jocelin experiences a dream that is his punishment for manipulating Roger Mason. He imagines himself lying in a Christus pose on the marshes like the model of the cathedral. But instead of sun streaming through the windows, Satan appears naked with red hair, an androgynous amalgam of the devil and Goody. The sight causes him to writhe on the marsh in "warm water," Jocelin's euphemism for semen. That the dream ended in ejaculation is clear from Jocelin's reaction to it: he is filled with such self-loathing that he flagellates himself.

Yet there are times when Jocelin speaks with the confidence of one who realizes his position in the divine scheme of things. In his speech to Roger Mason, he is quite specific about the role he is playing in the execution of the divine will: "When such a work is ordained, it is put into the mind of a, of a man. That's a terrible thing. I'm only learning now, how terrible it is. It's a refiner's fire. . . . You and I were chosen to do this thing together. It's a great glory. I see now it'll destroy us of course. What are we, after all?" (83). And again: "You're not in my net. . . . It's His. We can neither of us avoid this work" (115).

The Tragic Process

The Spire not only recreates the spirit of classical tragedy; it also recreates the tragic process. Golding has taken Jocelin along the same course that Oedipus traversed, as a comparison between *The Spire* and Sophocles' *Oedipus the King* reveals. Both works exhibit the following:

The tension between conscious motivation and unconscious desire.
   The spire, originally conceived as an adornment for a house of God, becomes a monument to frustrated sexuality and an indomitable will. Oedipus's conscious attempt to find the murderer of Laius runs parallel to, and ultimately coincides with, his unconscious attempt to uncover his origins. The erection of the spire and the investigation of the murder are both conscious endeavors and manifestations of the characters' unconscious.

Fusion of hero and mission.
   Jocelin's relation to his vision is described as a "necessary marriage." Oedipus's mission is not much different: it is a merging of identities, of quester and quest. Immediately after Oedipus learns that the murderer must be expelled from Thebes, he begins his investigation, vowing to champion the dead king as if he were his own son. His identification with his cause grows until he discovers the murderer; however, the one he has been seeking is himself. Oedipus is the object of his own investigation.

Change in the personality of the king-figure.

As Jocelin's goal becomes an obsession, he changes from a priest to a visionary, subordinating and sacrificing everything and everyone to the spire. He turns the cathedral into a home for fornicators and sodomites, condones adultery, practices deception, tolerates murder, and is indirectly responsible for the deaths of two people and another's madness. Oedipus, who originally regarded himself as a father-king bound by cosmic sympathy to his children-subjects, evolves into a tyrant; hence the play's Greek title, *Oedipus Tyrannus*. His insistence on clarity becomes a nagging literalism. He taunts Teiresias, whose veiled language infuriates him; he even vents his wrath at Creon and finally at Jocasta, who, he suspects, is afraid the investigation will prove him illegitimate.

Tragic knowledge.

In *Oedipus the King*, the final stage in the tragic process is the protagonist's realization that he has accomplished his purpose, but with an ironic and unanticipated outcome: Oedipus has succeeded in finding Laius's murderer, and in doing so, has passed from ignorance to knowledge. But the knowledge Oedipus acquires is not merely factual; the facts themselves are part of the fabric of Oedipus's life. In learning about the past, he has learned about himself. He has reconstructed his own biography. Or rather, he has composed his autobiography, for in autobiography, subject and object coincide.

Jocelin's knowledge is more complex. He knows early in the novel that he is an executor of God's will. In itself this is not cosmic knowledge but orthodox Christianity, which teaches that the minister of the Gospel is a servant of Christ and a steward of God's mysteries (1 Cor. 4:2). The real knowledge Jocelin acquires is deathbed knowledge. To make certain that the reader understands the difference, Golding italicizes Jocelin's insights so that they stand apart from the narrative and are not confused with his visions or utterances. For these are Jocelin's final thoughts (not last words since they remain unspoken): "*How proud their hope of hell is. There is no innocent work. God knows where God may be. It's like the apple tree!*" (214–15).

There is something rhetorical about his first realization; "proud hope" is an oxymoron, a juxtaposition of two seeming opposites. Jocelin is making a universal statement about pride and hope, not about the proud and hopeful. Previously, he had imagined humankind wrapped in parchment. To a modern reader, the vision might seem curious, but not to a medieval priest who read from parchment. Humanity, then, is a book, a manuscript of pride, a readable text. If pride brings humans to hell (and as the deadliest of the seven deadly sins it should), the proud have willed it; if their beings tends toward hell, they naturally hope to achieve it, just as the righteous hope to gain heaven. If pride is sinful, so is the hope of the proud; for them, hope is not a virtue but a vice.

Jocelin, however, is one of the proud. He is, in fact, so proud that when he overhears some deacons speaking about him, calling him proud and ignorant, he assumes they mean someone else. Yet Jocelin is proud and ignorant, although not one of the parchment people. Jocelin's pride is not "the never failing vice of fools" as Pope terms it in *An Essay on Criticism*. Jocelin may be a fool, but he is God's fool. Originally, he is swollen with self-importance, but he is deflated when he finds it was not his learning that made him dean of the cathedral but the whim of the king, whose mistress was Jocelin's aunt. The position was a plum that the king tossed to Jocelin at his aunt's urging.

Such a plum would naturally make a man like Jocelin proud. But his pride is not hybris; it is not arrogating to oneself what is God's. Jocelin knows he is "a, a man" but not "a learned man," as he himself admits. Unfortunately, Golding forgets that Jocelin could barely read the "Our Father" and, on his deathbed, has Jocelin utter the name of Berenice, who dedicated her hair to Ptolemy III. Jocelin is thinking, as he constantly does, of Goody's hair. Still, the allusion is inappropriate. The only way a medieval priest could have known of Berenice would have been through Catullus's poem, *The Lock of Berenice* (*Coma Berenices*). But familiarity with Catullus, much less with his most difficult poem, would have been impossible in the fourteenth century. First, Catullus was not part of the medieval trivium; second, even if he were, Jocelin's Latin was so bad (he has trouble, after all, with the *Pater noster*) that he could have scarcely made it past the first line. Irony and allusion have pitfalls that Golding is generally able to avoid. While, in this instance, he falls into the trap of double irony, he manages to extricate himself, however implausibly, through Father Adam's response when he hears the name Berenice. "Saint?" Father Adam asks. To humor him, Jocelin answers, "Saint."

Jocelin's insights are like the movements of César Franck's Symphony in D Minor, in which despair struggles with hope—one winning, then the other—until reconciliation is achieved, neither being victorious. Thus Jocelin's vision of a proud race hoping for hell is tempered by a sobering insight into the ways of God: "*There is no innocent work.*" There is nothing that does not bring evil in its wake, even the *opus dei*, the work of God. What matters only is that the good outweigh the evil.

"*God knows where God may be.*" Even if "God knows" is interpreted as an expression of doubt ("God knows when we shall meet again"), the basic concept of an omniscient and immanent God remains: God is present everywhere and in everything, even in a man chosen to do His work despite a mind bursting with fantasies and a tuberculosis eating away his spine.

"*It's like the apple tree!*" is the coda, drawing together the strands of Jocelin's thought as well as crystallizing an earlier vision in which Jocelin sees the spire as something that began simply, like a single green shoot that first bourgeoned into tendrils and finally into branches. In this image,

Jocelin sees the divine as well as the demonic, for among the leaves is a "long black thing," the serpent. To understand the full meaning of the serpent in the tree is to realize that even in Eden before the Fall, there was the possibility of a fall; and to separate the tree from the serpent is to misunderstand both God and humankind. Redemption has not driven the serpent from the tree, any more than baptism has eradicated original sin. To realize this is to accept humankind with all its greatness and limitations, and life in all its glory and horror. The spire, with its complementary and contradictory meanings, is humankind's dialectic. One meaning that can never be lost is the erotic, for the inspiration to glorify God can be as much the result of sexual as of spiritual energy. Jocelin's last thought of the spire is that it is "as slim as a girl," rising up to the sky with a "silent cry," never able to reveal what brought it to its height.

Despite the cost, the spire is still a work of art that reminds Jocelin of an upward flowing waterfall. That the last image is an inversion is not surprising; it is the inversion that resolves the others. The spire, while it came from the Fall, is not *of* the Fall; it does not look down, like the waterfall in *The Inheritors*, but upward. The spire is a symbol of hope, not for the proud, for theirs is the hope of hell; but for the humble, for whom it is an act of faith. To accept something as a product of the Fall but unable to fall is to understand the great paradox of human nature: humankind's ability to soar into infinity from the most finite of bases.

Notes

1. See William Dodsworth, *An Historical Account of the Episcopal See and Cathedral Church of Sarum, or Salisbury* (Salisbury: 1814), 153.

2. "An Affection for Cathedrals," in *A Moving Target*, 17.

3. Lillian Feder, *Ancient Myth in Modern Poetry* (Princeton, N.J.: Princeton University Press, 1971), 10–11.

4. *The Spire* (New York: Harvest Books, 1964), 3. Subsequent references in the text are to this edition.

Perspectives   Mark Kinkead-Weekes and Ian Gregor*

I

He holds him with his glittering eye —
The Wedding-Guest stood still,
And listens like a three years' child:
The Mariner hath his will.

*Reprinted by permission of Faber and Faber Ltd. from *William Golding: A Critical Study* by Mark Kinkead-Weekes and Ian Gregor (London: Faber, 1967).

Ultimately, the appeal of every literary artist must be that of Coleridge's Mariner. He is there for us to talk about only because he has caught and held our imaginations. So far in this study of Golding we have been trying to describe the effect of the "glittering eye" as it has revealed itself in the particularities of individual works; in this final chapter we hope to shift the perspective and see the particular kind of "will" that Golding has exerted over us. How, in other words, do we judge the imaginative features of the Golding novel?

To put the question like that is to feel a special sympathy for Blake's dictum that to generalize is to be an idiot, and reasons for this feeling are not far to seek. The trouble lies initially in the concept of "the novel" itself. Over the two and a half centuries of its existence, the novel has come to cater for so many different needs and pressures of the imagination that it cannot accommodate them meaningfully under a single label. Nevertheless the range and disposition of a particular imagination tend to elude us if we concentrate our attention exclusively on its specific manifestations. A novelist's *oeuvre* becomes something more than an aggregation of books; it can reach a point of definition where seeing one book in the light of another gives us new insight into the nature of the imagination which is operating. To describe this body of work takes us immediately into describing the kind of novel which this imagination instinctively offers. And at once we have to deal in a vocabulary which has had to do duty for so many purposes that it can be used only if it is buttressed by closer definition and example. We hope to distinguish Golding's particular kind of novel by bringing together the terms "fable," "history" and "myth," and trying to make clear our understanding of them and their relevance to the five books we have discussed.

Literary concepts are precipitated by impressions, so we might turn first to the impressions made by a Golding novel. We might think of it as something heavily patterned, uniformly intense, severely exclusive. The patterning can be observed even in the externalities of length and chapter division, virtually the same in every novel. The general form is so markedly dialectical that we are invariably led into describing each novel in terms of different worlds brought into stark confrontation. The moment of confrontation is of high dramatic intensity, though as the novels progress the "moment" becomes less precise, and consequently less stark in its effect. The books are uniformly intense in that the mood in which each is written hardly changes; though there may be violent shifts in the point of view. The central characters may interrogate themselves remorselessly, may indeed alter, but always they remain the eye of a storm. Related to this homogeneity of mood is the dominant impression of exclusiveness. The shaping spirit of the imagination seems always at work in the foreground of our attention. There is a determination to follow what is thought to be the main road, so that we can only glimpse the possible extensions of a relationship, a place, a sub-topic. Hence we feel that, however densely imagined a particular character or episode may be, everything has been pared down, stripped of irrelevant detail. Bringing these impressions together, we might say that a Golding novel gives the effect of something dedicatedly made, every strain and stress calculated and overcome, so that the final product leads us to think in terms of a sculpture.

This however is only half the story. Our impressions are formed not only by the shape of the fiction, but also where its movement takes us — and here we seem to be faced with paradox. These books, so emphatic in pattern, so exclusive in structure, have as an increasingly dominant theme the limitations of the pattern-maker and the tragic consequences of his vision. This is already present in *Lord of the Flies*. Piggy and Jack try to press their patterns of human nature into action; but neither can bear to see man as he is. Only Simon achieves a vision more inclusive and accepting, but he is destroyed by the excluders who translate the boy into the Beast. The problem of pattern becomes the overt theme of *Free Fall*, it is Sammy's obsession: "I have hung all systems on the wall like a row of useless hats. They do not fit. They come in from outside, they are suggested patterns, some dull and some of great beauty. But I have lived enough of my life to require a pattern that fits over everything I know; and where shall I find that? Then why do I write this down? Is it a pattern I am looking for?" It is there most complicatedly in *The Spire*, where Jocelin seeks explanation or comfort in one pattern after another, until, "knowing nothing", he is left staring at an object, seeing it, as it is, for the first time.

Our general impressions are founded on paradox: books of calculated and obtrusive design work towards the creation of a mysterious centre, visionary eyes have to learn to see, novels of purpose insist on the importance of discovery. Basically a Golding novel grows through the tension between its form and his imagination. To describe this tension we must enlarge the context of discussion and the terms "fable", "history" and "myth" help to establish a useful perspective.

Fable brings Aesop to mind as a point of departure. Broadly speaking, the fabulous world is one that is made up. It exists deliberately outside the world which we inhabit, and fidelity to common experience is a very minor or even an irrelevant consideration. Aesop's world is inhabited by animals with human traits; other fabulists may write of giants and monsters, or, if they write of men, it is in the mode of dreams and vision, or of an "un-country" where the boundaries of probability can be crossed and recrossed at will. Yet if the world of fable is quite unlike the world of everyday, it has direct bearing on it. We enter the other world to analyse our own with greater clarity and freedom. We look continually for point; so that the process of reading involves a continuous need for translation. Our awareness of meaning depends on our awareness of correspondence. Nothing is offered for its own sake. Situations, relationships, protagonists, figures are selected, controlled for a purpose beyond themselves, serving an analytic design or debate.

Curiosity rather than analysis is the motive behind the imagination we describe as history. This is the imagination which Virginia Woolf sketches in her essay on Arnold Bennett:

> Mr Bennett "would keep his eyes in the carriage. He, indeed, would observe every detail with immense care. He would notice the advertisements; the pictures of Swanage and Portsmouth; the way in which the cushion bulged between the buttons; how Mrs Brown wore a brooch which had cost three-and-ten-three at Whitworth's bazaar; and had mended both gloves — indeed the thumb of the left hand glove had been replaced. And he would observe, at length, how this was the non-stop train from Windsor which calls at Richmond for the convenience of middle-class residents, who can afford to go to the theatre but have not reached the social rank which can afford motor-cars, though it is true, there are occasions (he would tell us what) when they hire them from a company (he would tell us which.)"

Virginia Woolf is polemical; but setting this aside, we can see the kind of imagination involved. History recognizes no other level of "reality" than the phenomenal or contingent. It is anti-formal; not in the sense that it attempts to escape form, which would be impossible for art, but in the sense that it rejects any idea of imposing form on multifarious experience. It seeks always by complicated interrogation to expand, extend, or even subvert what it feels to be the restrictions of pattern. It wishes to include everything and willingly pays the price. It cheerfully accepts "bagginess" and "monstrosity" in the service of faithful representation. Since its horizons tend theoretically to infinity, its ending — a death, a marriage, a birth — will be an arbitrary pause rather than a conclusion. By definition, history can never tell all there is to be told, there is always another story. History as fiction begins with historians themselves filling in the lacunae between facts, writing scene or dialogue by inference to lend plausibility to "what must have been," while remaining true to the facts as they have found them. Fiction as history tries to persuade us that it is merely a transparency through which we view a complicated phenomenal world, its persons and places empirically "true." Such fiction may be weighted towards the portrayal of individuals, or societies, or epochs. In the first case we have fictive biography whose basic shape is the shape of a man's life. In the others, a number of such biographies are made to interact. But whatever the weighting there is the same fundamental drive towards inclusiveness — "Mr Bennett would observe every detail with immense care."

Of the structure of anthropological myth we can predicate nothing; each story of Gods and their dealings with men has the shape of its own vision. But literary myth so deals with men as to reveal an archetypal "truth" hidden below the surface of everyday life. This cannot simply be "made," it must be discovered. If fable suggests Aesop, myth takes us back to Aristotle and his citation of *Oedipus Rex* as the perfect tragic *mythos*. In

Oedipus we have an imaginative mode quite different from either fable or history. The rhetorical structure is not designed for translation into correspondences; equally, it is not concerned with the self-sufficiency of the phenomenal world. Rather, we begin with the world we know, and examine it in such a way that we no longer seem to know it. The essence of literary myth is process, and, more precisely, reversal and discovery. *Oedipus* opens with the assertion of a stable world (I am Oedipus of Corinth, savior of Thebes, this is my wife Jocasta, these are my children), but it dissolves in the acid of a different truth. Swellfoot of Thebes, deformed bringer of plague, patricide, incestuous husband and father-brother, puts out the eyes which had persuaded him that the world was the explicable world of man and not the inscrutable world of the gods. Myth is history seen through an X-ray lens which reveals a more basic structure than that of the surface body of life.

Fable, history, myth — it is important to insist that nothing qualitative is implied in these terms. They are three different ways of looking at life, each of which has a different stance towards "truth." Myth may seem to make larger claims than the others, but there are as many realities and truths as there are ways of looking; and we are concerned with modes of imagination, not philosophical views. Each has a fundamental strength of a different sort, but when looked at from an angle other than its own, each has also fundamental limitations. From the viewpoint of history, myth and fable seem too rigidly patterned, taking too exclusive a grip on the complex processes of life. From the viewpoint of fable, history is a baggy monster, capable of testifying only to its own muddle; while myth is mystification, depriving itself of intellectual freedom through its pretensions to a historical reality. From the viewpoint of myth, history tries to include too much, fable too little. Each mode affords a definably different satisfaction as it proceeds from a different imaginative urge. Fable offers the pleasures of analysis, history those of recognition, myth those of revelation.

To see the varying treatments of character in these different modes is to see from another angle their distinctive emphases. It is history that gives us our normative idea of fictional character, an idea typified, for example, in the opening of *Emma*:

> Emma Woodhouse, handsome, clever, and rich, with a comfortable home and happy disposition, seemed to unite some of the best blessings of existence; and had lived nearly twenty-one years in the world with very little to distress or vex her. She was the youngest of the two daughters of a most affectionate, indulgent father; and had, in consequence of her sister's marriage, been mistress of his house from a very early period. Her mother had died too long ago for her to have more than an indistinct remembrance of her caresses; and her place had been supplied by an excellent woman as governess, who had fallen little short of a mother in affection. Sixteen years had Miss Taylor been in Mr Woodhouse's family. . . .

The mode is established: the heroine is put before us, age, disposition, upbringing. Her relations with her family, the indulgence of her father, the early death of her mother, the maternal affection of her governess — it is out of this material that the novel will be woven. The assumptions governing fictional character here are almost too familiar for us to be able to recognize them. There is no theoretical limit to the facts that we ought to know, and our knowledge of characters presented in this way (in terms of family, relationships, education, outlook) is analogous to our knowledge of people in daily life. Or, more strictly, it is analogous to a convention of expressing that knowledge to ourselves or to others. A character-sketch such as Jane Austen gives us of Emma, and the "reference" we might be asked to give for such a person, assume a similar structure, a similar vocabulary.

We could not say the same for the presentation of Mr Gradgrind.

> "Now, what I want is, Facts. Teach these boys and girls nothing but Facts. Facts alone are wanted in life. Plant nothing else, and root out everything else. You can only form the minds of reasoning animals upon Facts: nothing else will ever be of any service to them. This is the principle on which I bring up my own children, and this is the principle on which I bring up these children. Stick to Facts, sir!"
>
> The scene was a plain, bare, monotonous vault of a schoolroom, and the speaker's square forefinger emphasized his observations by underscoring every sentence with a line on the schoolmaster's sleeve. The emphasis was helped by the speaker's square wall of a forehead, which had his eyebrows for a base, while his eyes found commodious cellarage in two dark caves, overshadowed by the wall. The emphasis was helped by the speaker's mouth, which was wide, thin, and hard set. The emphasis was helped by the speaker's voice, which was inflexible, dry, and dictatorial. . . .

We are immediately presented not with character, but with attitude, a stance deliberately posed for purposes of argument and analysis. We sense that every detail of scene and speaker, no matter how tiny, is not descriptive but pointed; and we begin at once to translate them into their point. The predominant impression is of the artifice of the author. The rhetorical performance rivets our attention to his design. We know that action will be important, but will not be the inevitable outcome of character so much as of careful plotting; and that the total pattern will be created not by the way the characters act upon one another but by the way they fit in with one another as functional components of a single informing analysis. With this we know that we are in the world of fable.

Interestingly, and of necessity, myth eludes such brief illustration. It begins in a way indistinguishable from history; but its underlying structure is only gradually discovered by the special ordering of the narrative. Like history, myth has to persuade us that its characters are real people in real places, but it has links with fable in that it persuades us to question the nature of this reality. Unlike fable, however, the revelation of myth will be gradual, unobtrusive, taking shape beneath the surface. As far as the presentation of character is concerned, this means that individual features fade to reveal archetypal forces, like those classified by the great psychologists. But just as these forces, however archetypal, cannot be truly conceived apart from this and that individual, so myth can only be expressed in personal terms, and never in the abstract terms of fable. It is possible to go further and say that the more myth is concerned with isolating the archetype, the more banal it becomes, because it has lost contact with the complexities of the individual, without whom this imaginative process can have no life. Oedipus again will indicate the kind of interest in character we find in myth. He begins in a world of history, so that we can talk of his character in terms of leadership, assurance, hot temper; but then this alters to reveal the "character" or "signature" inscribed upon him by the gods, one not peculiar to him but a part of the human condition. The complexity of Oedipus is refocused in the light of the sphinx's riddle "what is man?", but it is this man in this situation which gives the riddle all the imaginative life it has. If we try to see myth in terms of its "message," it trembles on the edge of the received, or even the trite. But it is a sense of the powerful imaginative resonance of the archetypal that drives an author to seek to capture it in fiction, as it is the imaginative power and richness of the capture that makes the fiction valuable and not the thesis we could abstract from it.

Perhaps these varying treatments of character are sufficiently distinct to require a different terminology, so that "character" might be reserved for history, "type" or "attitude" for fable, and "archetype" for myth. But this terminology should be purely descriptive in purpose. If we see the mode of history dominant in *The Prelude, War and Peace, A la Recherche du Temps Perdu*, the mode of fable in *The Faerie Queen, The Pilgrim's Progress, Gulliver's Travels*, the mode of myth in *Oedipus Rex, The Ancient Mariner, Moby Dick*, then it becomes clear that by no earthly standard could we want to rank imaginative works of this order. We have been using history, fable, and myth in an attempt to characterize certain modes of the imagination, hence they are anterior to specific literary genres. They may be found in poetry, drama, and fiction. Further, there is no reason why these modes should not co-exist within a single work of art, and they often do. The imagination, though it may travel one line more than another, is not confined to a single track. (Allegories, for example, often combine fable and myth, novels—like Jane Austen's—history and fable.) Nevertheless, the recognition of these varying predilections of the imagination, whatever labels we pin to them, should prevent us from applying to one predominant mode criteria appropriate to another.

With these terms in mind we can return to our general impressions of a Golding novel. If his five books are considered collectively, they seem to constitute a phase of work which we might reasonably consider complete.

This is not to say that they are a step-by-step achievement in which each step must be "higher" than the last. Rather, they provide a series of variations on a problem, which within his own terms he now seems to have resolved, and this series of variations can be plotted in terms of fable, history, and myth; the twelve years' work can be seen as an exploration of the problem of disengaging myth from fable, and of giving it a sufficiently historical location.

To think of *Lord of the Flies* is to think of the qualities of immediate accessibility, clarity of design and intention, which mark it off from the novels which followed, and explain its popular success. The island setting, isolated from the complexities of society; the exclusiveness of its characters, not merely children but boys before puberty; the firm direction of its plot; all minister to that creation of a deliberate artifact which is the hallmark of fable. It affords the satisfaction of a ship-in-a-bottle, it is a world of equivalences, of meticulous scaling-down. We seem to be able to review it in its detail and in its total design simultaneously. The author seems in conscious control, doing with virtuoso skill and success what he has obviously set out to do. *Lord of the Flies* is in fact the closest of Golding's novels to fable.

Our criticism however has attempted to show how much the novel differs from any such account. There is an important openness in the presentation, especially of Piggy and Simon, which raises questions about the overt design of the book; in one sense making it considerably less definitive than it seems, in another, giving it a new dimension of interest. Looking back now, we can see that this dimension is the stirring of myth imagination in a world primarily fabulous.[1] Golding's imagination is more complex and less articulate than his design and structure. His basic art is already one of revelation rather than demonstration, and what is eventually revealed is more mysterious than author or reader expected. Also, although the novel is calculatedly isolating both in setting and in its characters, it depends on our acceptance of a psychological reality "true to life." The boys have to be entirely credible as boys as if we are to respond to the novel's vision, and in the imagination of the island and its inhabitants there is a pronounced drive towards the mode of history which plays against the thesis, the translation and the analysis of fable. *Lord of the Flies* in retrospect reveals the myth-imagination already seeking to liberate itself from a mode which, from its viewpoint, is too confidently analytic, too restrictive.

In that respect *The Inheritors* is a long leap forward. In one sense, at the level of "subject," Golding takes a world so completely "other" that it might seem unequivocally to invite the description of fable, taking its place with Utopia, Brobdingnag, Erewhon. Moreover he seems to have begun from a thesis-quarrel, a conscious design to demonstrate the inadequacies of Wells. But Golding establishes the novel's "otherworld" by employing all his imaginative resources, not as More, Swift and Butler do, to manoeuvre analytically between "their" world and "ours," but rather to make us forget our world and become imaginatively immersed in the dense mystery of his. The essential element in the writing is the discovery of a procedure which inhibits analysis and judgement, becoming for the first time essentially exploratory and tentative. In other words, the datum of *The Inheritors* seems to belong to fable, but its whole realization belongs to history in which myth is located by imaginative exploration. This is not to say that Golding's interest is that of the historical novelist trying to recapture the past, though his anthropological knowledge continually tethers his imagination to fact. His mode is not history but myth, in that it seeks to reveal archetypal truth within history; it is not fable, in that the myth is demonstrably discovered by the process of writing the novel, could be discovered in no other way, and turns out to be far more complex and difficult to grasp than the novelist thought when he started.

In *Lord of the Flies* we are continually made to look *at* a scene in order to pinpoint its significance within the whole analysis; in *The Inheritors* we are drawn into the scene, incapable of seeing where we are going, but immersed in a mysterious act of discovery. A comparison of the death of Simon with the death of the Old Woman may illustrate this better than a general statement can do:

> The water rose further and dressed Simon's coarse hair with brightness. The line of his cheek silvered and the turn of his shoulder became sculptured marble. The strange, attendant creatures, with their fiery eyes and trailing vapours, busied themselves round his head. The body lifted a fraction of an inch from the sand and a bubble of air escaped from the mouth with a wet plop. Then it turned gently in the water. Somewhere over the darkened curve of the world the sun and moon were pulling; and the film of water on the earth planet was held, bulging slightly on one side while the solid core turned.

Although, as we argued, the total imaginative context of this surrounds it with a more ambiguous suggestiveness than is apparent, the first response is to its clarity and the certainty of its design, the serene confidence with which Golding relates the fraction of an inch and the wet plop with the ordered and beautiful processes of the cosmos. At this moment he seems exactly sure of the placing of Simon's death against the "darkened curve of the world" and the phosphorescent tide pulled by sun and moon. In contrast with the two scenes with the pig's head, Golding seems to tell us exactly how to see. What we are most aware of is the conscious artistry of the novelist.

In *The Inheritors*, Lok is confronted suddenly by the dead body of the Old Woman coming up at him as he hangs "upside down" over "deep water":

> The weed-tail was shortening. The green tip was withdrawing up river. There was a darkness that was consuming the other end. The darkness

became a thing of complex shape, of sluggish and dreamlike movement. Like the specks of dirt, it turned over but not aimlessly. It was touching near the root of the weed-tail, bending the tail, turning over, rolling up the tail towards him. The arms moved a little and the eyes shone as dully as the stones. They revolved with the body, gazing at the surface, at the width of deep water and the hidden bottom with no trace of life or speculation. A skein of weed drew across the face and the eyes did not blink. The body turned with the same smooth and heavy motion as the river itself until its back was towards him rising along the weed-tail. The head turned towards him with dreamlike slowness, rose in the water, came towards his face . . . She was ignoring the injuries to her body, her mouth was open, the tongue showing and the specks of dirt were circling slowly in and out as though it had been nothing but a hole in a stone. Her eyes swept across the bushes, across his face, looked through him without seeing him, rolled away and were gone.

The immediate effect of this is to create an experience of bewildered incomprehension. We are no longer looking at a dead body so much as entering a mind for whom violent death is inconceivable. Hence detail, unrelated, finely particularized, is everything, pattern nothing; the rhetoric keeps "significance" at bay. There is significance, but it comes to us unstated and unstatable, released in our imaginations with the rhythm of nightmare. "Upside down," "deep water": the disorientation involved here will be stabilized only at the end of the last chapter. And the writing in this passage strikes an obsessive note,[2] quite unlike the conscious artistry of *Lord of the Flies*.

Paradoxically, however, it is *The Inheritors* which first focuses Golding's attention on the nature of his art—so much so that it is given an almost conceptual description in the closing chapter,[3] as Tuami prepares to carve his ivory, and in the particularity of that "shape" senses the destiny of the People and of the Inheritors. But the explicitness with which this is done shows that Golding is in danger of slipping back into fable, this time the fable of the artist as myth-maker. For what *The Inheritors* as a whole has made plain is that the novel as myth, unlike the novel as fable, can never be aimed at directly. If it is, it will tend to become fable. The three novels that follow are increasingly profound recognitions that Hamlet's plan, by indirections to find directions out, must be Golding's also. More and more clearly, we shall find conscious artistry replaced by an art of discovery.

In *The Inheritors* Golding tried to reveal the nature of man by imagining his origins; in *Pincher Martin* he looks at his end. There is a significant change, however, which prevents these accounts from being complementary. In *The Inheritors* he is concerned with a group; in *Pincher Martin* he comes for the first time to look at individual man, not mankind. A sense of "shape" has to be found, not in the emblematic figure of the artist carving the ivory, but in the particularities of a personal life.

With *Pincher Martin* Golding confronts for the first time the problems that "character" presents for the writer of myths.

In *The Inheritors* Golding was concerned with the way things "fit," and consequently with a moment of discovery—not in the sense of a fleeting moment, but rather that given the right moment, a whole lifetime can be caught within it. Obviously, no moment offers itself more dramatically than the moment of death, and Golding avails himself of this to show "what we are." Choosing an individual character, however, inevitably raises the past and the question of its relation to the present. Man may be the sum of his actions, but we need to know how. So Golding writes on two levels, giving us Pincher's struggles on the rock in the mode of history, and giving us also the background to his being in the series of flashbacks from his past. Because he is so concerned with being, however, these flashbacks are in the mode not of history but of fable.

Neither of course represents the true mode of the novel. On a second reading the myth is discovered beneath the encounter of history and fable, with its own hidden structure of days and nights behind the chapter divisions, its own tentativeness of explanation behind the clarities of Chris-Greed, or the self-dramatizing of Prometheus-Faust, its disclaimer of official views.

This myth is a powerful and extraordinary achievement. But the clash of history and fable on the surface raises explicit problems for the reader, and also raises implicit questions about the myth's exclusive concern with being, as we tried to show. In this retrospective summary we need only emphasize again how the difficulties spring from Golding's first encounter with the precise problem of character. Dissatisfaction arises from the insufficiency of the "stills" in the mode of fable to explain how the man on the rock becomes his being. For Golding, Martin's past has only an emblematic and analytic connection with his present, but this translates itself for the reader into Golding's indifference to the character of the man whose struggle he creates so marvellously. The design is now unhappily at odds with the imagination. Although Golding has moved from the group to the individual, he treats Pincher as an attitude, capable of being rendered in a series of analytic vignettes. Though he has realized, properly enough, that the myth-writer must come to terms with the individual, the individual he presents us with is allowed to breathe only in an oxygen chamber of the author's devising. The glass jar is a world, but the more Golding has tried to get a character into it, the more it becomes clear that the atmosphere is too rarified for human life. It could not be extended. It will have, somehow, to be broken open.

The three years that separated *Pincher Martin* from *Free Fall* obviously constituted an artistic stocktaking. As he moved away from fable towards myth the treatment of character had become of crucial importance. Abstractly, it was a question of reconciling the essential being of a character with that process of becoming without which no character can satisfactorily exist. However much the myth-maker may be concerned with a moment of definition, he must include in his process of discovery a past for his character that has the reality of his present, and can satisfactorily account for it. These are the considerations that shape *Free Fall*. The ambiguity of the title itself suggests the abandonment of all claim to the certainty implicit in the title of its predecessor. The new novel is explicitly about the problems of writing a novel. "How shall I understand my art?" becomes for Golding both his subject and his object.

Golding chooses a central character who can be an *alter ego*: a successful artist in one mode trying to understand himself, in another, a pattern-maker resolutely interrogating his own experience. With Sammy Mountjoy, the crucial "moment" of his life is now something to be searched for, not merely shown. Consequently he is genuinely involved from the outset in his own history. But his search is to explain a pattern of being already definite and known to him. So Sammy's purpose and Golding's seem more or less the same; but both the difficulty and the way forward lie precisely in that "more or less." For Sammy the novelist remains always, inescapably, a pattern-maker. Although Golding succeeds in creating a character of a depth and resilience that were lacking in *Pincher Martin*, the world of Sammy's novel never frees itself from the collision of differing patterns. The dominant experience of the novel he writes is of learning to "tune" the differing frequencies, until in his "conclusion" the worlds of being and becoming are starkly opposed, irreconcilable. But "two worlds without a bridge" is itself a pattern; the last of Sammy's "hats" and the only one that will fit for him. The imagination of myth is there in Sammy's novel in the mysterious experience of revelation in the "being" sections. The imagination of history is there in the particularized experience of the "becoming" sections. But, because Sammy always seeks an explanation, both are always stratified by the patternings and analytic formulations of fable. As we argued, Golding can use the painter's eye or the myth experience to take Sammy beyond his conscious knowledge; but in Sammy's novel there is no fusion of an art of becoming with an art of being into one vision. Of that novel, as much as of Sammy's paintings, we must finally say that the art is one of "islanding in pictures" out of the complexity of living.

Golding's long and difficult exploration of the problem through his *alter ego* does however show him, at last, a way beyond, though he can only indicate its direction, not follow its path. His purpose does eventually separate itself from his protagonist's. The final page of the book tries to challenge us to glimpse the complexity of living, upsetting Sammy's certainties. Not only is all hope of an inclusive pattern abandoned, but all pattern is seen as reductive. In other words, Golding in *Free Fall* comes to realize that myth cannot be satisfactorily located in history until a way is found to circumvent fable altogether. There can be no "answer" to the Sphinx's riddle; what myth must aspire to is the revelation of the nature of the riddle. It is not enough to create a character who can lead a fictive life free from mere author-manipulation. The myth-writer must also create a historical world fit for him to live in; a world similarly free from reduction.

In *The Spire* Golding finds such a world. Once again he takes as central figure the artist as pattern-maker, though with a much greater assurance than in *Free Fall*. Jocelin is less self-conscious than Sammy and there is no danger of identifying his explanations with Golding's. There is a return to third-person narration with a corresponding gain in objectivity. Jocelin doesn't talk about seeking patterns, his whole behaviour enacts them. Golding is now quite clear about the nature and limitations of the world of fable—and it is this world he gives to Jocelin. But the world of fable is circumvented, neutralized, in two different ways. It is tethered to the world of history because they have a point of common reference—the spire itself. Seen from one point of view, the spire is the diagram of prayer (or the tree of evil); but from another it is "a skin of glass and stone" . . . with the builders "bartering strength for weight or weight for strength, guessing how much, how far, how little, how near." And as soon as we think about the spire, built in faith, in heavy stone, in sin, the very diversity of explanation means that an explanation is impossible. By the end of the novel fable disappears, as Jocelin dies. We look at the spire the novel has built, and glimpse its mythic revelation because we know all we need to know.[4]

The building of the spire pierces every level of the novel, so that fable is taken up into history. To look at the spire is to see Jocelin, to look at Jocelin is to see the spire: "The singing of the stones pierced him, and he fought it with jaws and fists clenched. His will began to burn fiercely and he thrust it into the four pillars, tamped it in with the pain of his neck and his head and his back, welcomed in some obscurity of feeling the wheels and flashes of light, and let them hurt his open eyes as much as they would."

There is no question now of self-consciously feeling for the shape in the ivory. Jocelin is shaped by the spire as surely as he shapes it. This perfect fusion between the inner and the outer world is what gives the novel its immense solidity. The building of the spire becomes different at every level, and presents new problems both physically and metaphysically. It is not history, for it seeks the revelation of archetypal truth, but it founds itself satisfactorily in historical process, gradually unfolding.

It is in the process of discovery within history that the essence of the myth also lies, using the insights of fable, but allowing its clarities and exclusions to cancel one another out. There is no final analysis or formulated wisdom, the emphasis is on the journey and not on the arrival. Hence again and again in *The Spire* we balance faith against the cost of faith, and explanation against explanation. Is it tubercular euphoria that drives Jocelin on? Is it religion—the saint's vision? Is it psychological—

sexual sublimation? Is it moral — the blindness of human pride? Is it social — the privilege of secular advantage? As the questions mount and cut across one another, the answers become a matter of increasing indifference to us. What matters is to realize, in Sammy Mountjoy's words "the unnameable, unfathomable, and invisible darkness that sits at the centre." But, as Golding's novels have developed into this stage, the "darkness" has also lost its definite label, it is opacity rather than blackness. It is no longer simply associated with evil and violence, but also with good. It is shrouded in mystery, alien to definition, the most we can hope for is momentary insight. Yet mystery is not muddle. The spire against the sky is a solid object with a solid history, and it reveals, though we cannot "explain" what it reveals. It leans askew, in constant danger of falling. The myth-maker has realized that he can present, no longer a moment of absolute definition, but only a transitory moment of revelation glimpsed from the corner of the eye. But it also cascades to infinity, "fixing" the otherwise incomprehensible in a moment of time. In one way it is "nothing like" the novelist's original conception, a failure; in another it is a successful discovery of a far more difficult and complex truth. Golding has rid himself of fable and achieved, not history, but that satisfactory location in history without which myth is still fabulous.

Looking back over the novels we can see the change not only in form, but in the nature of the insight which has required formal development to express it. The fable-like structure of *Lord of the Flies* insisted on the darkness of man's heart. In *The Inheritors* the darkness is no longer simply evil, though it is still fearful. Yet Tuami's eyes, unlike the officer's resting complacently on the trim cruiser, or Ralph's weeping, "peer forward . . . to see what lay at the other end of the lake (but) there was such a flashing from the water that he could not see if the line of darkness had an ending." It is the strength of *Pincher Martin* that there is no definite "official view" about where the line of darkness is to be drawn. From one point of view, Pincher lies awake in the night "helpless on the stone floor, trying to run back, run away, climb up," a victim of his own nature; from another, his darkness is the darkness of depravity; from yet another, he is not Judas but Prometheus struggling against extinction. Though on the level of its flashbacks it is more simply fabulous than *Lord of the Flies*, on others it is more mysterious than anything Golding had written. The new feeling for character it gave him is built on in *Free Fall*, dramatizing his new problems. The door of the cell where Sammy had entered into himself in darkness eventually opens onto a genuinely ambiguous world. "There is a mystery in you which is opaque to both of us," Dr. Halde had remarked, but the psychology of the cell itself is the too simple design of the Doctor who does not know about peoples. The spirit of the remark however shapes the art of *The Spire*. Where Sammy's novel had been programmatic about "mystery," *The Spire* reveals it, and we can no longer talk of "darkness." All of Golding's novels have been concerned in one way or another with the Sphinx's riddle, but, as they have developed, the emphasis has shifted from the necessity of getting the right answer to the necessity of posing right questions, setting the riddle in the right way. As explanations have given way to explorations, fable has gradually been assumed into myth located in history.

Put in these terms, we might incline to regard Golding's achievement from *Lord of the Flies* to *The Spire* as a continual progress, in that in his last novel he seems to have found a satisfying shape for myth. In a way this is true, but we are saying less than we might think about the actual achievement in fiction. The solution of artistic "problems" is something that can be seen only in retrospect, and consequently it is an abstraction from the individual works of art. To think of "solutions" as synonymous with "achievements" would be to misunderstand the nature of the artistic process – to become, in fact, a pattern-maker without the imaginative strength of the art of fable. All we can say, as we look at the various transformations which Golding's imagination has undergone in the last twelve years, is that it would seem that *The Spire* marks the end of a phase in his work; the resolution established in that work is of such a kind that it is not easy to see how it can be extended. In saying this, the critic can claim no foresight. He can only try to learn to see what is there already, and what is there in Golding's case seems to be a body of work which has resolved what seem to have been its predominant tensions, leaving the artist free for further exploration. Criticism itself constantly aspires to the condition of fable. It is the lesson derived from working on Golding's novels that it should recognize the limitations of its patterns and welcome opacity, remembering Eliot's words:

> . . . *knowledge imposes a pattern, and falsifies,*
> *For the pattern is new in every moment*
> *And every moment is a new and shocking*
> *Valuation of all we have been.*

Criticism can speak only of "all we have been"; but in doing so, it seeks to prepare us to understand the "new and shocking valuation" when it comes, as it surely will for a writer who has shown the imaginative vitality and resourcefulness of Golding.

Notes

1. In "Fable," *The Hot Gates*, pp. 98–9, Golding records how his imagination seemed to him to "get out of hand" in the first episode with the pig's head. What he there regards as a fault "of excess," however, we regard as a point of growth.

2. P. N. Furbank in a review of *The Spire, Encounter*, 22 May 1964, pp. 59–61, observes that the image of a broken or suffering body in water is found in all the novels. Here, as in *Pincher Martin* (especially p. 96, pp. 144–5), *Free Fall* (p. 130), and *The Spire* (pp. 59–60), but not in *Lord of the Flies* (pp. 189–90, 222–3), the image occurs in a context connected with dream.

3. See our mention of the difference between the manuscript and the final version, Ch. 2, p. 117.

4. This would not be true if the mode *were* history. For example, we know virtually nothing of Goody, not even her name, and little of Jocelin's early relationship with Anselm. Golding cut out, as irrelevant, an account of the latter. Without seeing this, it is impossible to know whether he was right, but it seems likely. We know all we need to know for myth *in* history. By "historical" criteria myth will always be seen as exclusive, but our argument is that we must not blur the differing criteria. Golding may have set out to subvert Trollope, as he had done Ballantyne and Wells.

The Pyramid: Innovation, Rediscovery, Challenge

Arnold Johnston*

In the final chapter of their study of Golding, Mark Kinkead-Weekes and Ian Gregor sum up his first five novels as follows: "the twelve years' work can be seen as an exploration of the problem of disengaging myth from fable, and of giving it a sufficiently historical location." They conclude that in *The Spire* Golding finds such a historical location for his symbolic vision, and that the novel resolves the "predominant tensions" of his work, "leaving the artist free for further exploration." Though *The Spire* does approach more closely than its predecessors the particularity and substance of the mode that Kinkead-Weekes and Gregor call "history" and which John Peter calls "fiction," its medieval setting and tragic intensity seem to set it somewhat apart from the main currents of the contemporary novel.[1] *The Pyramid* (1967) may be seen as resulting from Golding's "further exploration" of the fictional mode, and especially from his confrontation of the more purely social aspects of reality.

The novel comprises three overlapping but essentially independent sections, each set in the tiny English village of Stilbourne and narrated by the protagonist, Oliver, whose growth from childhood to middle age is the book's main connecting thread. The independence of the parts is underscored by the fact that two of the three had appeared in periodicals as long short stories, the first in *Kenyon Review* as "On the Escarpment," the third in *Esquire* as "Inside A Pyramid."[2] The first part of the novel finds Oliver on the verge of entrance into Oxford in the early 1930s, torn between his love for music and the prospect of a career in chemistry, between his chaste and hopeless passion for the soon-to-be-married Imogen Grantley and his desire for the accessible body of Evie Babbacombe, the "local phenomenon."[3] His seduction of Evie is accompanied by his first real consciousness of guilt, and the section ends with his realization of the opportunity he has

*Reprinted from *Of Earth and Darkness: The Novels of William Golding* by permission of the University of Missouri Press. Copyright 1980 by the Curators of the University of Missouri.

lost to "discover" her true humanity. The second, previously unpublished segment covers Oliver's unwilling involvement in the petty quarrels and rivalries of the Stilbourne Operatic Society at the end of his first Oxford term, and his encounter with Evelyn De Tracy, the grotesque and probably homosexual professional director hired to produce the Society's version of *The King of Hearts*. At the conclusion of this episode, during a comically disastrous performance of the sentimental operetta, Oliver loses another opportunity for human discovery through his immature and insensitive response to a drunken but well-meant gesture of self-revelation by De Tracy. *The Pyramid* is completed by the middle-aged Oliver's return to Stilbourne in 1963, a visit that triggers a chain of reminiscences dating back to his childhood, of his relationship with his former music teacher Miss Dawlish, better known as "Bounce," and of her role in determining his future. This section, wider ranging than the first two and less centrally concerned with Oliver, also treats Bounce's relationship with Henry Williams, a mechanic who turns the lonely spinster's love for him to his own advantage, though in a process too ambiguous to invite simple moral judgment. The novel does conclude with another demonstration of Oliver's lack of humane insight. This time, however, he is ultimately granted recognition of his failing; and the self-knowledge brings with it not only a sense of guilt and resignation, but also an awakening of his human sympathies that softens somewhat the book's otherwise bleak conclusion.

The Pyramid is informed throughout by the prevailing note of irony that is so apparent in all of Golding's work; but the narrative tone, perhaps best described as tragicomic, is new — at least in the degree to which it is employed here. Golding once characterized *Pincher Martin* as "a blow on behalf of the ordinary universe," and perhaps his subsequent novels may also be identified as such.[4] However, as one may conclude from the direction of his development through *Free Fall* and *The Spire*, Golding has come to believe that such blows may best be struck by attempting to recreate that universe in terms more comprehensive, less symbolically intense. Denis Donoghue, in a review of *The Pyramid*, goes even farther, proposing that Golding would perhaps "like nothing better than to write a loose baggy monster of a novel, possessed of life to the degree of irrelevance." Donoghue's judgment is that as an attempt, even on a more modest scale, to write such a novel, *The Pyramid* is "an embarrassment, a disaster," because Golding's imagination is "alien to memory."[5]

In dealing with a writer of Golding's stature, one feels compelled to reexamine his apparent failures — like *Free Fall* — to avoid judgments based on misunderstanding of their purposes, and to measure their possible contributions to the further development of his art. *The Pyramid* does seem to represent an effort by Golding to explore the life of social man through fuller commitment to the mode of fiction, or as Donoghue would have it, memory. And memory is indeed an appropriate term in relation to *The Pyramid*. Oliver's story is an exercise in reminiscence; and more importantly, the novel is full of correspondences to Golding's life and earlier works. In *The Pyramid*, as in his previous novels, Golding reexamines the sources of the insight that motivates the work at hand; this time those sources are traceable in large part to his own past. Knowing Golding's methods, one may be less than surprised that his first real "autobiographical" novel was written only after it could be sufficiently justified by thematic and technical necessity.

Oliver and his family live in a cottage much like the boyhood home in Marlborough that Golding describes in "The Ladder and the Tree" (*The Hot Gates*, pp. 166–75); and Marlborough is clearly the counterpart of Oliver's Stilbourne, sharing with it a number of geographical features, including its proximity to Barchester, the fictionalized Salisbury of *The Spire*. Oliver's uneasy poise between the attractions of music and chemistry parallels that of the young Golding between science and literature; and his entry into Oxford to pursue a scientific career is mainly influenced, as was Golding's similar course of action, by the gentle and diffident rationalism of his father. Indeed, one may trace to "The Ladder and the Tree," and to another autobiographical essay called "Billy the Kid" (*The Hot Gates*, pp. 159–65), numerous details in *The Pyramid*: Oliver's father's fascination with the wireless and the gramophone (compare *The Pyramid*, p. 156, and *The Hot Gates*, pp. 168–70); the scholastic crisis that leads to Oliver's commitment to science (*The Pyramid*, pp. 165–66; *The Hot Gates*, pp. 172–75); the character of Oliver's mother (*The Hot Gates*, pp. 159–60, 163); the pervasive sense of social hierarchy that paralyzes life in Stilbourne (*The Hot Gates*, pp. 167–68). Even Golding's frustrated poetic ambitions are allusively incorporated in *The Pyramid* when Oliver retreats in confusion from an attempt to read a modern poem. Reflecting on his earlier consignment of music to the status of a hobby, he observes: "I was a scientist with one private vice. I was expecting too much if I thought myself clever enough for two" (p. 93). In fact, Oliver, who goes on to become a successful scientist, may well be Golding's projection of what he might have become had he not switched from scientific to literary studies after his second year at Oxford.

Oliver, unlike Golding, follows a typical line of development, both in his choice of career and his ultimate regard — albeit touched with a sense of frustration and loss — for the arts as diversions, hobbies, not to be confused with the seriousness of everyday life and work. One need only compare Oliver with such atypical protagonists as Christopher Martin, Sammy Mountjoy, and Dean Jocelin to recognize the high degree of Golding's commitment in *The Pyramid* to examining the "ordinary universe." Striking, too, in comparing the novel with its three immediate predecessors, are its echoes of various features of the earlier works, some merely incidental, others more substantial, but all contributing in some way to the creation of *The Pyramid*'s ordinary world.

The structure of *The Pyramid* invites comparison with *Pincher*

Martin and *Free Fall*, since all three novels incorporate discontinuous time schemes and flashbacks. Golding's purposes differ, of course, from one novel to the other: the flashbacks in *Pincher Martin* are hardly intended as a coherent, substantial study of Martin's life and times; and *Free Fall*, too, is ultimately more concerned with Sammy than his surroundings. But the fact remains that both novels were assailed for their failure to create a sufficiently convincing sense of social reality, a sense that is definitely present in *The Pyramid*. The time scheme of *The Pyramid* is much less puzzling, less liable to misunderstanding than those of the earlier books: unburdened like Chris by the fear of reality, or like Sammy by the desire for significance, Oliver narrates clearly and at a leisurely pace; the self-completeness of each episode leaves the reader free to draw parallels and infer thematic relationships at will, without obvious authorial manipulations. Indeed, *The Pyramid* seems much like a second version of *Free Fall*, with more substantially realized — because more autobiographical — plot and characters and less overt concern with the problems of significance and communication that were apparently resolved in *The Spire*.

Oliver's seduction of Evie is a more complex process than Sammy's attempt to possess Beatrice, since Oliver's is a real social world, inhabited by mothers, fathers, rivals, gossiping neighbors, uninterested bystanders, full of the complications and distractions of everyday life and work in a small town. The preliminary sparring between Oliver and Evie, and the actual seduction scene itself, involve the most explicit sexual descriptions (pp. 55–56, 62) that Golding had written prior to *Darkness Visible*, realizing graphically an image that had appeared more tentatively in both *Free Fall* and *The Spire*. In *Free Fall* the child Sammy's innocent drawing of rolling hills and woodlands is distorted by the sexually frustrated Rowena Pringle into a libidinous fantasy (pp. 205–6); and in *The Spire* Jocelin's similar frustration produces a like response to the wooded landscape that he sees from the tower (p. 101). *The Pyramid* transforms these internal projections into external reality, as for Oliver the clump of trees on the escarpment that overlooks Stilbourne is the "hot and sexy" haven where he wishes to have Evie.

The erotic passages in *The Pyramid* are notably different from those of *Free Fall* in their exploration of the complexity of both characters involved. Indeed, though Oliver is as concerned with exploitation as was Sammy, he is overwhelmed by Evie's womanhood like "a small boat in a deep sea" (p. 62), and is himself personally humiliated when she uses him as an object of revenge against Stilbourne, forcing him to make love to her on the bare escarpment in full view of the town, and particularly of Oliver's father, who sees the couple through his binoculars.

The final meeting between Oliver and Evie, two years later, after his entry into Oxford and her establishment as a woman of the world in London, leads to a violent quarrel and the inadvertent self-revelation by Evie of an earlier incestuous relationship with her brutal father. In the midst of his anger Oliver suddenly realizes that Evie has acquired for him "the attributes of a person rather than a thing," that he and she might have "made something, music, perhaps, to take the place of the necessary, the inevitable battle." But Evie leaves to disappear forever from Oliver's life, and he returns home "confounded, to brood on this undiscovered person and her curious slip of the tongue" (pp. 90–91).

The "making of music" mentioned by Oliver becomes, as the novel progresses, more than a romantic cliché. The inscription on the cross that Evie wears—*Amor vincit omnia*—merges with an oft-quoted pronouncement of Miss Dawlish's father—"Heaven is music"—and the combination of music and love takes on a symbolic significance, opposing the exaltation of science represented mainly by Oliver's father.

The central part of *The Pyramid*, involving Oliver with Evelyn De Tracy and the Stilbourne Operatic Society, takes up thematically where the first leaves off, dramatizing the Stilbourne syndrome, the inability of the townspeople to "make music together." *The King of Hearts* is a disharmonious fiasco that De Tracy is powerless to rescue; his theatrical knowledge is irrelevant here, since the real problem lies in the snobbery, small-mindedness, and essential selfishness of the assembled representatives of English society. Though much of the episode aims at being humorous, the underlying theme is clearly serious, a fact emphasized by the conclusion, in which the homosexual De Tracy responds to Oliver's youthful desire to know "the *truth* of things" (p. 123) by showing the young man a photograph that pictures the director in a ballerina's costume. Oliver's laughter drowns out all hope of communication, and masked in the grotesquerie of the scene is the fact that the two are playing in a different key: Oliver wants to know the truth of things like a scientist; De Tracy proffers a greater truth—about people—emphasizing the need for perception. Oliver's perception at this point, however—a year away from his last meeting with Evie—is unequal to an understanding of De Tracy. And though the producer does awaken him to the stupidity, vanity, and insensitivity of his romantic ideal, Imogen Grantley, the section ends not with a real increase in Oliver's perceptiveness, but with his smug confidence of his superiority to the disharmonious throng.

The third part of *The Pyramid* emphasizes both the music-love-science symbolism and the novel's relationship to *Free Fall*, fusing the two elements and integrating them skillfully into the central symbol of the pyramid. The child Oliver, shuttling back and forth across the street between his father's rationalism and Miss Dawlish's music lessons, parallels the child Sammy, torn between the gentle scientism of Nick Shales and the fierce religiosity of Rowena Pringle. The paired adult characters are certainly similar: Nick is a science teacher and Oliver's father a chemist; both Rowena and Bounce are love-starved spinsters teaching spiritually oriented subjects. In one scene, after he has seen Oliver and Evie on the escarpment, Oliver's father echoes closely Nick's vehement sentiments on sex: "—this man what d'you me call him—these books—cinema—pa-pers—this sex—it's *wrong, wrong, wrong!*" (p. 81; compare with *Free Fall*, p. 231). But Oliver's father is a more complex character than Nick, more human and less clearly functional; from an autobiographical stand-point one may see Nick as an idealization of Golding's father, and Oliver's father as a more realistic portrait. Bounce Dawlish, too, is far deeper and more various than Rowena Pringle; a mannish, pipe-smoking old maid whose own ambivalent love for music has been sternly inculcated in her by an eccentric father, Bounce is in fact *The Pyramid*'s most interesting character.

Bounce's musical relationship with Oliver (whom she nicknames "Kummer" in a rare joking mood) is intertwined with her frustrated love for Henry Williams, an itinerant young Welsh mechanic who persuades her to buy the town's first car, and after endearing himself to her eventually settles in Stilbourne as a general handyman, mysteriously producing a wife and child in the fashion of many an old ballad. The Williamses finally move into Bounce's house as lodgers, and for years Oliver's music lessons afford him glimpses of the strange ménage, of Bounce's frustrated and pathetic attempts to capture Henry's attention, of Henry's use of Bounce's money to establish himself as a prosperous garage owner. But Oliver betrays the same insensitivity to the unattractive Bounce that he had shown in his encounter with De Tracy, though again he may be partially excused by his youth, the influence of the Stilbourne environ-ment, and his parents' persistent and irritating assertions of his devotion to his music teacher.

Bounce's thwarted love for Henry diminishes her capacity for love of music. And in turn she plays her part in turning Oliver from music to science, unexpectedly seconding his father's advice while prophetically equating him with Henry: " 'Don't be a musician, Kummer, my son. Go into the garage business if you want to make money. As for me, I shall have to slave at music till I drop down dead' " (p. 163). On his last visit to Stilbourne, while seated at her grave, Oliver concludes that his assumed devotion to Bounce has actually been hatred, stemming from his child-hood fear of her Gothically gloomy house and her own forbidding exterior; from his oppression at her role in turning him from music and at the grotesque relationship between her and Henry's family. Oliver laughs at the irony of the inscription that Henry has had cut on her tombstone: her father's unctuous epigram, Heaven is Music. But shortly afterward, while visiting her empty house, he comes upon the smashed, burnt ruins of Bounce's music, and he is jolted by the realization that Bounce has destroyed it out of despair, out of her inability to find solace in the harmonies so inhumanely taught by her father or the selfish love that Henry rationed to her like dividends from the capital she had invested in his business. The pyramid of the title becomes symbolically one with the defeated possibilities of music and love in the ruins of Bounce's pyramid-shaped, crystal-encased metronome (pp. 150, 182). And Oliver realizes that he, like Henry, has evolved into a selfish rationer of love, incapable of reaching out to another human being, of paying the "unreasonable price" of himself as Bounce did on the day when her mind snapped, when in her last all-out attempt to win Henry's attention she paraded naked down the streets of Stilbourne (pp. 174–75).

The theme of human blindness to the necessity for selfless love is explicitly identified in *The Pyramid*'s epigraph, taken from the *Instructions* of Ptah-Hotep, the primal Egyptian deity, creator of gods and men and, significantly, the patron of art and science and builder of the first pyramid: *If thou be among people make for thyself love, the beginning and end of the heart.* Both the epigraph and a further dimension of Golding's symbolic use of the pyramid are present in germinal form in *Free Fall*: in Sammy's aphorism, "Love selflessly and you cannot come to harm" (p. 33), and in a remark upon his adolescent sensitivity to "the shape of our social pyramid" (p. 193). And the overall symbolic aspect of *The Pyramid*'s theme is foreshadowed in Sammy's fascination with the kings of Egypt.

Perhaps the most useful source of insight into Golding's symbolism in *The Pyramid* is "Egypt from My Inside" (*The Hot Gates*, pp. 71–82), in which he discusses his lifelong interest in Egyptology.[6] Here, he identifies modern man with the ancient Egyptians in the capacity for banality, greed, and cruelty, and speaks of "our ant-like persistence in building a pyramid of information" (p. 81), drawing a parallel between modern man's exaltation of science and the purely scientific aspect of the Egyptian pyramids. But despite these similarities, and despite the social tyranny and "ponderous self-advertisement" (p. 73) represented by the ancient pyramids, Golding nonetheless accepts them as the stuff of vision, "the thumbprint of a mystery" (p. 81). For it is the secret within the pyramid that makes it, like Jocelin's spire, a true symbol, "that which has an indescribable effect and meaning" (p. 74). In the depths of the tomb is the puzzling answer to the Sphinx's riddle of *Free Fall*: "Man himself . . . timelessly frozen and intimidating, an eternal question mark" (p. 74).

Turning to *The Pyramid*, one sees clearly how it embodies the ideas that Golding discusses in "Egypt from My Inside." The novel treats the social aspect of the pyramid — its banality and hierarchical preoccupation, its exaltation of science over art — from base to apex. But it focuses, too, on the mystery, the human enigma that Oliver, bound by artificial social strictures and his growing faith in science, ignores until almost too late. With De Tracy, Oliver misses the mystery almost entirely; with Evie, he senses it incompletely, and merely in relation to her. Only with Bounce Dawlish, appropriately enough after a visit to her grave, while seated amid the relics of her life, does Oliver get inside the pyramid to confront the "eternal question mark" that is man. Only from this confrontation does he gain a measure of insight into his own humanity and that of others, the knowledge that in looking at Henry Williams he sees his own face, that of a man who will "never pay more than a reasonable price" (p. 185). But though Oliver drives away from Stilbourne as a man who cannot "love selflessly," he is at least aware of his condition. And the bleak consolation of self-awareness is the most that Golding's novels offer to the majority of men as a possible source of qualified salvation.

Clearly, *The Pyramid* is much more complex than most of its early reviewers and critics have found it to be. The book is as symbolically dense as any of Golding's previous novels while at the same time dealing more extensively with the contemporary world and exploring new dimensions of characterization and human interrelationship. Much of the added social breadth and detail of the novel stems from its autobiographical aspects; much remains in Oliver's story, however, that cannot be easily traced to autobiographical sources, or to the working out of its intricate symbolic pattern. A close reexamination of the book reveals that here again, as in *Free Fall*, Golding's imagination apparently challenges the vision of a towering literary figure: *The Pyramid*, Golding's first real attempt at a social novel, seems to parallel ironically *Great Expectations*, by England's greatest social novelist, Charles Dickens. Oliver's story corresponds, in a number of important respects, to that of Pip, the protagonist of Dickens's book.[7]

The parallel is suggested even by general likenesses: both novels deal with the central theme of spiritual blindness, as caused both by the pressures of society and individual obsession; both emphasize in similar ways the power of selfless love and count the cost in guilt and wasted lives of blindness to its necessity; both are first-person narratives of a young man's journey in such darkness to a somber self-awareness of his guilt in middle age; both possess an anecdotal flavor and a tendency to derive both humor and insight from human eccentricity and the ironic possibilities of an immature narrator. The books even have a similar history of publication, appearing first in parts and later as completed works, a common practice in the eighteenth and nineteenth centuries, but notably less so today.

More specific correspondences are numerous. *The Pyramid* opens, like *Great Expectations*, with the protagonist's coerced involvement in a clandestine errand of mercy to a nearby marsh: Oliver is persuaded by Evie to help push Bounce's car, in which Evie and his neighbor Bob Ewan have been joyriding, out of a pond. Oliver's home life is much like Pip's, since his mother is as dominant as, if less offensive than, Mrs. Joe. Like Pip, Oliver, infatuated with a shallow, vain girl of higher station — Imogen Grantley — fails to see the worth of an accessible girl of lower station — Evie — and loses both. In a scene highly reminiscent of the low-born Pip's questionable triumph over Herbert Pocket for the attentions of Estella, Oliver employs roughhouse tactics to best Bow Ewan, his social superior, in a fight for Evie's favors. Much of Oliver's inner life is dominated, like

Pip's, by a rejected spinster who lives in a house of Gothic proportions and atmosphere, a house he returns to in later life to acknowledge his hatred of the woman, only to find her earthly remains—in Bounce's case, her music—ravaged by fire, softening his attitude and causing him to "forgive" her. On Oliver's return from London to his hometown he also confronts Henry Williams, whose tradesman's homespun manner and ultimate success seem to indicate his correspondence to Joe Gargery, and whose profession—garage mechanic—is the twentieth-century equivalent of Joe's. Indeed, Henry is the one person who suspects, but keeps, the secret of Oliver's involvement in the affair of Bounce's car, paralleling Joe's silent knowledge of Pip's thefts on behalf of Magwitch. Occupying a central place in both novels, though Golding treats it at greater length, is the protagonist's encounter with a grotesque actor, an encounter that crystallizes the theme of each novel: Wopsle's self-deceiving "great expectations" are a more ludicrous version of Pip's, and the entire episode, like Oliver's experience with De Tracy, demonstrates the young man's lack of perception and human sympathy. There are other parallels, even extending to such minor details as Oliver's name (recalling one of Dickens's best-known child heroes), and his being dosed, like Pip, with "opening medicine" at the slightest sign of emotional instability.

The intent of such a relationship would seem twofold: to render Golding's criticism of the modern world more trenchant; and more importantly, to revise Dickens's novel, both thematically and technically. On the one hand, Golding underscores by comparison with Dickens's fictional world the banality and meanness of his own; in almost every instance described above, the modern characters are distinctly diminished in moral or dramatic stature by comparison with their nineteenth-century counterparts, and their world, consequently, is a duller, less hopeful place. But this is precisely Golding's point. For the world of *The Pyramid*, unlike that of *Great Expectations*, is carefully pruned of any sentimentality that might soften its somber theme. Conversely, however, the issue of guilt is deliberately clouded in *The Pyramid* to emphasize the complexities that plague modern man's attempts either to affix or accept moral responsibility.

For if Golding's characters suffer by comparison with those of Dickens, they are in a sense more realistic: Bounce Dawlish, for all her grotesqueness, is much less bizarre than Miss Havisham, and Bounce's role in determining her young pupil's future is far smaller, his hatred of her far less justified; and Henry Williams, unlike Joe Gargery, is hardly selfless and simple, though these are traits that he attempts to project. Indeed, in the sort of switch that Golding is so fond of, Henry Williams is a more plausible villain of *The Pyramid* than is Bounce. One can imagine Golding's reasoning here: "Who is more likely to hold sway over people's lives in modern society, an eccentric old lady or an entrepreneur?" Even here, however, the issue is complicated, for Henry's sin is, like Oliver's, merely his inability to "pay more than a reasonable price" in his dealings with his fellows.

And just as there are no clearcut villains in *The Pyramid*, there is an absence of Dickensian melodrama and coincidence, digression and repetition. Golding's novel is trimmed of Orlicks and Magwitches: they contradict the real universe. And *The Pyramid* avoids entirely the city of London, which provides much of the sprawling populousness of *Great Expectations*, concentrating instead on Stilbourne, which like Pip's boyhood home is the ultimate repository of revelation, guilt, and atonement.

But though *The Pyramid* succeeds in presenting a more realistic and concentrated embodiment of its themes than does *Great Expectations*, it does so at considerable cost in other important fictional elements. Golding's apparent reduction of Dickens's world to a size that corresponds to the world of his own vision demonstrates not only the persistent single-mindedness of that vision, and his confidence in his own powers, but also his evident limitations as a writer. For if *The Pyramid* creates a world more typical than that of *Great Expectations*, and presents an accurate picture of modern man's isolation from his fellows, it also sacrifices Dickens's wider sense of humanity, his love of eccentric, larger-than-life types, and his delight in weaving a complex and fascinating web, not primarily of symbols, but of human action. And perhaps more important, *The Pyramid* sacrifices the high dramatic tension, not only of Dickens's novel, but of Golding's own earlier works.

The Pyramid shows Golding once more in a state of artistic flux, expanding his own vision beyond its former limitations, but at the same time unwilling to abandon himself completely to chaos. Unlike Dickens, he is not yet, and perhaps will never be, a writer who "revels in the vitality of the ordinary universe." *The Pyramid* is incisive in its portrayal of Stilbourne and its people; and the subtlety of its symbolic patterns stands as an impressive technical achievement. Donoghue clearly overstates when he says that Golding "writes of ordinary things with extraordinary awkwardness."[8] But the fact does remain that, compared with the human riches of Dickens, Golding's characters and their relationships seem somewhat tritely conceived and his novel more akin to such narrow chronicles of small town banality and eccentricity as *Main Street* and *Winesburg, Ohio* than to *Great Expectations*. Then, too, Golding's attempts at humor in *The Pyramid* compare badly with Dickens: the irony that Golding uses so well as an element of tragedy seems heavy-handed when he applies it to the creation of comic effects, a fault also notable in his play, *The Brass Butterfly*; his attempts at more boisterous comedy—as when he describes in sexual imagery Oliver's frantic attempts during *The King of Hearts* to get onstage through a narrow passageway with his beefeater's halberd—are often so flatfooted as to be embarrassing.[9] Despite its faults, however, *The Pyramid* does represent a definite extension of Golding's range, and perhaps may best be regarded, like *Free Fall*, as a necessary stage in his developing fictional confrontation of the contemporary world.

Perhaps the major difficulties that Golding faced in working out his expanded vision may best be seen by focusing on two related features of his first six novels. The first of these features was his tendency, as in *The Pyramid*, to use works by other writers as ironic foils of his own, his tendency to say, like Sammy Mountjoy, "Not that — but this!" (*Free Fall*, p. 102). John Bowen sees in Golding's assertive individualism a kind of arrogance, "as if all his fellows walking their more usual technical paths but lighting them with their own personal lights were doing something he scorned to do."[10] Golding's novels sometimes do give this impression; and a further indication of such an attitude was Golding's initially steadfast refusal to recognize readings of his novels based on such studies of human nature as the works of Freud and Frazer.[11] Of course, a writer must stand or fall not by what he reacts to or by what he intends, but by what he creates, and Golding's creative record is impressive. But one must conclude that in *The Pyramid* Golding's reactive tendencies — whether arrogant or not — betray him somewhat: the parallel of *Great Expectations* causes him to fall between two stools, since the obviously reductive process involved acts in opposition to his equally obvious attempts to extend his fictional range.

The second feature of Golding's works that needed resolution if his new approach to fiction were to succeed was his apparent inability to find in the contemporary social world more than the vitiated drama and tragedy of such characters as Oliver and Sammy Mountjoy. Of his first six novels, only *The Spire*, which is far from contemporary, seems to offer a fully integrated blend of the historical and the tragic. Perhaps, though, the answer lay not, as Martin Green had it, in Golding's "sullen distaste for the contemporary," but in his choice of protagonists.[12] Golding's art, reactive as it is, seems to require as a protagonist a foil of sufficient stature to allow his vision the detachment it needs to realize its full dramatic power. In his latest three novels through 1967, only one protagonist, Jocelin, was a successful foil; Sammy and Oliver — perhaps because of their autobiographical aspects — seem too close to Golding to lend themselves to such treatment. This requirement of a foil, so much akin to his use of literary parallels, is at once Golding's most striking limitation and a major source of his unique power.

The Pyramid seemed to represent, for most critics, another crucial stage in Golding's career, one that would demand of him continued widening of his vision, continued exploration of the technical resources of his craft, perhaps even an attempt to break free from the reactive pattern that had held him throughout his writing life. The ordinary universe, as Donoghue observed, might prove to be "beyond [Golding], or beneath him."[13] Perhaps, however, Golding's new declaration of oneness with the ancient Egyptians — with their "unreason, spiritual pragmatism, and capacity for ambiguous belief" (*The Hot Gates*, p. 82) — gave promise of a new commitment to the everyday world.

Notes

1. Compare Mark Kinkead-Weekes and Ian Gregor, *William Golding: A Critical Study*, pp. 239–57, and John Peter, "The Fables of William Golding," *Kenyon Review*, p. 557.

2. William Golding, "On the Escarpment," pp. 311–400; and "Inside a Pyramid," *Esquire*, pp. 165–69.

3. William Golding, *The Pyramid* (New York: Harcourt, Brace & World, 1967), p. 7; further parenthetical references in the text are taken from this edition.

4. Frank Kermode and William Golding, "The Meaning of It All," *Books and Bookmen*, p. 10. See also Leighton Hodson, *William Golding*, pp. 101–9, for a discussion of Golding's use of the "tragicomic" mode.

5. Denis Donoghue, "The Ordinary Universe," pp. 21–22.

6. Significantly, this essay first appeared as "Egypt and I" in *Holiday*, several months before the publication of "Inside a Pyramid" (see note 2 to this chapter).

7. Golding acknowledges Dickens's greatness in Jack I. Biles, *Talk: Conversations with William Golding*, p. 9; and Virginia Tiger, *William Golding: The Dark Fields of Discovery*, p. 202, notes that "the sturdiest literary furniture of his imagination dates from the nineteenth century — Wells, Dickens, Thackeray, and the robust popular tradition of Henry, Ballantyne, and Burroughs." She also (p. 215) points out Trollopeian qualities in *The Pyramid*. The parallels to *Great Expectations*, however, are numerous and pervasive.

8. Donoghue," The Ordinary Universe," pp. 21, 22.

9. Compare this scene with *The Inheritors*, pp. 200–4, and with *Free Fall*, pp. 20–21.

10. John Bowen, "Bending Over Backwards," *Times Literary Supplement*, p. 608.

11. See James Keating, "Interview with William Golding," Casebook Edition of *Lord of the Flies*, p. 195, Frank Kermode, "The Meaning of It All," *Books and Bookmen*, p. 9, and Biles, *Talk*, pp. 18, 53–58, 75.

12. Martin Green, "Distaste for the Contemporary," *The Nation*, p. 454.

13. Donoghue, "The Ordinary Universe," p. 21.

[*The Scorpion God*: Sending Up the Idea of History]

James R. Baker and William Golding*

BAKER: Is it true you first began to develop an interest in ancient Egypt and in hieroglyphics through an early encounter with a mummy at eleven or twelve years of age in the Bristol museum?

GOLDING: I think now I was interested before then. I mean the fact

*This exchange first appeared in "An Interview with William Golding," *Twentieth Century Literature* 28 (Summer 1982) and is reprinted by permission of *Twentieth Century Literature: A Scholarly and Critical Journal*.

that I was in the museum and had that strange encounter was because I had been interested in Egyptian things.

BAKER: You mean the encounter described in "Egypt from my Inside"?

GOLDING: Yes. Very odd encounter. The interesting thing is I just discovered that that encounter is now taking place, so to speak. They are unwrapping that mummy in the museum. They did it some sixty years ago, but they're doing it all over again. Very weird. However, one mustn't make too much of such things, though one does since the temptation is overwhelming.

BAKER: But so far as I know it wasn't until you wrote *The Scorpion God*, published in 1971, that Egypt and Egyptology came directly into play, although it's implied, I suppose, in *The Pyramid* as well.

GOLDING: To some extent, yes. But I had the Egyptology up my sleeve all the time. I was quite sure I was going to write something about it sooner or later. But I didn't know what it would be, and of course, the story "The Scorpion God" is Herodotus's view of Egypt more than anybody else's, it's not received archaeological opinion.

BAKER: Does that connection with Herodutus apply to just the one story in the volume?

GOLDING: Yes, I think so. Herodotus didn't have anything to say about primitive man and obviously nothing about the Roman Empire. But he did have a lot to say about Egypt. He is the first Egyptologist, they say, followed its history and all that.

BAKER: But the tales in *The Scorpion God* are also anthropological fables? Again we've returned to the theme of patterns in history or lack of patterns and to the theme of evolution.

GOLDING: You mean change, let's not call it evolution. Evolution, presumably, implies progress in one direction or another. I see change rather than progress.

BAKER: Change, it appears from the stories, is often a matter of accident, circumstance, chance, and therefore the changes or patterns that we might observe in history are more often a result of coincidence.

GOLDING: Yes, also you've got to remember, to some extent, I'm sending up the idea of history, and have my tongue in my cheek much more often than people ever suspect because I have this kind of solemn reputation. My tongue is in my cheek an awful lot of the time, and it was in those stories, it was tucked in there firmly. Herodotus says that the Egyptians do everything in public that other people do in private, and everything in private that other people do in public, so that was good enough for me. I simply tied that to the story.

BAKER: Well, in the story itself we see tradition and the sequence of God-rulers interrupted by the sexual attraction between Princess Pretty-flower and the Fool. Then in the second story, "Clonk, Clonk," it is the crippled male who purely through accident escapes being put to death as a child and again, through accident, wins the sexual attention of Palm and becomes one of the accepted Leopard Men, the tribal cult for brave males, and one of the tribal leaders.

GOLDING: Yes, that's right.

BAKER: And thirdly, in "Envoy Extraordinary," Phanocles, the Greek inventor who threatens to usher in the entire modern age a thousand years too soon, is sent to China by a wise Caesar.

GOLDING: It delays the industrial revolution by about a thousand years. I remember the brave Leopard Men are actually based on an incident one day when I was in an American university, a very eminent university, and I looked out — there was the university football team going off with the band playing them to their bus, or whatever it was, and it was wonderful. My eyes came out at the picture of this kind of gross maleness marching to their bus — rah, rah, give me a "D." They became the Leopard Men, you see, so my tongue is really often much further in my cheek than you think.

BAKER: Looking at those three tales, then, one might conclude that history is comedy.

GOLDING: Well, for God's sake, let's have fun with something. You can't change history. You can't change what's happened, but you can have a little gentle fun at its expense.

BAKER: And patterns, or the patterns therefore that we perceive in the past, are really largely the result of accidents.

GOLDING: I should think accidents have an effect on them, and I think it makes a good story when an accident does affect history. If Cleopatra's nose had been an inch longer, as somebody once said, the history of the world would have changed. If it'd been *half* an inch longer, history would have changed. Suppose Saint Paul hadn't survived his first shipwreck, shall we say. Supppose Caesar had been drowned crossing the channel to Britain, either way, going or coming, the history of the world would have been very different. And the number of times that Alexander the Great must have been missed by an arrow or a spear!

BAKER: Does this explain why you chose *The Scorpion God* as the title for the whole volume?

GOLDING: I think I chose that title because it's a good title.

BAKER: But he's a Scorpion God because he hurts. The high priest and other devouts who believe in systems and in structures and in their continuity are always stung by the Scorpion God, is that the proper metaphor?

GOLDING: The king is the earliest. You probably know this as well as I do, the first recorded Pharaoh, the one who united the whole of Egypt, united upper and lower Egypt, was called Menes. Now, I don't know what the name means, but there was another Pharaoh and there's a huge Egyptological argument going on as to whether the name Scorpion, which they found on a slate palette, is an alternative name for this chap, or whether it is an unknown Pharaoh before him. I choose to make the scorpion Pharaoh the one who unites the whole of Egypt, so when the dying high priest says "he stings like a scorpion," that names the Pharaoh. He is going to unite Egypt, make it a great power. He's nothing like an Egyptian at all. And so he is Scorpion, and he is God. There was a "Scorpion God."

BAKER: But the book has a kind of unity, nevertheless?

GOLDING: It was not intentional. Years separated the stories. I think I had the first story hanging about and I wanted to preserve it because it was published in a volume with two other stories by two other people. I wanted to keep it for myself, so I thought, I can't publish it by itself, I have to have a story to go with it, and so I wrote "The Scorpion God." Then I wrote "Clonk, Clonk" to keep the other two stories apart, and also make it a book which was wide and big enough to be put on sale as a book and not a pamphlet. So it was very much more ad hoc, and if it has a unity it is one of the accidents of history.

Darkness Visible

Don Crompton*

Although Golding has consistently refused to talk about *Darkness Visible*,[1] its central position in the canon of his work is immediately apparent, for this is the novel where he has explored unflinchingly those subjects that trouble and fascinate him most — the extremes of behaviour of which men are capable, their propensities for absolute good or evil, their endlessly, paradoxical saintliness and sinfulness. And behind these lie the mysteries of the spiritual world that continually surround us but are largely closed to us, invisible, forgotten or ignored for much of most men's lives. It is these mysteries that Golding penetrates, this darkness that he attempts to illuminate, using two characters who live primarily in a spiritual dimension although at opposite poles within it. The first section is concerned with the nature and visions of Matty who, though physically disfigured, is, in his unworldliness, self-dedication and selfless love, some kind of saint. Opposed to Matty is Sophy, young, beautiful and an agent of the powers of evil, whose impulse towards destruction and primal chaos she advances as far as she can. The book's third section brings the two into direct conflict in the familiar everyday world (now 1978) where the majority of averagely sensual men and women muddle on, neither saved nor damned except by their own triviality. The confusion and dislocation of the modern urban wasteland are vividly conveyed; the high street of the ironically named Greenfield is filled with the incessant noise of jets and juggernauts, broken up into distinctive racial groups, disintegrated by the failure of traditional communal life, a failure epitomised by the conversion of the parish church into a so-called "community centre."

The still small voice of the spirit that alone gives life a meaning beyond itself, informing it with energy and beauty, can scarcely be heard amid this babel, so that Matty is forced to communicate instead by means of touch and silence. When he examines Sim's palm, Sim "fell through into an awareness of his own hand that stopped time in its revolution. The palm was exquisitely beautiful, it was made of light. It was precious and preciously inscribed with a sureness and delicacy beyond art and grounded somewhere else in absolute health." This delicate revelation echoes that of William Blake who, like Matty, communicated with angels and Old Testament prophets. Blake, too, understood what it meant

> To see a World in a Grain of Sand
> And a Heaven in a Wild Flower,
> Hold Infinity in the palm of your hand
> And Eternity in an hour.

*This essay first appeared in Don Crompton, *A View From the Spire: William Golding's Later Novels*, edited and completed by Julia Briggs (Oxford: Basil Blackwell, 1985) and is reprinted with permission of Basil Blackwell, Limited, Oxford, England.

In *Darkness Visible* Golding has plunged into spiritual mysteries which at best may only be seen through a glass darkly, at worst may be looked on at one's peril. Small wonder, then, that he has been unwilling to discuss them further, has indeed prefaced his book with Virgil's prayer as he set out to describe Aeneas's descent into the underworld and the forbidden sights he there beheld: "sit mihi fas audita loqui" — may it be allowed to me to speak what I have heard.

Darkness Visible spans Golding's career not only in terms of the centrality of its concerns but also in terms of its starting-point — a firestorm in the docks during the war. A similar scene of sickening destruction and conflagration, at once horrifying and luminously beautiful, had provided the starting-point of *Lord of the Flies*, though it was later cut before publication.[2] The book originally began with a description of the atomic explosion out of which the children escaped, an event recapitulated exactly but in miniature by the fire that is destroying the island at the end of the book; in a comparable way, the naval officer's uniform and sub-machine gun are reproduced on a small scale by the children's war-paint and pointed sticks. Perhaps the description in *Darkness Visible* is the more powerful for having waited all those years to find its appropriate context; its hauntingly vivid detail probably springs from a wartime experience that had not been fully exorcised. But if *Darkness Visible* begins in a man-made inferno, it also begins with a miracle, for out of the fire and the bombs exploding along the street walks a small child. The first response of the fire watchers is incredulity, not only because small children do not normally walk out of fires that are "melting lead and distorting iron," but because children had no reason to be there at all; they had been the first to be evacuated from the area. And the boy, in spite of all the horrible burns he has suffered down one side of his body, is neither running nor apparently afraid, but walking with a "kind of ritual gait." During his subsequent hospitalisation, attempts are made to identify him but it is eventually decided that he has "no background but the fire" and that "he might have been born from the sheer agony of a burning city." Having no name, he is first given a number — seven, the mystic number of the Apocalypse or Book of Revelation; then, two Christian names — Matthew Septimus. When read as a biblical reference, this alludes to Matthew, chapter 7, whose opening verse provides what is to be a major theme of the book: judgement, both in the straightforward sense provided by the verses themselves — "Judge not, that ye be not judged" — but also in the sense of the final judgement, the judgement day promised in St John's Revelation. From the outset, everything about the child, known as Matty, is uncertain; for example, his surname is left deliberately vague. He is to be misnamed Windy, Wandgrave, Windrap, Wildwort, Windwort, Wildwave, Windgrove, Windrove, Windgraff, Windrave, and Windrow until finally, in the last few pages, he is called Windrove, the most appropriate version for a character who from the first seems to have the ability to disappear, to "become unnoticeable like an animal." At times those around him wonder, as Mr Pedigree does, whether he is "all connected with everything else or does he kind of drift through."

In the first chapter other hints prepare the reader for other possibilities. One of the firemen is, in his normal profession, a bookseller, and as he watches the holocaust over which the firemen have no control, he ponders its significance: "The bookseller was saying nothing and seemed to be staring at nothing. There was a memory flickering on the edge of his mind and he could not get it further in where it could be examined; and he was also remembering the moment when the child had appeared, seeming to his weak sight to be perhaps not entirely there—to be in a state of, as it were, indecision as to whether he was a human shape or merely a bit of flickering brightness. Was it the Apocalypse? Nothing could be more apocalyptic than a world so ferociously consumed. But he could not quite remember." Why does the child flicker like this? In what sense is he "real," and if he is, how can he remain unconsumed by the fire? On the first page, the firestorm which is consuming the city is compared to a "burning bush," a reminder that God himself spoke to Moses out of the fire of a burning bush, a bush that burnt but, miraculously, was not consumed. As in Eliot's *Little Gidding*, the fire of the Blitz may be purifying, purgatorial as well as simply destructive, like the annihilating "black lightning" that threatens Pincher Martin.

Whatever was flickering on the edge of the bookseller's mind, however, it was not only Moses's burning bush. And though the Apocalypse includes many allusions to fire, and provides the most important single reference point for the whole novel, it does not include a comparably flickering figure. The German bombers spraying incendiaries over London have a biblical counterpart in the prophecy of Ezekiel (10:2) where avenging angels scatter coals of fire over the doomed city of Jerusalem. The emergence of Matty from the flames is also reminiscent of an incident in chapter 1 of the same prophecy when Ezekiel beholds a mysterious being: "And I saw as the colour of amber, as the appearance of fire round about within it, from the appearance of his loins even upward, and from the appearance of his loins even downward, I saw as it were the appearance of fire, and it had brightness round about." Later in chapter 8, this spirit carries Ezekiel up to heaven. And if Matty walks into the book like a spirit of fire, so he walks out of it, "waist deep in gold" and taking the dying Mr Pedigree with him, as "the gold grew fierce and burned" and Matty vanishes "like a guy in a bonfire."

But the Bible is by no means Golding's only point of reference in this opening chapter. The description of the holocaust, which so effectively conveys the agony of a dying city, also has a certain magical quality in all the destruction, a strange brightness, almost a beauty, as though one were looking at a city of the underworld containing "too much shameful, inhuman light . . . so much light that the very stones seemed semiprecious, a version of the infernal city." The burning streets become Hell, their glowing stones recalling the building of Pandemonium in *Paradise Lost* (I, 688–730) from which the novel's title is derived. They also suggest the classical underworld with its rivers of flame to which Golding's epigraph has already drawn attention: its words occur just before Aeneas, in the company of the Sybil and carrying the sacred golden bough of mistletoe in his hand as a protective talisman, enters the underworld. Significantly, it is the poet Virgil himself, not Aeneas, who prays to the dark gods to allow him to penetrate the depths and make darkness visible, rather as Golding hopes to penetrate the depths of his society and of human nature.

This patchwork of associations is an indication of how the book is to be read. For the first book of *Paradise Lost*, the sixth book of the *Aeneid* and the Apocalypse have something in common: they are all concerned with twilight zones where judgement is awaited but has not yet been meted out, where things are neither this nor that, and where it is difficult to identify at what point darkness ends and light begins. In this respect both *Darkness Visible* and *Rites of Passage* seem to owe something to Arnold Van Gennep's classic work on ethnography, *The Rites of Passage* (1909), which explores the part neutral zones play in the rituals of passing from one human state to another. It could be argued, however, that much of Golding's work has been preoccupied with situations or states of mind where things are in equipoise. Free fall, in the scientific sense of the term (that is, when gravitational forces no longer operate) is a condition which has always interested him — the point when Neanderthal man died out and *homo sapiens* began in *The Inheritors*; the point when the hero is dead but has not yet submitted to judgement in *Pincher Martin*; the point when paganism ended and Christianity began in "The Scorpion God"; *Free Fall* and *The Pyramid* may also be said to examine the transition from childhood to manhood. *Darkness Visible* offers more, simply because it attempts more — nothing less, in fact, than an exploration of the most crucial no-man's land of all, where the final battle is to be joined between right and wrong, between good and evil, between darkness and light, and between God and Satan.

Darkness Visible is divided into three parts and, like *The Pyramid*, clearly derives some of its strength from the threefold division, the Hegelian form of thesis, antithesis and synthesis being particularly appropriate for the type of work it is. Of the three parts of the book, the first — "Matty" — is probably the most complex and difficult to understand. The construction is picaresque, the eponymous hero wandering from place to place, undergoing a variety of adventures whose significance is not always immediately obvious. At the simplest level it can be read as a kind of pilgrim's progress, with Matty seen as the strange waif of the firestorm who, because of his injuries, lives out an unnatural and unwanted childhood; in maturity, he receives a call to put the world aside, including sex, and to become a sort of prophet—a mission which takes him to Australia and then back to England; finally he becomes a charismatic figure exerting a strange power over the men who earlier in his life had ignored or rejected him. Such simplification, however, robs the character of the very thing that Golding in a variety of ways insists upon—his unreality, his capacity to merge into the background—even to disappear, his other-worldliness, his sense of being prophet, priest, king, and suffering servant all at the same time—in a word, his intense spirituality.

Matty, we are told, is not very bright but is skilled "pre-eminently, in Bible-studies"; his habitual mode of thought, his repeated questioning of his nature and purpose, and many of his actions are shaped and conditioned by his passionate and literal faith in the Bible. On one occasion, for instance, retreating in haste from the temptations of the flesh embodied in Mr Hanrahan's seven beautiful daughters, he uses the words of the Bible almost as a talisman or protective spell, reciting the whole of the Book of Revelation from the first verse to the final "Amen."[3] Matching Matty's knowledge, Golding himself, with considerable virtuosity, incorporates elements of the Bible, from Genesis to Revelation, in his novel so that it seems that sometimes deliberately, sometimes accidentally, Matty acts out a series of biblical roles, himself becoming a changing exemplar of biblical typology. The young boy who limps from hospital, one side of his face destroyed by the fire, has some of the characteristics of Cain in the Genesis story, but even in the first episode at Greenfield a metamorphosis takes place as Matty slips from being Cain to Esau, and then takes on some of the characteristics of Moses.

At the Foundlings School at Greenfield he comes under the influence of a fading former classics master, Mr Pedigree, a man whose name suggests that, whatever else, his lineage is significant; a man who, in the larger context, seems to be the ironic counterpart of the Bible's great progenitor, Adam. Mr Pedigree differs from Adam in having no children, and by reason of his sexual inclinations which are the source of this fall, is never likely to. But he indulges, nevertheless, in a fantasy in which "he pretended to himself that he was always the owner of two boys: one, an example of pure beauty, the other, an earthy little man!" In his fantasy world, Matty seems marked out for the second role. He is simple and uncultivated, "his hands and feet were too big for his thin arms and legs. His sexuality was in direct proportion to his unattractiveness," a fact which, because he is a true innocent, is easily and cruelly exploited by his school fellows. It is the other type of child, the Abel figure, that Mr Pedigree lifts on to a pedestal and on whom he bestows all his special favours; he is exemplified by the boy Henderson, "a child of bland and lyric beauty." Under the impression that when Mr Pedigree sarcastically calls him "a treasure" he really means it, Matty thereafter dogs Mr Pedigree with absolute devotion and cannot conceive that the relationship is based on a joke. In his primal innocence, Matty is literal-minded and unresponsive to the nuances of language. If Mr Pedigree asks him to sit in a corner, keep quiet and tell him when his class fellows do not behave, that is what he does, even though it results in his being despised for sneaking. If Mr Pedigree calls Henderson "ghastly" and seems to be in great agony of soul because Henderson keeps coming to see him, then Henderson must be "evil." Uncomprehendingly, Matty responds to Mr Pedigree's pleas for help against Henderson's loving persecution — with disastrous results.

Soon afterwards Henderson is found dead, having fallen from the school roof, and Matty's gymshoe is found beneath his body. The roof is reached by means of the fire escape, the symbolism of which may now be apparent to the reader, but necessarily escapes the Headmaster and an Inspector who comes to investigate. But the gymshoe is a different matter, raising the question of how it came to be beneath the child's body when he fell. Pressed to explain how it got there, Matty mutters something which the school solicitor mishears as "Eden" so that he asks the child "What's Eden got to do with a gymshoe?" Only later, after the Headmaster has retired and has the leisure to think about it, does he feel he begins to understand. Matty was heard to say something about the shoe being "cast" to which the headmaster had reacted with irritation, remarking that "it had been thrown, not cast, it wasn't a horseshoe." But the old-fashioned term comes back to him as he goes over "the dim fringes of the incident" in his mind and remembers the Old Testament quotation: "Over Edom have I cast out my shoe," a primitive curse found in two of the Psalms (60:8; 108:9). Now he begins to wonder whether he has "the key to something even darker than the tragedy of young Henderson," but he reassured himself that "to *say* is one thing: but to *do* is quite another."

This is, of course, exactly where he is wrong. What happened to Henderson is clear enough because Golding tells us: "No one . . . ever knew . . . how Henderson had begged to be let in and been denied and gone reeling on the leads to slip and fall, for now Henderson was dead and could no longer reveal to anyone his furious passion." In an obvious sense his death is accidental, the result of extreme distress. In another sense, it is not. Matty had thrown his gymshoe and uttered the biblical curse, and then, as his journal for 26/11/66 reveals, he had watched Mr Pedigree's window — "the one at the top that opens on to the leads and where I saw Henderson come away after I had followed him and waited." Matty had willed Henderson's death and because he possessed a spiritual power that at that stage he did not understand or recognise, his curse was fulfilled and the child fell to his death on the very spot where Matty had flung his gymshoe.

On this dark note the second chapter ends. But there is a further undercurrent that links the misheard Eden with Edom and primitive curses. It lies in two of the Bible's early stories, each concerned with two brothers, and in each of which the elder feels himself to have been unjustly treated as compared with the younger. One is Cain who slew Abel because the Lord paid no regard to the offering he had made, whereas Abel's offering was accepted; the other is Esau (whose other name was Edom and from whom the Edomites were reputedly descended), who is cheated out of his birthright by the smooth trickery of his younger brother, Jacob. The subsequent fate of both elder brothers is that they become fugitives and wanderers on the earth, though in neither case does judgement seem to have fallen on them. Esau is an innocent beguiled; and the mark which God put on Cain was not, as is commonly supposed, to indicate his guilt but as a protection to warn those who saw it that if they attacked Cain, God's vengeance on them would be sevenfold.

The notion of judgement in both these Bible stories is thus as obscure and elusive as the question of who was responsible for the death of young Henderson. To complicate matters even further, there is in Matty's relationship with Mr Pedigree a hint of yet a third early biblical wanderer whose restless journeyings had also begun with the killing of a man— Moses in his youth had slain an Egyptian and concealed his body (Exodus 2:12). Many years later, when Moses communicated with God on Mount Sinai, we are told in Exodus (34:29) he "wist not that the skin on his face shone while he talked with him." In the same way, whenever Matty talks to Mr Pedigree the good side of his face, which had escaped the original burning, shines like the sun and indeed when he is trying to give Mr Pedigree an alibi after the death of Henderson, Golding records that the "sun shone . . . positively ennobling the good side of his face."

The establishment of a biblical context and a spiritual dimension in the early pages of the book is clearly part of Golding's purpose, not just as an ironic counterpoint, but to suggest the stages of growth that go towards the production of a type of goodness (or Godness) which finally breaks down the partitions that divide ordinary men. The "Sophy" section works as a contrast; it shows the same principle operating in reverse, thus developing a tension between positive and negative spiritual power, between good and evil forces, between God and Satan, and between light and darkness, which will not be resolved until the final section, "One is One."

Sophy's development strikingly parallels Matty's in several particular episodes. Just as his spiritual powers which he does not yet understand become apparent in the episode of Henderson's death, so Sophy's spiritual powers are evident in her throwing the stone that kills the dabchick, an act which an ordinary small girl could not perform if she tried. The incident presents itself to her "as if it were a possibility chosen out of two, both presented, both fore-ordained from the beginning," involving "a sort of silent *do as I tell you.*" In other words, like the death of Henderson, it is an act of will operating spiritually or, from another point of view, magically. Of these two acts of untried and indeed unrecognised forces, the cursing and consequent death of Henderson is obviously on a very different scale; yet, deeply wrong though it was, it was prompted by misunderstanding and misguided love for Mr Pedigree. Matty atones for it in full, not only in terms of self-inflicted ordeals (including stabbing his palm with a nail), but in finally giving his life to save another boy of about Henderson's age, and returning after his own death to fetch Mr Pedigree whom he had loved with constancy in the face of total rejection. Sophy's act, trivial by comparison, is nevertheless an act of gratuitous destructiveness. The chick meant nothing to her, yet she took its life wantonly. With similar powers, Sophy and Matty are already developing in opposite directions. Interestingly, near the end of the book, Matty's elders say of Sophy "Many years ago we called her before us but she did not come."

Meanwhile Matty must figuratively follow the path that leads from Eden to Apocalypse, suffering along the way the fate of the prophets who warn men in a language that none seems capable or desirous of understanding. Having left the Foundlings School under the heaviest of clouds, he has a short spell as a delivery boy and general odd-jobber for Frankley's the ironmongers, an establishment which is poised between two worlds, one ancient and one modern — an "image in little of the society at large."[4] On the one hand there is the nineteenth-century building with its ancient system of accounting and its wing-collared elderly assistants, who live in gloom and have achieved something approaching perfect stillness; on the other there is the new girl in her brilliantly lit bower of artificial flowers, plastic screens, trellises, and whimsical garden furniture, intended to bring Frankley's into the twentieth century and solvency. Into this environment Matty fits like a frenetic Quasimodo or thwarted Vulcan, living in the old coachhouse over the smithy and, in his rare moments of spare time, scrambling about the lofts of Frankley's, trying to catch a glimpse through the skylight of the fair Miss Aylen below, whose scent, grey eyes, and shiny curtain of hair are beginning to put all thoughts of Mr Pedigree out of his mind.

But the veil of Miss Aylen's hair divides him from the Holy of Holies as surely as if it were the veil of the Ark of the Covenant. Other people, at later stages of the book, are to be responsive to the fact that life can rarely be comprehended or, indeed, lived as a whole; that partitions are always there; that "One is one and all alone, and ever more shall be so." At this point, the barrier for Matty partly lies in his own realistic assessment that any romantic approach to a girl like Miss Aylen from such a misshapen beast would be a farce and a humiliation; but more significantly, it lies in his sense of guilt for Henderson's death, and in his response, made in prayer and white-hot anguish, to a call which comes to him as he is looking into the window of Goodchild's Rare Books. The catalyst for this experience is a fortune teller's ball or scrying glass which, we are later told, was placed there for reasons that remain obscure by Sim Goodchild's rationalist father. Even though the day is cloudy and dull, the ball blazes as though it contained "nothing but the sun." It acts on Matty almost as a revelation, like the mystic moment in *Burnt Norton* when the dry concrete pool seems filled out of "heart of light." If the scrying glass blazes magically as a "heart of light," the Rorschach ink blots that throw Sophy into a fit at a party may be seen as an equivalent "heart of darkness." The scrying glass affects Matty the more powerfully simply because it does not *say* anything, is not made up of a whole store of frozen speech as books or churches seem to be, but simply *is* – glowing, illuminating, transforming. Kneeling in Greenfield Parish Church, Matty knows that he has received a call, that he must put the desires of the flesh behind him and try to discover himself and his purpose. He leaves for Australia.

The fact that Matty received his prophetic call from a fortune teller's scrying glass rather than through the frozen words of books, or the conventional medium of the Church, suggests that his subsequent mission to discover himself and his purpose may not follow conventionally religious or biblical paths, may indeed take a more mysterious, even a more magical direction. In his adventures in Australia, one of the main lessons Matty has to learn is the danger of his own literal-mindedness; things are not always as they seem. The Sweets, who employ him in Melbourne, are kind enough, but the girls who work in Mr Hanrahan's sweet factory are far from sweet to him. The wilderness where Matty is stranded on his progress north, with its symbolic "scrubby thorns" and "low humps of three trees" is not really the outback, but lies close to the suburbs of Darwin. More particularly, the aborigine who subjects him to near emasculation and mock crucifixion turns out not to be a genuine Abo at all, but simply Harry Bummer, who has "a fat little woman expecting and two nippers," and has never been the same since they made a film about him. Bummer's pretence at rain-making with the "small polished stones" is strictly for the tourists. The rain-making "mumbo jumbo," does however, have its serious aspect. It can be no accident that the dust jacket of the novel carries a reproduction of one of Russell Drysdale's paintings, showing a figure that might almost be Matty emerging from the fire, but is actually called "The Rainmaker." And after a period in hospital in Darwin, Matty studies with great absorption the practices of the Abos with their pebbles, before conducting his own strange ceremonies on the State House lawn, building first a tower of matchboxes and then adding, after seven days, twigs and a clay pot. Where the ceremonies differ is that Matty's do not promote rain, but warn against a coming conflagration. He then moves to a large patch of wasteland and sets light to it, and a number of his audience are singed in the ensuing fire. He is called before the authorities because of the trouble he has caused. The secretary, who questions him after this episode is a civilised, highly intelligent man. He knows that ignorant people (those who stand idly round the fire and get burnt; the "ignorant fellahin" whose first-born were destroyed at the time of the Exodus; the doomed charioteers of Pharaoh's army in the Red Sea episode) will never understand "predictions of calamity" until it is too late and they are on the point of being engulfed. He carefully explains to Matty that it is precisely the informed and the educated, men like himself, who understand "the content of the message," but they are also the likeliest to escape its effects: "The whirlwind won't fall on government; . . . neither will the bomb."

The nature of Matty's calling and his reason for coming to Australia now begin to become apparent, though how far Matty himself understands them at this stage remains uncertain. As well as watching the rain-making activities of the Abos, Matty closely consults his Bible before building the tower of matchboxes, and it is clear from a comment he later makes in his diary that he derives his inspiration from Ezekiel: "I had thought that only me and Ezekiel had been given the way of showing things to those people who can see (as with matchboxes, thorns, shards . . . etc.)."

In chapter 4 of the Book of Ezekiel, the prophet is encouraged to foretell in visual form the destruction of Jerusalem:

> take thee a tile, and lay it before thee,
> and pourtray upon it the city, even Jerusalem;
> And lay seige against it, and build a fort
> against it, and cast a mount against it . . . and
> set battering rams against it round about.
> Moreover take thou unto thee an iron pan,
> and set it for a wall of iron between thee
> and the city . . .

At this point, Matty seems to have moved forward through the Old Testament and is now identified with the prophet Ezekiel: like him, he is in exile (in Australia); like him he communicates through signs rather than through speech; he is very concerned to stay away from images of lust and other abominations (Matty's own "particular difficulty"); and he only finds the power of speech when the Lord has something for him to say. In this case, the words that finally burst, like golf balls, from Matty's twisted lips, are "I feel!"—a repudiation of the secretary's unfeeling fluency; his language, pernickety and precise, is inadequate to explain what Matty sees.

Yet the secretary's comments, true enough in their own right, tell us what Matty can see but cannot say. His conflagration of piled-up match-boxes topped with a clay pot are a warning against the "meteorological gamble" taking place in Australia where Britain had been testing its first atomic bombs. These tests raised alarming questions not only as to their effects in terms of atmospheric pollution, but also concerning the danger of their use in a future conflict amongst the major nations. The Apocalypse that Matty foretells is not just a warning against those particular tests or even just for Australia. England, as the secretary rightly says in advising his return, needs Matty's warnings more than Australia does.

For the remainder of his time there, Matty's prophetic work is in any

case effectively over. There is just one more symbolic act to perform before
he shakes the Australian dust off his feet. This incident, in which he goes
in search of a place, low down, hot and fetid, and where there is water, is
difficult to interpret. Matty's subsequent actions — waiting for darkness,
stripping, weighting himself down with chains and heavy steel wheels,
and wading through muddy water which at one point completely im-
merses him, while at the same time carrying a lighted lamp high over his
head, does nothing to lessen its mystery. As he performs these actions,
Matty loses his individuality, becoming "the driver," "the man." As if
watching him from a long way off, Golding suggests that it was all
"inscrutable except inside of the man's head where his purpose was."
Certainly there are strong overtones of a descent into an underworld,
whether classical or biblical, in Matty's ritual, particularly as he chooses
to enact it in a place where "even at noon the sun could scarcely pierce
through to the water." The chains and wheels and Matty's heaving up of
the lamp to the four points of the compass after he has undergone his
ordeal also suggest a ritual cleansing — possibly even a form of self-
baptism — before going on to the next stage of his mission. Matty notes in
his diary that he has committed a "great and terrible sin" probably to be
interpreted as a reference to his responsibility for the death of the child
Henderson. The gospel of St Matthew (18:6) warns that "who shall offend
one of these little ones which believe in me, it were better that a millstone
were hanged about his neck, and that he were drowned in the depths of
the sea." Possibly Matty's literal mind suggests to him that an appropriate
method of atonement would be to hang millstones (or their nearest
equivalent, wheels) around his waist and to immerse himself in that which
most closely resembles the depths of the sea. Alternatively, like Dante or
Aeneas before him, he may be symbolically crossing from one world into
another, and his elaborate ritual might thus be interpreted as some kind of
rite of passage, anthropologically speaking.

    In the years following his return from Australia, Matty, convinced
that he is "at the centre of an important thing," commits himself to a life of
self-dedication, foregoing food and drink, following the precise practices
laid down in the Old Testament (in making heave offerings, wave offerings
etc.) and preparing for the final judgement which he is sure will come "in
the twinkling of an eye" when the last trumpet sounds. Reading the Book
of Revelation one day after his return to England, he becomes convinced
that the sixth day of the sixth month of 1966 must be the precise day of
judgement forecast in the Apocalypse. The "awful number" 666 in
Revelation is the mark of the beast associated with Rome, and particularly
of the Emperor Nero in whose reign the persecution of the early Church
was so severe. Matty sees it as his duty to paint the dread number in blood,
wear it on his forehead (in fact in his hat band) and to carry it as a
warning through the Cornish streets. But nothing happens. At the end of
the fateful anticlimactic day, he suffers greatly at the thought of being the

only one to feel "the dreadful sorrow of not being in heaven with judgement all done." Once again he asks himself "What am I for . . . If to give signs why does no judgement follow?

After his return to England, Matty begins to be visited by spirits—one robed in blue and the other in red, both wearing what he naively refers to as "expensive hats." Instead of offering him consolation, they warn him that "Great things are afoot" and tell him that he must throw away his Bible, a direction that makes Matty wonder temporarily whether they are Satan in disguise. It is a kind of obedience test. The discarding of the Bible does indeed seem to be a symbolic putting aside of the Old Testament, the Book of the Law and the Prophets, as a preparation for the New. Matty now seems to take on some of the characteristics of John the Baptist. His spiritual face is scarred by his sin, but he is "the best material that can be obtained in the circumstances." The fact that he seems to be, at this stage, a combination both of the voice in the wilderness, and also a type of the Christ John preceded and heralded, reflects yet again the way in which Matty's biblical roles tend to slide into one another and overlap.

Matty's discarding of his Bible emphasises the change of direction the book is now taking. The final section carries the title "One is One" a phrase taken from "Green Grow the Rushes O," or the "Dilly Song"—an old medieval mnemonic to aid children in remembering some of the basic truths of the Church. In this song the two "Lily white boys" are the Old and New Testaments in the persons of John the Baptist and Christ. And the change from the Old to the New, beside being hinted at in Matty's discarding the Bible of the Law-givers and the Prophets, is also suggested by the attendant spirits who tell him "Judgement is not the simple thing you think." Their warning once again reinforces the message of Matthew 7, the point in the Sermon on the Mount where Jesus condemns the hypocrite who wishes to cast out the mote from his brother's eye without first attending to the beam in his own.

Returning to Greenfield, Matty feels compelled to prophesy against the town that has allowed heathen temples and mosques to grow up alongside the Church of the Seventh Day Adventists. "Thou Jerusalem that slayest the prophets" he begins, echoing the words of Jesus denouncing the Scribes and Pharisees in Matthew 23:27. Matty claps his hand over his mouth, but the messianic theme is reinforced when his spirits tell him that his mission has to do with a child born on the day when Matty had expected the day of judgement, at which time a black spirit was cast down. Their words may recall both the fall of Satan and the birth of Adam in *Paradise Lost*, books 6 and 7, as well as the defeat of the dragon and the birth of the child who is to be the Messiah in the Book of Revelation. Structurally, this particular passage is crucial as it establishes a direct link with the "Sophy" section and anticipates the confrontation between the forces of good and evil in the final chapters. At this stage, though, Matty cannot see the way things are going and is quite unconscious of any threat from the two little girls he sees entering Mr Goodchild's shop. Quite the reverse, in fact: "They were so beautiful like angels," he writes, "I could not help wishing that they were who I am for." His attendant spirits are a bit severe with him for getting it so wrong, but like all the best demonic protagonists, the Stanhope twins can make themselves appear like angels of light, and project an outward appearance so attractive in both looks and behaviour as to prove irresistible to the Goodchilds, to Roland, to Fido and even, momentarily, to distract the enlightened Matty from his purpose.

Much later, Sophy, the dark-haired twin, appears to Matty in a dream that seems to be occasioned by "my bad thoughts about Miss Stanhope," and causes him to defile himself. Soon afterwards Matty becomes the sole witness of Sophy's pretended discovery of her engagement ring, an event which he interprets as a sign or warning. But he does not pursue its obvious significance — that Sophy is a liar and must have had some further purpose in pretending to lose the ring. Rather he sees it as a symbolic action, translating it to mean "she does not care if her jewel is lost," a statement true at another level. Sophy's "jewel" could stand for her virginity which she deliberately set out to "get rid of," but it may also signify her soul. In *Macbeth*, a play whose concern with the powers of darkness makes it particularly relevant, Macbeth speaks of the loss of his soul in terms of "mine eternal jewel / Given to the common enemy of man." Sophy embodies the temptations of the flesh which Matty has learnt to see as a Satanic device to divert him from his mission. Matty's dream explicitly identifies her with the Whore of Babylon in the Apocalypse, a figure generally assumed to represent Rome (this connection is reinforced in the novel by the characterisation of Sophy's father, who has an eagle-like head and sits in his columned room with the remote air of an effete and decadent Roman patrician). St John's purpose in introducing the Whore was to suggest that, after the dragon had been defeated by the archangel Michael, Satan had turned his attention to earth, encouraging the Roman Empire to seduce the early Church from virtue. In a comparable way Milton's purpose in *Paradise Lost* was to show how Satan, defeated in the wars in Heaven, destroyed God's newest creation, Adam and Eve, by undermining their primal innocence. Golding's purpose is more obscure. But Matty's identification of Sophy with the Whore of Babylon alerts us to the fact that she is a figure of unequivocal evil. Her progression from childhood to maturity is as clearly charted as Matty's and her understanding of the process of darkness is as deep and long maturing as Matty's understanding of fire and light.

Sophy's advance towards evil is closely connected with her pursuit of "weirdness," a concept that even confuses Sophy herself since she recognises that it has several possibilities and is a word that can be used in several ways. The first time Sophy has a "passionate desire in the darkness to be weird," even though the impulse comes from the unexplored dark tunnel leading to the back of her head, it finds expression in what are on the surface little more than schoolgirl pranks—breaking bad eggs in the drawer of her father's bedside table as a childish protest against his proposed remarriage to Winnie; trying to give Winnie nightmares by "aiming the dark part of her head" at her when sleeping; later she envisages the unfortunate Winnie, magically incarcerated, Hansel and Gretel style, within her own transistor, to be switched on and off at Sophy's will. Childishly she links such actions with bad smells—"so eek, so stinky-poo, so oof and pah."

At this stage, Sophy's weirdness might still be seen as the natural fantasising of a disturbed childhood. But the hints of witchcraft and diabolic possession are there right from the start, and as she grows up, Sophy, like Matty, learns to understand that the pursuit of purity and simplicity, whether it be for good or evil, makes enormous demands. Merely breaking the rules is not enough. Sophy realises that one must "hunger and thirst after weirdness" with that dedication with which Jesus urged men to hunger and thirst after righteousness (Matthew 5:6). The inversion of the biblical injunction marks a turning-point in Sophy's pursuit of weirdness, as decisive in its own way as the call which Matty receives when he contemplates the scrying glass. Sophy recognises that "unless she did what had never been done, saw something that she never ought to see, she would be lost for ever and turn into a young girl."

In one sense Sophy is using "weirdness" as a synonym for evil, for no child of the 1960s would knowingly dedicate herself to such an archaic concept as "evil." But the word has been carefully chosen for a whole series of associations whose importance emerges gradually. Sophy herself feels "weird" in the sense of strange when she is caught up in enacting an evil that seems to reach her from outside herself—just as Matty feels the hair rising on his head and goes cold all over in the presence of his spirits. Sophy is also the "weird" sister, and thus linked with the witches of *Macbeth* whose prophecies of the future teach Macbeth to make them happen by evil means. And this sense of somehow inexplicably knowing the future, knowing what is going to happen next, is another important element in her weirdness, what the child Sophy experiences as "the 'of course' way things sometimes behaved." She feels that "as soon as the future was comprehended it was inescapable." The Old English meaning of "weird" was "fate." Sensing the future in some way, even being able to shape it to some extent, is, both for Sophy and Matty, bound up with the spiritual powers. It can be no accident that it is the scrying glass, conventionally used for foretelling the future, that becomes the medium for Matty's vision, the call that sends him to Australia.

It is through the dark tunnel at the back of her own head that Sophy knows herself to be different, and recognises, without having words for it, the powers of evil waiting to be exploited—the "stinky-poo bit, the breaking of rules, the using of people, the well-deep wish, the piercing-ness, the—the what? The other end of the tunnel, where surely it joined on." By using people, by denying her common humanity, Sophy can explore the nature of that dark tunnel. And so she embarks on a process of breaking through the partitions into darkness in a way alarmingly reminiscent of Lady Macbeth:

> Come, you spirits
> That tend on mortal thoughts, unsex me here,
> And fill me from the crown to the toe topful
> Of direst cruelty!

In Sophy's case the unsexing is achieved by an act of will. She gives her body as a useless, unnecessary and unregarded thing to anyone who wants it. And in the same way that Lady Macbeth, by stopping up the "access and passage of remorse," allies herself with the powers of darkness and becomes identified with the Weird Sisters, so Sophy's weirdness now becomes more obviously associated with the traditional picture of witches and witchcraft — an identification accidentally suggested to her after Gerry's libidinous love-making, but denied by Sophy with revealing force:

> "One day, Gerry, you'll be the filthiest old man."
> "Filthy old woman yourself."
> The grey light washed through Sophy like a tide.
> "No. Not me."
> "Why not you?"
> "Don't ask me. You wouldn't understand anyway."

What Sophy might have become had she not made her deliberate commitment to weirdness is clear. She would have developed like Toni. The duality residing in each individual, the uneasy fusion of the spirit which aspires and the flesh which drags down, has always interested Golding. For him human nature is nearly always dual, and Golding usually explores its dichotomies in a characteristic and easily recognisable way, often indicated by the two names which his central characters have or are given (e.g. Christopher/Pincher in *Pincher Martin*; Sammy/Samuel in *Free Fall*). In *Darkness Visible* the nurse who lovingly brings Matty through his worst period of recovery as a child is surprised because Matty thinks of her as two people — she seems to "bring someone with her." Matty himself has a good side and a bad side to his face; and there are two Sophys, one who presents a fair face to the world, and the other who sits at the mouth of a black tunnel inside her own head. But now Golding introduces a refinement — twins; girls who, in the eyes of the world, are "everything to each other," are both beautiful, both of "phenomenal intelligence" and can both make adults go "soppy" over them and thus use them for their own purposes. Underneath, however, they are "as different as day and night." Toni is the cold one, the intellectual who thinks and is "out of the whole business of feeling," while passionate Sophy "broods," cherishing the memory of a rare moment of intimacy with her father.

The main difference between the two sisters is that Toni always lives outside herself (sometimes she seems just to drift away), and Sophy inside. Toni's eyes can see through the back of her head quite easily, as Mr Pedigree finds to his cost when he is stealing books in Goodchild's. But that is because in the back of Toni's head there is nothing. Wild, independent, eccentric, though she can be, she is as transparent as her lint-white hair, and as hollow inside — an easy prey for empty causes like freedom fighting, since she is unable to recognise that such concepts of freedom are a snare and delusion — as much a delusion indeed as believing that by putting on a black wig, she can give depth and substance where no substance exists.

If freedom means anything to Sophy, it is something which involves putting aside all silly posturing and pretending and simply being, simply taking the brake off and allowing the spring to uncoil, because that, in her view, is to be in sympathy with the process of untangling and running down which is the universal law. In its cosmic form she sees this in terms of physical unwinding, or entropy: "The long, long convulsions, the unknotting, the throbbing and disentangling of space and time, on, on, on into nothingness . . . the hiss and crackle and roar, the inchoate unorchestra of the lightless spaces." Like Matty, Sophy sees this process as full of significance, a significance which extends even to the pattern of numbers formed by dates. Just as Matty thought 6.6.66 must be the day of judgement, so Sophy sees the date 7.7.77 as no coincidence, but rather part of a larger progress towards unbeing: "What it wants, the dark, let the weight fall, take the brake off — ." Where Matty senses divine energy, feels himself "at the centre of things," with time winding itself up to the promised and longed-for fulfillment, Sophy feels exactly the opposite, feels she must collude with collapse and disintegration. And she pictures the end as annihilating waves, "arching, spreading, running down, down, down — ," monstrous versions of the tidal wave that frightened her and Toni when Winnie took them to the seaside. If Matty's element is fire, Sophy's is water. She lives by the river and many of the most important incidents of her life are linked with it.

In human terms the unwinding and running down is reflected in Adam's fall and the apparent triumph of the powers of darkness. And the only way to achieve the final simplicity, to ensure that triumph becomes final victory, is, Sophy recognises, through outrage. It has an inevitability about it, an "of courseness," a "weirdness" which, right from earliest childhood when her one-in-a-million throw killed the dabchick, Sophy has learned to recognise as conditioning her destiny. Gerry and his friends might see the kidnapping of the wealthy child as an adventure, an exciting crime suited to mercenary spirits. Toni and her friends might attempt the same thing for political ends. To Sophy, both are profitless, not effectively different from their childhood sport of stealing sweets from the Pakistani shops. Her mind finally comes to dwell on the only thing that really matters, the equivalent of Lady Macbeth's plucking her nipple from the boneless gums of the child that milks her and dashing its brains out; to achieve the final simplicity through outrage. Sophy's sadism is already evident from the episode where she has her first orgasm, brought on not by love-making but by stabbing her boyfriend Roland in the shoulder. At the climax of the story, she fantasises that she has the kidnapped child at her mercy, that she is sliding the knife into his body, that she can feel the sacrificial blood flow and watch the "black sun" rising in the sky. This final identification of Sophy with Satan, bringing sin and death into the world as a second challenge to God's authority, prepares the way for the last act of Golding's Apocalypse — the saving of the child and the triumph of the forces of good.

The third section of the novel opens in another twilight zone which again throws up echoes of Aeneas's wanderings among the spirits of the underworld who are in limbo and still awaiting final judgement. Sim Goodchild and Edwin Bell are two elderly men, one a bookseller (perhaps the same as that of the opening chapter), the other a schoolmaster. Both are poised between a past that is dead and a future waiting to be born. They represent contrasting types of unknowing and unawareness. Repelled by the noise and confusion of the real world outside, with its jets and juggernauts, ill at ease with the new customs, the new social and cultural grouping of "the Pakis and Blacks, the Chinese, the Whites, the punks and layabouts" whom they see thronging around them, each in his own way is waiting for a sign. Like Simeon in the gospel of St Luke (2:25) they await "the consolation of Israel"; unlike him they are not just or devout and will not understand salvation when they see it.

Sim Goodchild, the bookseller, is not, at the conscious level, as aware of this as Edwin. Despite his attempts to think about "First Things," his waking thoughts are more concerned with fighting fat, inflation, the problems of an old family business going to the dogs, the apathy of a non-book reading public, and his own shortcomings as a man — particularly his "furtive passion," his interest in the attractions of very young girls. He is cultured in the way of the world, living his life out amongst books, and has a strong literary turn of mind, though an entirely conventional one. All his responses, even at the deepest level, are conditioned by his reading. If Edwin mentions the man in black (Matty, in fact), his mind automatically responds with Wilkie Collins's *Woman in White*. The mere mention of the word "transcendentalism" touches off the appropriate literary response — "the great wheel . . . the Hindu universe . . . skandhas and avatars, recession of the galaxies, appearance and illusion." And just as easily, his illicit feelings for the Stanhope twins are insulated by invoking Wordsworth. In his heart he is conscious that there *is* something else, but "it is a kind of belief which touches nothing in me. It is a kind of second-class believing. My beliefs are me; many and trivial." The brute fact of being, the brute fact of believing really comes down to his contemplation of himself alone, locked in the Cartesian tower of his own self-consciousness and other people's words. A rationalist by conviction and president of the local philosophical society, his greatest moment was to act as chairman for a lecture by Bertrand Russell on "Freedom and Responsibility"; but he is conscious that freedom for him is still only a word, part of a faded poster on the wall.

Edwin Bell, the schoolmaster from the Foundlings, "cultivated, cultural and spiritually *sincere*," is at the other end of the spectrum from Sim Goodchild. Edwin's line is not mind but spirit (or so he thinks), and he bubbles over in pursuit of the esoteric and the mystical, with the enthusiasm of a schoolboy chasing butterflies. Pursuing the perfect form of all-knowing, when speech will be unnecessary and only the pure language of the spirit will remain, he rarely stops talking long enough to consider the point his quest has reached; clearly, in Greenfield at least, there is as little need for Edwins' gush of words as for Sim's books.

Into Edwin's sad, distracted world comes Matty—the gardener's odd job man at the rich boys' school to most people, but to Edwin the long-expected one, the nameless Man in Black who has broken through the language barrier and communicates his mystic otherness by extra-sensory means—"ecce homo," the last hope of an old man desperate for salvation. Unwilling to accept Edwin's frothy protestations wholeheartedly, Sim Goodchild nevertheless allows himself to be led to the park to see Matty, and the subsequent encounter has overtones of the calling of the disciples, with Matty leading the way across the park, a rapturous Edwin and a still sceptical but nevertheless "interested" Sim trailing in his wake. Largely as a result of Edwin's importunity and Matty's silent acquiescence, the three men form themselves into a small group and Edwin decides that the silence which is so obviously part of Matty's make-up is to be the cornerstone of the group's search for truth. As water was holy to the early Church, so silence is now—"random silence, lucky silence, or destined." Such random silence is to be found in the Stanhopes' garden, a "private place farther down into the earth" where, fortuitously, even the noise of the jets roaring overhead seems muffled. To Edwin it is the obvious place to bring the expected one.

Paradoxically this haven of apparent spiritual peace is also the place where Sophy lives. The "pool of quiet" that even the rationalist in Sim Goodchild responds to and, in his "generation-long folly," sees as symbolising the "innocence" of the little girls who lived there, is in reality another version of the underworld. Sim Goodchild even compares descending into the garden to going under the sea. It is small wonder that Mr. Pedigree, who comes reluctantly with Matty to the first meeting and seems considerably more attuned to the reality of what is going on than the others, believes that he is being brought into some "kind of trap" and struggles to escape. For Matty too, as his journal records, it is a place of evil spirits, "green and purple and black," which he tries to hold off. The failure of Edwin and Sim to perceive them is a measure of their spiritual blindness or deadness. At another level, of course, Sophy's dwelling place is the home of a "known" terrorist, part of a genuine underworld of crime and one on which the police have their eye. As Matty and the two old men sit holding hands and sharing what to Edwin seems a magical experience, the hard camera eye above their heads is impartially recording, recording — and trial and judgement are just around the corner.

The scene in the upper room may have something of the mood of the Last Supper about it, for this is the last time that Sim and Edwin will ever again be directly in contact with the mysterious figure who so captivates them and yet whom they are so incapable of understanding. The next time they are to see Matty is in the film of their upper room séance when it is shown as part of the court proceedings following the attempted kidnap. "It wasn't like that" says Sim Goodchild, trying, like Peter when he denied Christ, to dissociate himself from the accusations and laughter of the gathering crowd, as he watches himself on the television in a shop window, back in the upper room and ridiculously trying to scratch his nose on the table. At the trial and judgement that follow, Sim realises that "the real public condemnation was not to be good or bad; either of those had a kind of dignity about them; but to be a fool and to be seen to have been one — ." Edwin continues to insist on their innocence, but Sim, in some ways more perceptive, replies "We're not innocent. We're worse than guilty. We're funny." Their final confrontation with Mr Pedigree in Sim's shop reverts to Matthew 7:1, "Judge not, that ye be not judged." For too long Edwin and Sim have been recognising the mote in the eyes of other people without heeding the beam in their own. Sim Goodchild has been quick to condemn Mr Pedigree for coming into his shop to steal books "as bait" for children, refusing to recognise that his placing of the children's books in the window to attract the Stanhope girls had exactly the same motive, and was the more culpable in that it was cloaked in pious platitudes about the children's cleanness, sweetness and innocence. He is not the "sentimental old thing" he pretends but is driven on by "the unruly member," as his fantasies about the twins reveal. And Edwin might say sanctimoniously about Mr Pedigree "There but for the grace of God" without seeing any connection with his own sexually ambivalent marriage, that of an effeminate man married to a masculine woman. "How do I know that I am not speaking to a very clever pair of terrorists?" says Mr Pedigree after the trial. "The judge said you were innocent, but we, the great British Public, we — how odd to find myself one of them! — we know, don't we?" Such a verdict is no less than they deserve. Both old men have been close enough to feel the warmth of Matty's presence and yet their eyes are not opened. Their fate is not merely to be laughed at, but to remain in the limbo of their own choosing, neither good nor bad. Sim Goodchild at least has some consciousness of the futility of it all, of a paradise that has been forfeited. Cynically convinced of the impossibility of breaking through the circumscribed bounds of life into something finer, convinced that one is one and all alone and ever more shall be so, he yet recollects that when

Matty looked into his palm in the upper room, it was "exquisitely beautiful" and "made of light." And the last reference to him sees him pondering on the significance of the whole episode, and "staring intently into his own palm."

A purer form of judgement has yet to be achieved — not one concerned solely with moral issues, but one which springs naturally from the spiritual conflict between good and evil. Throughout the book, good has become more and more concentrated in Matty, and evil in Sophy. Now, in a section drawing heavily on the Apocalypse of St John, battle is joined. By this time, Matty recognises that Sophy is to be identified with the Whore of Babylon — provocative, tempting, and very much to be feared. Supporting him in his resistance to her are not only his attendant spirits, increasingly identified with the elders sitting round the heavenly throne, but also other beneficent supernatural forces associated with the magical number seven (Edwin links Matty with "sevenness"), in turn connected with the healing, generative powers of music and dance. Matty is filled with transports of joy as he listens to Beethoven's Seventh Symphony being played to the children in their music appreciation lesson.

In a final transcendent vision, Matty is shown that he has to become a burnt offering — a necessary sacrifice to be paid so that the forces of evil can be defeated and the child saved who will be the new Messiah and "bring the spiritual language into the world." Matty's spiritual face, of which his maimed and two-sided face was a reflection, will be healed, and he too will become an elder. A wonderful being appears "all in white with the circle of the sun round his head." He is the angel of the first chapter of Revelation (I:16), out of whose mouth "went a sharp two-edged sword: and his countenance was as the sun shineth in his strength." This is the spirit who guards the child, and whose servant Matty has now become. With the elders, he eats with Matty, participating in a form of communion, but when Matty raises his eyes to the angel's face, he is overcome, just as St John had been, and, in John's words, "when I saw him, I fell at his feet as dead."

The book now comes full circle. Born out of the fire of a doomed city, Matty endures his personal Calvary as, with his last act, he rushes from the burning school ablaze from head to toe to rescue the child the terrorists are seeking to abduct. Fire imagery increasingly dominates the closing section, warning of the judgement to come and the purgatorial flames through which all must go to achieve salvation. Sophy, on the other hand, is gripped by an uncontrollable rage in which she bitterly recognises that not only has she been thwarted of her prey, but also deserted by her lover for her sister Antonia. But she soon resumes her appearance of calm, smooth-talking her way out of trouble with little apparent effort. The powers of darkness after all can only be controlled for a season and it is entirely appropriate that Sophy should pass from the story still looking like an innocent flower, as she callously betrays the lover who has abandoned her and the father who has spurned her.

It is Mr Pedigree—the man who throughout the book has been most criticised and punished by the standards of the world—who finally becomes the focus of the judgement of Heaven. Like Matty, he has consistently been presented as having a basic innocence of spirit: "Except for his compulsion" we are told,"—which in many countries would not have got him into trouble—he was without vice." Indeed Mr Pedigree's worship of beautiful boys might be seen as the beginning of learning to love goodness, though he never actually ascends the ladder of Platonic love. If he is no worse than Edwin or Sim, he has suffered more, having been sent to prison several times and being set upon by indignant housewives. Matty applies to him the biblical phrase "despised and rejected," and Mr Pedigree differs from the other characters in the book in being more honest, and having paid for his sins—he is more fully human, as he insists in his own defence: "There've been such people in this neighbourhood, such monsters, that girl and her men, Stanhope, Good-child, Bell even, and his ghastly wife—I'm not like them, bad but not as bad, I never hurt anybody." Matty's love for Mr Pedigree may have started as a childish thing but he continues to love the man whom above all others he has wronged. Such love seems to indicate that Matty believes him capable of being saved. Mr Pedigree's "compulsion" is such that his natural instinct is to resist such a process, and to clutch to himself the brightly coloured ball which is both the means of supporting his weakness and the symbol of his own cherished illusions. Because he senses the unique quality in Matty better than others, he inevitably sees him as a threat—an inimical force, comparable to the "black lightning" of *Pincher Martin*. Unlike the earlier book, however, the resolution is full of quiet acceptance. All passion spent, Mr Pedigree is in the park, seeming to himself "to be sitting up to his very eyes in a sea of light." Sunlight is everywhere, and when Matty comes across to him, he seems to be wading along, waist deep in gold. A "wonderful light and warmth" seems to surround Matty and as judgement draws near, Matty's face becomes "no longer two-tone but gold as the fire and stern." Everywhere there is "a sense of the peacock eyes of great feathers and the smile round the lips . . . loving and terrible." Mr Pedigree makes one last effort to resist, "Why? Why?" he asks, and receives from Matty one word—though not in human speech—"*Freedom*." The many coloured ball that Mr Pedigree holds against his chest is firmly drawn away and, in agony but also in ecstasy, he crosses the bridge separating one world from another and dies into Heaven—no longer the pathetic old pederast that the park-keeper finds crumpled on the seat, but a soul in bliss. The freedom Matty offers and that Mr Pedigree, however reluctantly, accepts, is starkly contrasted with the illusory freedom for which Toni and her fellow terrorists are fighting; it is closer to the idea expressed in the most famous of John Donne's holy sonnets: "Take me to you, imprison me, for I/Except you enthrall me, never shall be free,/Nor ever chaste, except you ravish me." It is also the freedom that Sammy Mountjoy, Golding's other flawed and vulnerable human representative in *Free Fall* so long sought for but never found. Viewed thus, *Darkness Visible*, like *The Spire*, is ultimately a hopeful novel, suggesting in its final resolution at least the possibility of escape from a world threatened by atomic bombs, cultural dislocation, ceaseless noise and the tyranny of words.

In another sense the ending of *Darkness Visible* finds Golding as pessimistic as ever about unredeemed man:

> "We're wrapped in illusions, delusions, confusions" . . .
> "We think we *know*."
> "Know? That's worse than an atom bomb, and always was."
> In silence then, they looked and listened; then exclaimed together
> "Journal? Matty's journal? What journal?"

Matty's journal represents the new gospel, the good news that a child has been born that "shall bring the spiritual language into the world and nation shall speak it unto nation." The child is guarded by an angel out of whose mouth a sword appears, and on earth by a man who has no certain name, and whose natural mode of communication is in signs, not words. When Matty does speak, it is with the utmost brevity and the words seem to burst out of his misshapen mouth not like swords, but golfballs. "He's not got a mouth that's intended for speaking" Edwin explains. Matty communicates rather in "the innocent language of the spirit. The language of paradise." Matty's elders never "speak" to him, they "show," holding out "beautiful white papers with words or whole books," which he translates into his journal. When Matty asks to be allowed to speak more than he has done, in an echo of the words of Revelation 8:1, "there was a silence in heaven for a space of half an hour"; then his elders show Matty "that in the time of the promise which is to come you shall speak words like a sword going out of your mouth," as the guardian spirit of the child does. Since the only noise coming from Matty at the moment of the child's rescue and his own death is that of burning, it seems that, after all, his journal may yet speak like a sword, but not in the old tainted language of fallen man that the novelist is compelled to use. The optimism of *Darkness Visible* consists in its acknowledgement of the possibility of a new order, of saints walking on earth, of a saviour, a new gospel and a new language. But the promise of a new revelation can scarcely be more than a wild surmise, "Leaving one still with the intolerable wrestle/With words and meanings." Like T.S. Eliot, Golding is left to struggle on under existing conditions, conditions in which the writer cannot escape the guilt of the only words he has to use, and where his fate is not to bear witness himself, but only to imagine the possibility that some day someone else might do so.

Notes

1. In a letter to Don Crompton, but Golding has made the same point in interviews with W. L. Webb and John Haffenden.

2. Charles Monteith, Golding's publisher, described *Lord of the Flies* as he first saw it in Raine's radio programme *Cabin'd, Cribb'd, Confin'd*.

3. Matty's old Bible with wooden covers which he found in Australia may also act as a kind of talisman for him. If so, this might explain why the spirits later test his obedience by making him throw it away, thus requiring him to trust himself entirely to their protection.

4. Craig Raine enlarged tellingly on this point and others in his review of *Darkness Visible* in the *New Statesman*, 12 October 1979, pp. 552–3.

William Golding's "Wooden World": Religious Rites in *Rites of Passage*   Virginia Tiger*

I

We carry with us the wonders we seek without us. . . . The whole creation is a mystery, and particularly that of man.
— Sir Thomas Browne,
Religio Medici, 1682

To assess any living author is to walk a fine high wire. To assess as established a living author as William Golding is to take an even greater risk; for the assessment must be balanced against the fact that the whole creative body of work shifts with the publication of each new novel.

Golding's most recent novel, *Rites of Passage*, appearing so soon after his long awaited seventh novel, *Darkness Visible*, raises anew the conundrum of having to evaluate yet another "new Golding" in terms of already hardened critical hypotheses about the nature of his fiction.

Although Golding's novels elude easy categorization, after nearly three decades of literary discussion it has become a critical commonplace to describe him as a religious writer. Even when he seems intent on fostering the illusion of actuality as in *Free Fall*, *The Pyramid*, or *Darkness Visible* (a novel so panoramic in its portrayal of 20th-century English society that it possesses characters enough to embarrass a Russian realist), he gives us a world unpopularly insistent upon the spiritual. Unlike much contemporary British fiction, Golding's occupies itself with what is

*This essay first appeared in *Twentieth Century Literature* 28 (Summer 1982) and is reprinted by permission of *Twentieth Century Literature: A Scholarly and Critical Journal*.

perennial in the human condition, looking at man in relation not alone to his society, but to his universal situation.

In truth, the longer one inspects the evolving *oeuvre*, the more one is struck by its increasing complexity, ambiguity, and equivocation: the mystery at the heart of things human. (As Golding himself remarked in a recent interview: "We understand that we are not only mysterious in ourselves but in a situation of bounded mystery. It's a controlling fact in my life and in what I write.")[1] The fiercely obdurate quality of Golding's imaginative achievement—what has been called his poetic intensity— derives from his ability to construct solidly patterned novels on founda- tions of the most daring verbal modes. His technical range is great, encompassing material as diverse as a sailor's sea-washed body, the befuddled encounter of prelapsarian creatures with rapacious interlopers, an 18th-century sea voyage across the equator. Yet, however heterodox his fictional topographies may be, his seminal themes, like those of other obsessional artists, are limited and homogeneous. Each of Golding's novels represents another face carved from his earliest, most deeply held convic- tion that the two signs of man are his belief in God and his capacity to kill.[2]

"I cannot *not* believe in God," he recently remarked, and warily continued:

> My guess is that there are infinite cosmoses . . . and beyond that is the thing I call the Good. It seems to me that there could be infinite modes of life, and that they would all be sustained by the beings that inhabit them. In other words, we have invented our own universe. We have discovered that there are black holes out there because we have Hiro- shima and Belsen in here: we have made black holes in here and then discovered them out there. . . . Maybe there are universes of awful suffering, maybe there are universes of awful pleasure, but I guess that beyond them there must be a Good which is Absolute. . . . So when you ask me if I believe in God, it's not even a matter of what I believe. It's what I suspect.[3]

To provide accounts of religious belief is one thing; to convince us of their urgency and their centrality is quite another. Golding has taken upon himself the formidable task of arousing the religious impulse and restoring to this recalcitrant time the spiritual dimension which is the stuff of vital religious mythopoeia. The problem for the novelist is to portray his notions about mysterious and multiple modes of spiritual life in concrete novelistic terms. To this end Golding early devised an ingenious narrative form: the ideographic structure.[4]

Controlling each Golding novel is a narrative technique whereby two points of view are turned on one situation. In *The Inheritors*, for example, events are viewed first from the perspective of the Neanderthal mind, a mind that cannot reason beyond sense data. Golding gives us, first a primitive world to inhabit, a world where ideas are images; then, abruptly, he places us in the world of the pragmatic logical mind of the Cro-Magnons. In *Pincher Martin*, we move from the necessarily solipsistic world of a shipwrecked sailor struggling for seven days of ever diminishing strength to maintain his sanity on a barren rock to a remote island in the Hebrides where we discover to our existential alarm that the corpse that has been rotting for a week bears the identity disc of the shipwrecked sailor.

The overall intention of Golding's ideographic structures is to make his readers embrace paradoxes of existence which his own characters cannot recognize. In the final scene of *Darkness Visible*, for example, where the dying Mr. Pedigree imagines golden light emanating from the disfigured face of Matty, Golding means us to intuit that even as debauched a creature as Pedigree can be granted the possibility of salvation. It is not the least of the difficulty in reading Golding that he expects his readers to reassemble narrative images, reconcile apparently opposing points of view, build bridges between contradictory perspectives—all in the service of imaginatively participating in his religious construct. *Rites of Passage*, Golding's eighth novel, raises the same difficult questions for the reader as does *Pincher Martin*, his third: do the many obstacles to intelligibility, indeed to clarity, posed by the formal device of the ideographic structure reward or retard the reader's progress to final understanding? For *Rites of Passage* is a canvas of grids, elusive shapes, and obscurities as puzzling at first as any painting from Picasso's Cubist period.

II

British seamen have long and justly been esteemed for a disinterested generosity toward others in distress.
— Robert Finlayson, *An Essay addressed to Captains of the Royal Navy*, 1824

Rites of Passage, borrowing its title from Arnold Van Gennep's classic study of initiation rituals, plunges the reader into the Napoleonic era of the 1820's, just as the splendor of the spacious days of His Majesty's Royal Navy is beginning to wane. We are aboard a converted British war ship whose passengers are bound for Australia, long the dumping-ground for criminals, bankrupts, and assorted undesirables. Traditionally, stories set on ships at sea permit a host of literary associations, including those present, for example, in Alexander Barclay's *Shyp of Folys* (1509) where the ship itself becomes a cautionary tale of good and bad government and the hard task of piloting a precarious society—both temporal and spiritual—through the shoals, rocks, wrecks, and storms of life. By locating his ship's sea voyage in the 19th-century—with its pervasive themes of hierarchal rank, social privilege, snobbery, true and sham gentility—Golding is able to investigate such subjects as justice, moral responsibility, social class, and the uses and abuses of authority. The stratified world of his ship serves as a social microcosm, encapsulating as it does a whole society.

In *Rites of Passage* the ancient wooden vessel, constructed apparently long before the iron ballast frigates of the 1790's, carries in its stinking hull cargo, guns, animals, immigrants, the shipmen of the fo'castle, including a shadowy purser who gives truth to Pepys' comment that "a purser would not have twice what he got unless he cheated." Commanding the quarter-deck at the other end of the vessel is the ship's absolute ruler, Captain Anderson, barking orders to his standing officers: Cumbershum, Deverel, and Summers. In the cabins of the privileged reside a marine lithographer, a *"notorious* free thinker,"[5] Mr. Prettiman, and the caustic governess to whom he will become betrothed. Most significantly, aboard this "wooden world" (6) are the two characters whose respective journals will supple-ment each other to constitute the narrative of *Rites of Passage*: Reverend James Colley, a Church of England parson whose sad servility suggests he is very much the promoted peasant still, and — from the highest echelons of society — Mr. Edmund Talbot, godson to the brother of the governor of Van Diemen's Land, a British colony in the South Pacific.

Golding gives us first Talbot's sea journal to his influential godfather through whom he has secured an administrative post in Van Diemen's Land. The journal smacks of obsequious flattery and confident ambition: "You have set foot on the ladder and however high I climb . . . I shall never forget whose kindly hand first helped me upwards. That he may never be found unworthy of that hand, nor *do* anything unworthy of it — is the prayer — the intention of your lordship's grateful godson"(10).

Talbot, like Lord Chesterfield's son, is learning the patrician art of pleasing prettily for a purpose. (Especially revealing is Talbot's sentimental library of Richardson, *Moll Flanders*, *Gil Blas* and the then very popular *Meditations Among the Tombs* of the pious Hervey, all of which books will come toppling down when he ravages the ship's doxy.) The complacent, fastidious, patronizing, and utterly class-bound Talbot's awareness of his social rank combines with his sturdy vanity to assure him that the entire "floating society" (144) owes him homage. His voyage from England to the Antipodes, those rocky uninhabited South Pacific islands so named be-cause they are as far south, as Greenwich is north, of the equator, is Talbot's initiation — moral as well as geographical — into the underbelly of a hemisphere.

For all this, *Rites of Passage* is a funny book. Golding makes good his satiric intention to castigate social snobberies and vices in the manner of the picaresque voyages of Defoe, Fielding, Swift, and Smollett. His novel, like Sterne's account of his travels through France, parodies the voyage literature of that period which so tiresomely gives us so many of the unvarnished facts and so little of the living spirit of the journey. Clearly, Sterne's *Tristram Shandy* exerts an appealing influence on Golding, for

Talbot, like Tristram, is both chronically indisposed and when it comes to the art of storytelling chronically self-conscious: "Good God! Look at the time! If I am not more able to choose what I say I shall find myself describing the day before yesterday rather than writing about today for you tonight! For throughout the day I have walked, talked, eaten, drunk, explored—and here I am again, kept out of my bunk by the—I must confess—agreeable invitation of the page! I find that writing is like drinking. A man must learn to control it!" (29).

Eager Talbot may be to write like "lively old Fielding and Smollett," rather than "sentimental Goldsmith or Richardson" (3), but his journal—in its sudden starts and stops—echoes Tristram's digressive narrative, a resemblance which the Oxford-trained Talbot himself is quick to see: "I wrote that yesterday," Talbot scribbles to his godfather in reference to a brief, breathy complaint about his colic of the day before. "My entries are becoming short as some of Mr. Sterne's chapters!" (72). Golding even mocks Sterne's famous chapter headings: Talbot, in an unsuccessful attempt to number his journal entries, scrawls Alpha, Omega, Beta, Gamma. And the hobby-horse which Talbot gallops full tilt is his absorption in the nautical tactics and language of the Tarpaulin, which he studies assiduously in his copy of William Falconer's *Universal Dictionary of the Marine*, a 1769 sourcebook for the technical terms and phrases of the ship. Though he can little understand how ironic this entry will prove to be, Talbot notes early in his journal: "Summers is to explain the main parts of the·rigging to me. I intend to surprise him with a landman's knowledge—most collected out of books he has never heard of! I also intend to please your lordship with some choice bits of Tarpaulin language for I begin . . . to speak Tarpaulin! What a pity this noble vehicle of expression has so small a literature!" (74).

As readers of Golding's *Scorpion God* and *The Hot Gates* will well remember, this novelist has always been much absorbed by history, cutting sweeps wide and assured into distant times, shaping and fitting historical detail like the timbers of a great ship, to a moral purpose.

To this end, Golding in *Rites of Passage* once more adopts his characteristic paraphrase of the Old Masters. In varying degrees, the novels have all had as part of their genesis a quarrel with another writer's view of the same situation. Golding, by deliberately subverting literary models, intends his reader to judge the moral distance between, say, Ballantyne's complacent view of small boys in *Coral Island* and his own somber recasting in *Lord of the Flies*. In *Free Fall*, this sublative technique underwent something of a sea-change, but even there Golding used Dante's *Vita Nuova* as an ironic model for Sammy Mountjoy's love of Beatrice Ifor.

There is no such simple scenario underpinning *Rites of Passage*. Its provenance is Wilfrid Scawen Blunt's two volume work, *My Diaries: Being a Personal Narrative of Events, 1888–1914*, wherein Blunt mentions an acquaintance's reference to an episode in the 1790's involving the "iron" Duke of Wellington. En route to India, Wellington boarded an adjacent convoy, having been requested to buoy the spirits of a fellow seafarer sunk in a deep lethargy. The iron Duke's effort apparently failed—the man died.[6] "I don't understand it. But it's something that deeply interested me," Golding has said of the incident which clearly constitutes an intriguing, because inexplicable, determined death. "*Rites of Passage*," Golding continued, was "an attempt to invent circumstances . . . where one can see that this kind of thing can happen: that someone can be reduced to the point at which he would die of shame."

Of course, sea mysteries such as this have long fascinated and appalled Golding; indeed, in both *Lord of the Flies* and *Pincher Martin* the sea lurks as a palpable presence and atavistic force. The ocean is no imaginative stranger to the Golding who commanded a British Navy rocket cruiser during World War II and participated in the sinking of the *Bismarck*. He has sailed all his life and knows as well as any man that the sea is a graveyard of ships, the ocean floor a litter of wrecks, including the rusty remains of his own typewriter and all the rest of the gear from his ketch shipwrecked off the shores of Southampton in the mid-'Sixties. So the life and literature of sea voyages, *The Odyssey* and *The Aeneid* and the poetry of salt water, naval logs, sea shanties, memoirs, navigation manuals, accounts both fictional and real, have—to use a figure of speech with which he would feel at home—mulched down.[7] In their rich coalescence, *Rites of Passage* germinated.

Here he has reworked not so much the nautical literature of Melville, Stevenson, and Conrad as the travel literature of Smollett and Marryatt. These very British books, bombastic accounts of shipwrecks, mutinies, and murders, demand an innocence of approach which, as Golding noted in a review of Jules Verne, "while natural in a child amounts to a mark of puerility in an adult."[8]

Peter Simple, Frederick Marryatt's 1834 tale of a fool who rises to become a gallant and capable officer in His Majesty's Service, may be one of the literary models Golding recasts in *Rites of Passage*. For Marryatt's portrait of the frank, open-hearted tar whose fun-loving temper buoys him up in a sea of hard knocks is, as Golding has said of Wells' view of Neanderthal man, "too neat, too simple."[9] Literature may have it that the jolly tars of the fo'castle with their practical jokes were a fun-loving lot. In actuality, they were probably as ignorant, superstitious, and unruly as the tars Golding portrays in *Rites of Passage*. In his paraphrase of Marryatt's resolute, generous ever-courteous Captain Savage and the frigate world he commands (both a nursery and a school of the true spirit of British seamanship), Golding shatters once again a smug view of human nature. His cleric-hating Captain Anderson—who licenses the tars' persecution of poor parson Colley—is a genuine, not a counterfeit, Savage. And Golding's sea story has, as Talbot himself writes: "never a tempest, no shipwreck, no sinking, no rescue at sea . . . no thundering broadsides, heroism, prizes, gallant defences, and heroic attacks" (278). It does, however, sight an enemy, dark on the horizon: the guilt and shame gripping the heart of man.

III

I was never made so aware of the distance between the disorder of real life in its multifarious action, partial exhibition, irritating concealments and the stage simulacra that I had once taken as a fair representation of it!

Rites of Passage (110)

As a rule, in Golding's novels, the sheer magic of the storytelling lulls us into unguarded enjoyment. Our innocent delight is then darkly under-cut by an abrupt shift in narrative viewpoint; new revelations force us to modify our earlier sympathies and reconsider what — to our untutored hearts — had previously seemed innocuous. And *Rites of Passage* is no exception. Talbot's journal — which frames the story — disarms almost totally with its descriptions of the ship's pitching, thumping and groaning, of passengers staggering across dripping planks or bedding down sick with the sea in their fetid hutches. From his indeflectibly patrician point of view, we see the ship's motley society and later we even join him in ridiculing the cleric, who cuts such a lamentable figure in his ecclesiastical finery: "The surplice, gown, hood, wig, cap looked quite silly under our vertical sun! He moved forward at a solemn pace as he might in a cathedral. . . . But the sight of a parson not so much walking . . . as processing . . . amused and impressed me. . . . He lacked the natural authority of a gentleman and had absurdly overdone the dignity of his calling. He was now advancing on the lower orders in all the majesty of the Church Triumphant" (106).

The ideographic habit — with its practiced technique of calculated obscurity — is very much in evidence in *Rites of Passage*, where often we must piece together — even deduce — information which the self-absorbed Talbot simply does not apprehend. His myopia is with us from his first journal entry when he writes: "The month or day of the week can signify little since in our long passage from the south of Old England to the Antipodes we shall pass through the geometry of all four seasons!" (30). That he neglects to understand that the ship will, on passing through the seasons, cross the equator and so rest for some days in the equatorial belt of calms, marks an omission, all the more telling since Talbot will frequently allude to Coleridge's "Rime of the Ancient Mariner," savoring the refrain: "Alone, alone. / All, all alone, / Alone on a wide, wide sea."

A more significant bafflement is over a snatch of Tarpaulin slang, "badger bag," which Talbot hears sniggered about in the fo'castle: "I wonder what is meant by the expression 'Badger Bag'? Falconer is silent"

(84). This alerts us again to the presence of another important missing clue. Similarly, Talbot's confused registering of a creeper plant growing in the bilge's dark cellarage—"its roots buried in a pot and the stem roped to the bulkhead . . . wherever a tendril or branch was unsupported it hung straight down like a piece of seaweed" (78)—warns us that there may be yet another web of complex meaning, somewhere beyond his comprehension. For soon he will visit the captain's cabin and be astonished by the spectacle of this morose tyrant lovingly tending a rich garden with rows of "climbing plants, each twisting itself around a bamboo that rose from the darkness near the deck" (159).

It is left to the reader, not Talbot, to draw the connection between the plant struggling to survive in the vessel's noisome cellarage and these well-watered and blossoming flowers; and the connection, once drawn, can be linked to the fact, which has not gone unremarked by Talbot, that the ship is timber, indeed made from English oak. Colley's letter, comprising the second perspective on the story, likens "this strange construction of English oak" (223)—with "its complications of ropes and tackles and chains and booms and sails" (219)—to a massive English oaktree, and a preternaturally toothsome sailor strutting the bowsprit is fancifully compared to a "king, crowned with curls," balancing in the branches of "one of His Majesty's *travelling trees*" (218).

These oblique references to growing plants, wavering green weeds, "under the water from our wooden sides," (247) and the stinking cellar of the ship—which Talbot, in jest, calls "a graveyard" (5)—gradually produce narrative pressure as well as acquire symbolic meaning. For quite apart from its dramatic function in the plot, oak has a rich range of implications: among the ancients it was considered sacred and, so Graves and Frazer explain, it was associated with sacrificial killings in many primitive religions. Again, it is the reader, however—not Talbot, not Colley—who must discover that these plants, like the oak hull, represent the strange unmanageable tangled undergrowth of human impulses in this wooden world.[10]

Other seemingly impenetrable strands are woven throughout Talbot's journal. We learn of an "equatorial entertainment," (85)—an oblique piece of information, glancingly presented, since Talbot's journal at this juncture is much preoccupied with its author's hilarious sexual encounter with the doxy, Zenobia Brocklebank. At the crucial moment of Delirium, with perfect slapstick timing, a blunderbuss goes off on the quarterdeck. What, we wonder, has happened? Earlier, the notorious free thinker, Prettiman, had threatened to shoot an albatross to prove his freedom from superstition. And yet it was not he who fired the shot. The explanation is bound up in the puzzle of the equatorial entertainment but, for a full account we must consult Parson Colley's journal which will soon come shuddering into view.

IV

There are no grotesques in nature.

—Browne, *Religio Medici*

We move from Talbot's complacent narrative to Colley's exclamatory, tortured letter to his sister. Having long empathized with Talbot, we are hard put to shift our sympathies from him, even registering his limitations as now we do, toward Colley. A character in the long line of Golding's unworldly grotesques, Colley, despite his morbidity and grating sentimentality, is no longer Talbot's caricatured social misfit but emerges a man of deep sensitivity. Inhabiting his being through his letter, we understand his essential innocence and fervid spirituality as he records, for example, his awe before a storm:

> What has remained with me apart from a lively memory of my apprehensions is not only a sense of HIS AWFULNESS and a sense of the majesty of HIS creation. It is a sense of the splendour of our vessel rather than her triviality and minuteness! It is as if I think of her as a separate world, a universe in little in which we must pass our lives and receive our reward or punishment. . . . I remained motionless by the rail. . . . While I was yet there, the last disturbance left by the breeze passed away so that the glitter, that image of the starry heavens, gave place to a flatness and blackness, a nothing! All was mystery. It terrified me. . . .
>
> (191–92)

Colley's experience runs parallel to Talbot's but, while Talbot can arrogantly pull rank on the captain, Colley—who possesses even less worldly cunning than Sterne's Parson Yorick—is both socially and emotionally ill-equipped to grapple with the man's tyranny: "I am deeply suspicious that the surliness of the captain towards me is not to be explained . . . readily. Is it perhaps sectarianism? . . . Or if it is not sectarianism but a social contempt, the situation is serious—nay *almost* as serious! I am a clergyman, bound for an honourable if humble station at the Antipodes. The captain has no more business to look big on me—and indeed less business—than the canons of the Close . . ." (199).

As the voyage progresses, Colley finds himself increasingly excluded from the social world of the quarterdeck, quite at pains to comprehend why "a humble servant of the Church of England—which spreads its arms so wide in the charitable embrace of sinners," (199) should be ostracized by the ship's "gentry" (188). "The ladies and gentlemen at this end of the ship do not respond with any cheerful alacrity to my greetings," he writes, puzzling over their "indefinable *indifference*" (193).

Colley is of course the perfect social victim, woefully unschooled in the systematic snobberies of stratified society, appallingly ignorant of the ingrained contempt for persons of inferior rank which such as Talbot exhibit and therefore implicitly sanction in the ship world, "the shape of the little society in which we must live together for I know not how many months" (188). Indeed, Colley is so ingenuous that he sees Talbot as a true gentleman: "He is a member of the aristocracy, with all the consideration and nobility of bearing that such birth implies" (194).

The final effect of Colley's unworldly innocence — once we inhabit his journal and can compare it to Talbot's — is to make us aware of the latter's worldliness and indeed more ashamed of Talbot's moral blindness than he himself is. Colley's account of the voyage and the strange and gruesome rites into which he is initiated is, expectably, far different from Talbot's, though once again we must decode oblique clues in order to arrive at a complete understanding.

The captain, we discover, hates parsons and his animosity seeps insidiously through the ship. Should the cat-o'-nine-tails or grog fail to subdue his volatile men, a suitable object for derisive sport such as a parson could usefully divert. Sailors are a superstitious lot and the captain recognizes that to them "a parson in a ship" is "like a woman in a fishing boat — a kind of natural bringer of bad luck" (193).

At this dramatic juncture in the novel, the ship lies under a sultry sun in the equatorial belt of calms, the very doldrums to which the Ancient Mariner's vessel was dispatched because of his act of wanton cruelty. In the tumid air, the effluvia of the still ship mix with the stinking pestilence of the surrounding, soiled waters. The atmosphere is vividly enough described by Colley (and only by Colley — Talbot is too intent on playing Mr. B. to the ship's rather ironic Pamela): "Our huge ship was motionless and her sails still hung down. On her right hand the red sun was setting and on her left the full moon was rising, the one directly across from the other. The two vast luminaries seemed to stare at each other and each to modify the other's light" (233).

From both Colley and Talbot, we hear more whispers about the badger bag, which in Glascock's Naval Sketch Book (1825) is innocuously defined as: "Badger-bag, name given by Sailors to Neptune when playing tricks on travelers on first crossing the line."[11] The tars prepare for their "equatorial entertainment" by filling a huge tarpaulin with filthy sea water, dung, and urine — a badger bag to end all badger bags. The poor parson is seized by Cumbershum and Deverel and subjected to a scatological parody of mass and baptism in the bag. And before they inflict on him the mock rite of communion, and dunk him in the mock baptismal font, the tars force him to kneel in front of their primitive godhead, Poseidon: "As I opened my mouth to protest, it was at once filled with such nauseous stuff I gag and am like to vomit remembering it. For some time . . . this operation was repeated; and when I would not open my mouth the stuff was smeared over my face . . . each question was greeted with a storm of cheering and that terrible British sound which ever daunted the foe; and then it came to me, was forced in upon my soul the awful truth — *I was the foe!*" (237).

Poor Colley in extremity has not the means to comprehend that the "snarling, lustful, storming" (238) sport is no mere equatorial entertainment. This persecution of a sacrificial scapegoat amounts to a magico-religious ritual to exorcise fears about the seaworthiness of the becalmed ship. Covertly handled as the incident is, it recalls the ritual murders of *Lord of the Flies, The Inheritors,* and *The Spire* where the scapegoats — Simon, Liku, and Pangall respectively — are all sacrificed to ensure the terrified group's solidarity. It is only Summers' firing of the blunderbuss which stops the pack from committing a ritual murder here. For these pagan sailors venerate, as the ancients did, the oak of their wooden ship; they might well have killed Colley out of a generalized feeling that he would make a good guardian of the bilge. In mythic terms, his murder would represent the death of sterility and signal the release of generative power. That this ritual release of winds should occur during a Dionysian orgy of rum is another indication of the myth-enhancing power of *Rites of Passage.* Dionysus, whose original name, Tree-youth, links him to Colley's crowned king of the travelling tree, once made a ship seaworthy by causing a vine to grow from the deck and enfold the mast.[12] The sailors on his ship — like those of *Rites of Passage* with its creepers growing from the cellarage — became so intoxicated by wine and desire that they were metamorphosized into phantom beasts.

Colley participates in another Bacchanalian orgy, though neither his nor Talbot's journal directly recounts the "Make and Mend" festivity.[13] Its full implications for Colley's disgrace become clear only after the catastrophe (undescribed) and must be pieced together by Talbot and the reader. Having painfully resolved that "What a man does defiles him, not what is done by others — my shame, though it burn, has been inflicted on me" (235), Colley returns to the fo'castle intent, he believes, on God's mission: "Why — even the captain himself has shown some small signs — and the power of Grace is infinite. . . . I shall go forward and rebuke these unruly but truely loveable children of OUR MAKER. . . . I am consumed by a great love of all things, the sea, the ship, the sky, the gentlemen and the people and of course OUR REDEEMER above all! Here at last is the happiest outcome of all my distress and difficulty! ALL THINGS PRAISE HIM!" (247).

Unconscious of his growing infatuation for one of the deckhands, which he sublimates as a passionate longing to "bring this young man to OUR SAVIOUR" (218), he acts from confused and tangled motives. Stupefied with rum, he is driven to mad exuberance, though the entire episode is concealed from our view; we only see him exit from the fo'castle where, stripped of his canonical finery, he makes a spectacle of himself by pissing before an "audience,"[14] assembled on the quarterdeck. He is lugged back to his hutch from which he will never again emerge; he lies rigid, his hand clutching a "ringbolt" (127) — rigid until he dies. When an inquiry into his death is held, with Talbot in attendance, the captain interrogates a deckhand, Billy, and raises brusquely the issue of buggery, a delayed disclosure about Colley's unseen actions which is later confirmed when Billy laughs to another tar about "getting a chew off a parson" (273). We are meant to realize that Colley in drunken forgetfulness of self has committed fellatio on the deckhand, and to conclude, therefore, that he dies *literally* from shame at his defilement of himself.

V

You will observe that I have recovered somewhat from the effect of reading Colley's letter. . . . You will already have noted some particularly impenetrable specimens as, for instance, mention of a *badger bag* — does not Servius (I believe it was he) declare there are half a doxen cruxes in the *Aeneid* which will never be solved, either by emendation or inspiration or any method attempted by scholarship?

Rites of Passage (259)

Colley, then, is to be likened to Pentheus, who was driven mad and torn to pieces by the Bacchanals when he resisted the introduction of Dionysian worship into his kingdom; Colley, having been denied the quarterdeck, calls the fo'castle his "little kingdom" (209). But other conundrums are not so easily solved. Why does Talbot's servant, "omniscient, ubiquitous" (184) Wheeler, disappear mysteriously? Talbot assumes that he fell overboard, but can we not surmise, by way of Talbot's allusion to Palinarus who is flung from Aeneas' ship, that Wheeler may have known too much about the "Make and Mend" chewing, not to mention the dishonest dealings of the shadowy purser, who is yet another "impenetrable crux" (259) in *Rites of Passage?* For that matter, what is the unnamed ship's title with "her monstrous figurehead, emblem of her name and which our people . . . have turned colloquially into an obscenity" (34)? Could it sound like purser-grind, which is nautical slang meaning "coition bringing the woman no money, but consolation in the size of the member"?[15] Perhaps this is why Talbot jeers when Summers tells him that the infant born aboard ship will be named for her.

One riddle remains: the state of Colley's soul at its departure. It is not altogether clear whether Golding intends us to believe that Colley dies a self-flagellated sinner or whether, in his last moment, he is mercifully granted release from his guilt. Neither journal records the last moments. According to Talbot, Colley dies in a condition of despair and shame.

Golding's novels never conclude with one unequivocal meaning, however; they insist upon the intermingling of the visible and the invisible, the physical and the spiritual, the world of the burning candle and the burning bush, the cellarage and the spire. In the eschatology of *Free Fall* —

as in that of *Pincher Martin* — Mercy does operate in the world, although it
may be hidden from the eye of those who reject goodness. The drowning
Pincher imagines that he faces a bully and an Executioner while Sammy
despairs of the Judge, who he imagines stands on the other side of the cell's
door preparing to punish him for his guilt. Yet both novels suggest that the
punishment which each protagonist posits is the projection of his darkness.
("It's a whole philosophy, in fact," Golding explained, "suggesting that
God is the thing we turn away from and make a darkness there.")[16] When
the dying Jocelin is granted a momentary glimpse of a kingfisher and an
appletree Golding intends the reader to see the two emblems as symboliz-
ing the "my-godness"[17] of man.

Rites of Passage hints that Colley might have been granted release
from the cellarage of his deep sense of self-degradation. Recall, first, that
Colley has in his library a copy of Baxter's *Saints Everlasting Rest*,
devotional meditations on sudden death. Also, Colley fears "the Justice of
GOD, unmitigated by his Mercy!" (234); he believes that "the power of
Grace is infinite" (247); he believes that the "happiest outcome" of all his
"distress and difficulty" is "OUR REDEEMER" (247) — indeed, these are
the last words of his testament. Turning to Talbot's description of Colley's
posture in dying where his hand is barnacled to a "ringbolt"
(127;131;176) — "one hand still clutched what both Falconer and Summers
agreed was a ringbolt" (131) — one may surmise by way of the nagging,
reiterative (though unexplained) reference to the ringbolt that Golding
intends us to inspect it as a symbolic shorthand, like the verbal paradox of
Jocelin's "upward waterfall." Falconer may explain that a ringbolt "has
several uses . . . but particularly hooks the tackles by which the cannons of
a ship are secured."[18] We may (if we are spiritually inclined) imagine
another "use" and interpret it as that bolt from the blue — God's grace —
which hooks the penitent believer into the ring of God's everlasting Mercy.

Just as *The Inheritors* proffered the hint of sanctity on the level of the
plain beyond the Fall where the artist, Tuami, sculpted the death-weapon
into a life image, just as Pincher Martin is offered the chance to "die into
heaven," just as Mountjoy and Pedigree are mysteriously released from the
cell of their own unendurable identities, so too Colley may have been
granted everlasting rest. In the words of Sir Thomas Browne's meditation:
"the world, I count it not an inn, but an hospital; and a place not to live,
but to die in. The world that I regard is myself; it is in the microcosm of
my own frame that I cast mine eye on. . . . There is surely a piece of
divinity in us. . . . Thus it is observed that men sometimes upon the hour
of their departure do speak and reason above themselves."

In *Rites of Passage* Golding has again provided plunder enough for a
whole shipload of critics. Once again, he has constructed a religious
mythopoeia, the spur of a spiritual dimension — at least in the imaginative
realm — in which the reader can participate. For *Rites of Passage* is, among
many other things, about last rites. The novel's structure — with its partial

concealments, oblique clues, delayed disclosures — forces us to bring into focus Colley's conduct in the fo'castle farce as well as Talbot's role in Colley's final and appalling disgrace. We discover that it was Talbot who catalyzed the whole sordid sequence of humiliations, ending in the parson's death. Had Talbot not flaunted his rank, thus undermining the captain's sense of his own authority, the captain, in turn, might not have countenanced Colley's persecution. The final effect of *Rites of Passage* is to implicate the reader in the responsibility for the loss of innocence: Talbot's belated sense of shame becomes our shame, our guilt. We rest at one with him in the final entry he makes in his journal: "With lack of sleep and too much understanding I grow a little crazy, I think, like all men at sea who live too close to each other and too close thereby to all that is monstrous under the sun and moon" (278).

Notes

1. Golding to John Haffenden, "William Golding: An Interview," *Quarto Magazine*, Vol. II, No. 12, November 1980, p. 9.

2. "It is not too much to say that man invented war at the very earliest moment possible. It is not too much to say that as soon as he could leave a sign of anything, he left a sign of his belief in God." Golding, "Before the Beginning," *The Spectator*, 26 May, 1961, p. 768.

3. Golding, *Quarto Magazine*, p. 11.

4. For a full discussion of the term, see Virginia Tiger, *William Golding: The Dark Fields of Discovery* (London: Calder & Boyars, 1974), pp. 16–20.

5. William Golding, *Rites of Passage* (London: Faber & Faber, 1980), p. 93. Subsequent references to this edition appear in textual parentheses.

6. Golding explained that the genesis of *Rites of Passage* came from Blunt's diary. "When you read nineteenth-century life and literature it seems quite remarkable how many people subsequently died: Arthur Hallam, for instance, lay down on a couch and just died." Golding, *Quarto Magazine*, p. 9.

7. Golding's term for the imaginative process by which diverse literary fragments rot to compost in the fertile soil of the imagination.

8. Golding, "Astronaut by Gaslight," *The Hot Gates* (London: Faber & Faber, 1965), p. 111.

9. Golding to Frank Kermode, "The Meaning of It All," *Books and Bookmen*, August 1959, p. 9.

10. The metaphor recalls *The Spire* where images of bourgeoning plants and a growing mast-like spire symbolize the complexity of human effort.

11. William Nugent Glascock, *Naval Sketch Book; or the service afloat and ashore: with characteristic reminiscences, fragments, and opinions*, 3rd. ed. (1826; rpt. London: Whittaker & Co., 1843), I, 42.

12. Robert Graves, *The Greek Myths*, rev. ed. (rpt. Harmondsworth, Middlesex: Penguin, 1966), I, (27.h; 27.2), p. 106. And Frazer explains: "While the vine with its cluster was the most characteristic manifestation of Dionysus, he was also a god of trees in general. Thus we are told that almost all Greeks sacrificed to Dionysus of the tree. In Boetia one of his titles was Dionysus in the tree"; *The Golden Bough*, I Volume abridged ed. (1922; rpt. New York: Macmillan, 1960), p. 449.

13. The Make and Mend festivity has also an innocuous enough definition: it is "the naval half-holiday on Thursday, nominally for attending to one's clothes." Eric Partridge, *A Dictionary of Slang and Unconventional English*, 5th ed. (1961; rpt. London: Routledge & Kegan Paul, 1970), I, 506.

14. One reference alone does not adequately demonstrate how persistently theatrical images and metaphors are pursued in the novel. Talbot's first discussion of farce and tragedy — "Does not tragedy depend on the dignity of the protagonist. . . . A farce, then, for the man appears a sort of Punchinello" (104) — ironically foreshadows the real nature of Colley's drama while, at the same time, it indicates the narrative mode of *Rites of Passage* which is "by turns" (as Talbot later says of Colley) "farcical, gross and tragic" (276).

15. Partridge, I, 670.

16. Golding in letter quoted in John Peter, "Postscript to 'Fables of William Golding',", *William Golding's Lord of the Flies: A Source Book*, ed. William Nelson (New York: Odyssey Press, 1963), p. 34.

17. Golding's term (to Tiger, p. 208) for the *Scintillans Dei*, one's original God-given spirit.

18. William Falconer, *A Universal Dictionary of the Marine or, a copious explanation of the technical terms and phrases employed in the construction, equipment, furniture, machinery, movements and military operations of a ship* (1769; rpt. New York: Augustus M. Kelley, 1970), p. 245.

Nobel Lecture 1983   William Golding*

Those of you who have some knowledge of your present speaker as revealed by the loftier-minded section of the British Press will be resigning yourselves to a half hour of unrelieved gloom. Indeed, your first view of me, white-bearded and ancient, may have turned that gloom into profound dark; dark, dark, dark, amid the blaze of noon, irrecoverably dark, total eclipse. But the case is not as hard as that. I am among the older of the Nobel laureates and therefore might well be excused a touch of — let me whisper the word — frivolity. Pray do not misunderstand me. I have no dancing girls, alas. I shall not sing to you or juggle or clown — or shall I juggle? I wonder! How can a man who has been defined as a pessimist indulge in anything as frivolous as juggling?

You see, it is hard enough at any age to address so learned a gathering as this. The very thought induces a certain solemnity. Then again, what about the dignity of age? There is, they say, no fool like an old fool.

Well, there is no fool like a middle-aged fool, either. Twenty-five years ago I accepted the label "pessimist" thoughtlessly without realising that it was going to be tied to my tail, as it were, in something the way that, to take an example from another art, Rachmaninoff's famous Prelude in C sharp minor was tied to him. No audience would allow him

*Reprinted by permission of the Nobel Foundation. © THE NOBEL FOUNDATION 1983.

off the concert platform until he played it. Similarly, critics have dug into my books until they could come up with something that looked hopeless. I can't think why. I don't feel hopeless myself. Indeed, I tried to reverse the process by explaining myself. Under some critical interrogation I named myself a universal pessimist but a cosmic optimist. I should have thought that anyone with an ear for language would understand that I was allowing more connotation than denotation to the word "cosmic," though in derivation "universal" and "cosmic" mean the same thing. I meant, of course, that when I consider a universe which the scientist constructs by a set of rules which stipulate that his constructs must be repeatable and identical, then I am a pessimist and bow down before the great god Entropy. I am optimistic when I consider the spiritual dimension which the scientist's discipline forces him to ignore. So worldwide is the fame of the Nobel Prize that people have taken to quoting from my works and I do not see why I should not join in this fashionable pastime. Twenty years ago I tried to put the difference between the two kinds of experience in the mind of one of my characters, and made a mess of it.

He was in prison. "All day long the trains run on rails. Eclipses are predictable. Penicillin cures pneumonia and the atom splits to order. All day long year in year out the daylight explanation drives back the mystery and reveals a reality usable, understandable and detached. The scalpel and the microscope fail. The oscilloscope moves closer to behaviour.

"But then, all day long action is weighed in the balance and found not opportune nor fortunate nor ill-advised but good or evil. For this mode which we call the spirit breathes through the universe and does not touch it: touches only the dark things held prisoner, incommunicado touches, judges, sentences and passes on. Both worlds are real. There is no bridge."

What amuses me is the thought that of course there is a bridge and that, if anything, it has been thrust out from the side that least expected it, and thrust out since those words were written. For we know now that the universe had a beginning. (Indeed, as an aside I might say we always *did* know. I offer you a simple proof and forbid you to examine it. If there was no beginning, then infinite time has already passed and we could never have got to the moment where we are.) We also know or it is at least scientifically respectable to postulate that at the centre of a black hole the laws of nature no longer apply. Since most scientists are just a bit religious and most religious are seldom wholly unscientific we find humanity in a comical position. His scientific intellect believes in the possibility of miracles inside a black hole while his religious intellect believes in them outside it. Both, in fact, now believe in miracles, credimus quia absurdum est. Glory be to God in the highest. You will get no reductive pessimism from me.

A greater danger facing you is that an ancient schoolmaster may be carried away and forget he is not addressing a class of pupils. A man in his seventies may be tempted to think he has seen it all and knows it all. He may think that mere length of years is a guarantee of wisdom and a permit for the issuing of admonition and advice. Poor young Shakespeare and Beethoven, he thinks, dead in their youth at a mere fifty-two or -three! What could young fellows such as that know about anything? But at midnight perhaps, when the clock strikes and another year has passed, he may occasionally brood on the disadvantages of age rather than the advantages. He may regard more thoughtfully a sentence which has been called the poetry of the fact, a sentence that one of those young fellows stumbled across accidentally, as it were, since he was never old enough to have worked the thing out through living. "Men," he wrote, "must endure their going hence, even as their coming hither." Such a consideration may modify the essential jollity of an old man's nature. Is the old man right to be happy? Is there not something unbecoming in his cheerful view of his own end? The words of another English poet seem to rebuke him.

> King David and King Solomon
> Led merry, merry lives,
> With many, many lady friends
> And many, many wives;
> But when old age crept over them,
> With many, many qualms,
> King Solomon wrote the Proverbs
> And King David wrote the Psalms.

Powerful stuff that, there's no doubt about it. But there are two views of the matter; and since I have quoted to you some of my prose which is generally regarded as poetic I will now quote to you some of my Goon or McGonagall poetry which may well be regarded as prosaic.

> Sophocles the eminent Athenian
> Gave as his final opinion
> That death of love in the breast
> Was like escape from a wild beast.
> What better word could you get?
>
> He was eighty when he said that,
> But Ninon de Lenclos
> When asked the same question said, no
> She was uncommonly matey
> At eighty.

Evidently, age need not wither us nor custom stale our infinite variety. Let us be, for a while, not serious but considerate. I myself face another danger. I do not speak in a small tribal language, as it might be, one of the six hundred languages of Nigeria. Of course, the value of any language is incalculable. Your laureate of 1979 the Greek poet Elytis made quite clear that the relative value of works of literature is not to be decided by counting heads. It is, I think, the greatest tribute one can pay your committees that they have consistently sought for value in a work without heeding how many people can or cannot read it. The young John Keats spoke of Greek poets who "died content on pleasant sward, leaving great verse unto a little clan." Indeed and indeed, small can be beautiful. To quote yet another poet — prose writer though I am — you will have begun to realise where my heart is — Ben Jonson said:

> It is not growing like a tree
> In bulk, doth make man better be;
> Or standing long an oak, three hundred year,
> To fall a log at last, dry, bald and sere:
>   A lily of a day,
>   Is fairer far in May,
> Although it fall and die that night;
> It was the plant and flower of light.
> In small proportions we just beauties see,
> And in short measures, life may perfect be.

My own language, English, I believe to have a store of poets, of writers that need not fear comparison with those of any other language, ancient or modern. But today that language may suffer from too wide a use rather than too narrow a one — may be an oak rather than a lily. It spreads right round the world as the medium of advertisement, navigation, science, negotiation, conference. A hundred political parties have it daily in their mouths. Perhaps a language subjected to such strains as that may become, here and there, just a little thin. In English a man may think he is addressing a small, distinguished audience, or his family or his friends, perhaps; he is brooding aloud or talking in his sleep. Later he finds that without meaning to he has been addressing a large segment of the world. That is a daunting thought. It is true that this year, surrounded and outnumbered as I am by American laureates, I take a quiet pleasure in the consideration that though variants of my mother tongue may be spoken by a greater number of people than are to be found in an island off the west coast of Europe, nevertheless they are speaking dialects of what is still centrally English. Personally I cannot tell whether those many dialects are being rendered mutually incomprehensible by distance faster than they are being unified by television and satellites; but at the moment the English writer faces immediate comprehension or partial comprehension by a good part of a billion people. His critics are limited in number only by the number of the people who can read his work. Nor can he escape from knowing the worst. No matter how obscure the publication that has disembowelled him, some kind correspondent — let us call him "X" — will send the article along together with an indignant assurance that he, "X," does not agree with a word of it. I think apprehensively of the mark I present, once A Moving Target but now, surely, a fixed one, before the serried ranks of those who can shoot at me if they choose. Even my most famous and distinguished fellow laureate and fellow countryman Winston

Churchill did not escape. A critic remarked with acid wit of his getting the award, "Was it for his poetry or his prose?" Indeed, it was considerations such as these which have given me, I suppose, more difficulty in conceiving, let alone writing, this lecture than any piece of comparable length since those distant days when I wrote set essays on set subjects at school. The only difference I can find is that today I write at a larger desk and the marks I shall get for my performance will be more widely reported.

Now when, you may say, is the man going to say something about the subject which is alleged to be his own? He should be talking about the novel! Well, I will for a while, but only for a while, and, as it were, tangentially. The truth is that though each of the subjects for which the prizes are awarded has its own and unique importance, none can exist wholly to itself. Even the novel, if it climbs into an ivory tower, will find no audience except those with ivory towers of their own. I used to think that the outlook for the novel was poor. Let me quote myself again. I speak of boys growing up — not exceptional boy, but average boy.

> Boys do not evaluate a book. They divide books into categories. There are sexy books, war books, Westerns, travel books, science fiction. A boy will accept anything from a section he knows rather than risk another sort. He has to have the label on the bottle to know it is the mixture as before. You must put his detective story in a green paperback or he may suffer the hardship of reading a book in which nobody is murdered at all — I am thinking of the plodders, the amiable majority of us, not particularly intelligent or gifted; well-disposed, but left high and dry among a mass of undigested facts with their scraps of saleable technology. What chance has literature of competing with the defined categories of entertainment which are laid on for them at every hour of the day? I do not see how literature is to be for them anything but simple, repetitive and a stop-gap for when there are no Westerns on the telly. They will have a far less brutish life than their nineteenth-century ancestors, no doubt. They will believe less and fear less. But just as bad money drives out good, so inferior culture drives out superior. With any capacity to make value judgements vitiated or undeveloped, what mass future is there, then, for poetry, for belles-lettres, for real fearlessness in the theatre, for the novel which tries to look at life anew — in a word, for intransigence?

I wrote that some twenty years ago, I believe, and the process as far as the novel is concerned has developed but not improved. The categories are more and more defined. Competition from other media is fiercer still. Well, after all, the novel has no built-in claims on immortality.

"Story" of course is a different matter. We like to hear of succession of events and as an inspection of our press will demonstrate have only a marginal interest in whether the succession of events is minutely true or not. Like the late Mr Sam Goldwyn who wanted a story which began with an earthquake and worked up to a climax, we like a good lead-in but have most pleasure in a succession of events with a satisfactory end-point. Most simply and directly — when children holler and yell because of some infant tragedy or tedium, at once when we take them on our knee and begin shouting if necessary, "Once upon a time," they fall silent and attentive. Story will always be with us. But story in a physical book, in a sentence, what the West means by "a novel" — what of that? Certainly, if the form fails let it go. We have enough complications in life, in art, in literature without preserving dead forms fossilised, without cluttering ourselves with Byzantine sterilities. Yes, in that case, let the novel go. But what goes with it? Surely something of profound importance to the human spirit! A novel ensures that we can look before and after, take action at whatever pace we choose, read again and again, skip and go back. The story in a book is humble and serviceable, available, friendly, is not switched on and off but taken up and put down, lasts a lifetime.

But simply, the novel stands between us and the hardening concept of statistical man. There is no other medium in which we can live for so long and so intimately with a character. That is the service a novel renders. It performs no less an act than the rescue and the preservation of the individuality and dignity of the single being, be it man, woman or child. No other art, I claim, can so thread in and out of a single mind and body, so live another life. It does ensure that at the very least a human being shall be seen to be more than just one billionth of one billion.

I spoke of the ivory tower and the unique importance of each of our studies. Now I must add, having said my bit about the novel, that those studies converge, literature with the rest. Put bluntly, we face two problems — either we blow ourselves off the face of the earth or we degrade the fertility of the earth bit by bit until we have ruined it. Does it take a writer of fiction to bring you the cold comfort of pointing out that the problems are mutually exclusive? The one problem, the instant catastrophe, is not to be dealt with here. It would be irresponsible of me to turn this platform into a stage for acting out some anti-atomic harangue and equally irresponsible at this juncture in history for me to ignore our perils. You know them as well as I do. As so often, when the unspeakable is to be spoken, the unthinkable thought, it is Shakespeare we must turn to; and I can only quote Hamlet with the skull: "Not one now, to mock your own grinning? Quite chop-fallen? Now get you to my lady's chamber and tell her, let her paint an inch thick, to this favour she must come; make her laugh at that." I am being rather unfair to the lady, perhaps, for there will be skulls of all shapes and sizes and sexes. I speak tangentially. No other quotation gives the dirt of it all, another kind of poetry of the fact. I must say something of this danger and I have said it, for I could do no less. Now as far as this matter is concerned, I have done.

The other danger is the more difficult to combat. To quote another laureate, our race may end not with a bang but a whimper. It must be nearer seventy years ago than sixty that I first discovered and engaged myself to a magic place. This was on the west coast of our country. It was on the seashore among rocks. I early became acquainted with the wonderful interplay of earth and moon and sun, enjoying them at the same time as I was assured that scientifically you could not have action influenced at a distance. There was a particular phase of the moon at which the tide sank more than usually far down and revealed to me a small recess which I remember as a cavern. There was plenty of life of one sort or another round all the rocks and in the pools among them. But this pool, farthest down and revealed, it seemed, by an influence from the sky only once or twice during the times when I had the holiday privilege of living near it—this last recess before the even more mysterious deep sea had strange inhabitants which I had found nowhere else. I can now remember and even feel but alas not describe the peculiar engagement, excitement and, no, not sympathy or empathy, but passionate recognition of a living thing in all its secrecy and strangeness. It was or rather they were real as I was. It was as if the centre of our universe was there for my eyes to reach at like hands, to seize on by sight. Only a hand's breadth away in the last few inches of still water they flowered, grey, green and purple, palpably alive, a discovery, a meeting, more than an interest or pleasure. They were life, we together were delight itself; until the first ripples of returning water blurred and hid them. When the summer holidays were over and I went back again about as far from the sea as you can get in England I carried with me like a private treasure the memory of that cave—no, in some strange way I took the cave with me and its creatures that flowered so strangely. In nights of sleeplessness and fear of the supernatural I would work out the phase of the moon, returning in thought to the slither and clamber among the weeds of the rocks. There were times when, though I was far away, I found myself before the cavern watching the moon-dazzle as the water sank, and was comforted somehow by the magical beauty of our common world.

I have been back, since. The recess—for now it seems no more than that—is still there, and at low-water springs if you can bend down far enough you can still look inside. Nothing lives there any more. It is all very clean now, ironically so, clean sand, clean water, clean rock. Where the living creatures once clung they have worn two holes like the orbits of eyes, so that you might well sentimentalize yourself into the fancy that you are looking at a skull. No life.

Was it a natural process? Was it fuel oil? Was it sewage or chemicals more deadly that killed my childhood's bit of magic and mystery? I cannot tell and it does not matter. What matters is that this is only one tiny example among millions of how we are impoverishing the only planet we have to live on.

Well now, what has literature to say to that? We have computers and satellites, we have ingenuities of craft that can land a complex machine on a distant planet and get reports back. And so on. You know it all as well and better than I. Literature has words only, surely a tool as primitive as the flint axe or even the soft copper chisel with which man first carved his own likeness in stone. That tool makes a poor showing, one would think, among the products of the silicon chip. But remember Churchill. For despite the cynical critic, he got the Nobel Prize neither for poetry nor for prose. He got it for about a single page of simple sentences which are neither poetry nor prose but for what, I repeat, has been called finely the poetry of the fact. He got it for those passionate utterances which were the very stuff of human courage and defiance. Those of us who lived through those times know that Churchill's poetry of the fact changed history.

Perhaps, then, the soft copper chisel is not so poor a tool after all. Words may, through the devotion, the skill, the passion and the luck of writers, prove to be the most powerful thing in the world. They may move men to speak to each other because some of those words somewhere express not just what the writer is thinking about but what a huge segment of the world is thinking. They may allow man to speak to man, the man in the street to speak to his fellow until a ripple becomes a tide running through every nation — of common sense, of simple healthy caution, a tide that rulers and negotiators cannot ignore, so that nation does truly speak unto nation. Then there is hope that we may learn to be temperate, provident, taking no more from nature's treasury than is our due. It may be by books, stories, poetry, lectures we who have the ear of mankind can move man a little nearer the perilous safety of a warless and provident world. It cannot be done by the mechanical constructs of overt propaganda. I cannot do it myself, cannot now create stories which would help to make man aware of what he is doing; but there are others who can, many others. There always have been. We need more humanity, more care, more love. There are those who expect a political system to produce that; and others who expect the love to produce the system. My own faith is that the truth of the future lies between the two and we shall behave humanly and a bit humanely, stumbling along, haphazardly generous and gallant, foolishly and meanly wise, until the rape of our planet is seen to be the preposterous folly that it is.

For we are a marvel of creation. I think in particular of one of the most extraordinary women, dead now these five hundred years, Juliana of Norwich. She was caught up in the spirit and shown a thing that might lie in the palm of her hand and in the bigness of a nut. She was told it was the world. She was told of the strange and wonderful and awful things that would happen there. At the last, a voice told her that all things should be well and all manner of things should be well and all things should be very well.

Now we, if not in the spirit, have been caught up to see our earth, our mother, Gaia Mater, set like a jewel in space. We have no excuse now for supposing her riches inexhaustible nor the area we have to live on limitless because unbounded. We are the children of that great blue-white jewel. Through our mother we are part of the solar system and part through that of the whole universe. In the blazing poetry of the fact we are children of the stars.

I had better come down, I think. Churchill, Juliana of Norwich, let alone Ben Jonson and Shakespeare — Lord, what company we keep! Reputations grow and dwindle and the brightest of laurels fade. That very practical man, Julius Caesar — whom I always think of, for a reason you may guess at, as Field Marshal Lord Caesar — Julius Caesar is said to have worn a laurel wreath to conceal his baldness. While it may be proper to praise the idea of a laureate, the man himself may very well remember what his laurels will hide, and that not only baldness. In a sentence he must remember not to take himself with unbecoming seriousness. Fortunately, some spirit or other — I do not presume to put a name on it — ensured that I should remember my smallness in the scheme of things. The very day after I learned that I was the laureate for literature for 1983 I drove into a country town and parked my car where I should not. I only left the car for a few minutes but when I came back there was a ticket taped to the window. A traffic warden, a lady of a minatory aspect, stood by the car. She pointed to a notice on the wall. "Can't you read?" she said. Sheepishly I got into my car and drove very slowly round the corner. There on the pavement I saw two county policemen. I stopped opposite them and took my parking ticket out of its plastic envelope. They crossed the road to me. I asked if, as I had pressing business, I could go straight to the town hall and pay my fine on the spot. "No, sir," said the senior policeman. "I'm afraid you can't do that." He smiled the fond smile that such policemen reserve for those people who are clearly harmless if a bit silly. He indicated a rectangle on the ticket that had the words "name and address of sender" printed above it. "You should write your name and address in that place," he said. "You make out a cheque for ten pounds, making it payable to the Clerk to the Justices at *this* address written here. Then you write the same address on the outside of the envelope, stick a sixteen-penny stamp in the top right-hand corner of the envelope, then post it. And may we congratulate you on winning the Nobel Prize for Literature."

The Paper Men   Julia Briggs*

Golding's three most recent novels can be seen as a kind of triptych, with *Rites of Passage* at the centre, not only chronologically, but also because it was the most enthusiastically received, being more concerned than the other two (for all its historical setting) with everyday life, the "ordinary universe" in which most people live most of the time. It is thus the easiest of the three to place and keep in focus. Yet in different ways and to varying degrees, all three novels testify to spiritual truths that have no obvious part in the daily round. The less favourable reactions to *Darkness Visible* (widely acknowledged as a major novel, but a difficult one) and the largely unfavourable reception of *The Paper Men* (judged distinctly minor) seem directly related to the degree of tact with which Golding presents the manifestation of spiritual forces to a largely sceptical readership. In each of these books individuals bear witness, often setting down their experiences in journals or records of some kind, but in each the credence we are required to accord their documents varies, demanding more or less active levels of acquiescence. Matty describes his encounters with brightly-clothed spirits, but his naive goodness is balanced against Sophy's hyper-intelligent evil, and both are counteracted by the intelligent mediocrities, Sim and Edwin, who remain closest to the reader's experience and with whose responses the book ends. This tripartite structure of *Darkness Visible* is followed by the double perspective of *Rites of Passage*, where Colley's passionate responses to the spiritual world are mediated through the cheerfully prosaic scepticism of Talbot; his temperamental preference for reductive explanations tends to insulate the reader from having to accept unmodified symbolic or supernatural interpretations. But *The Paper Men* affords only one point of view, a single witness and one far less attractive in every way than Talbot who, though young and arrogant, was also responsive and deeply interested in the human world around him. The narrator of *The Paper Men* is old, callous and self-absorbed; at the same time the experiences of the spiritual world that he records are more direct and bizarre than anything that takes place in *Rites of Passage*. Disconcertingly, this narrator sounds and looks all too like his creator— Bill Golding metamorphosed into Wilf Barclay, an ageing novelist who had served in the navy during the war and whose earliest books had found immediate success, selling well enough to ensure him a permanent income (the first is entitled *Coldharbour*, for the significance of which see above, p. 50, and note 4 to chapter 1). Barclay has a straggly white beard and is irritated at finding himself the subject of an academic "light industry." He prefers to regard himself as a "moving target," eluding his critics' boss

*This essay first appeared in Don Crompton, *A View From the Spire: William Golding's Later Novels*, edited and completed by Julia Briggs (Oxford: Basil Blackwell, 1985) and is reprinted with permission of Basil Blackwell, Limited, Oxford, England.

shots. *The Paper Men* is in some sense his autobiography, and one of Barclay's motives in writing it is to be revenged upon his would-be biographer: "Think Rick — all the people who get lice like you in their hair, all the people spied on, followed, lied about, all the people offered up to the great public — we'll be revenged, Rick, I'll be revenged on the whole lot of them. . . ."

Of course such similarities are no more than traps for critical heffalumps, a form of crossed fingers that should avert further odious comparisons more than they invite them. Barclay resembles his creator only in his most public, that is to say his most superficial aspects. But at first these resemblances tended to deflect attention from the kind of novel that Golding had actually written, rather as Prufrock's resemblance to T. S. Eliot has sometimes hindered his Love Song from being approached as a dramatic monologue. The strictly limited viewpoint of *The Paper Men* requires us to understand what has really happened not only through what we are told, but also through what we are *not* told, to reconstruct events in the light of the narrator's narrowed vision. Thus it should take its place in the tradition of novels such as Henry James's *What Maisie Knew* or Ford Madox Ford's *The Good Soldier*, novels where the narrator's naive perceptions, whether the result of innocence or ignorance, only provide a part of the story. The rest must be pieced together by the reader out of his superior experience or understanding. But in both these examples the narrators' limitations lie in their inability to grasp the nature of sexual passion, a knowledge that adult readers can usually supply without difficulty. Golding in *The Paper Men* has created a narrator who is a man of exceptional intelligence of a worldly kind, but is morally and spiritually stupid. He is adrift in a universe of numinous forces, and we must identify his failure to understand or come to terms with that universe. Like T. S. Eliot, Golding does not want to hear "Of the wisdom of old men, but rather of their folly, / Their fear of fear and frenzy, their fear of possession, / Of belonging to another, or to others, or to God." Barclay, the narrator, is "suggestible," attuned to receiving mystically transmitted messages, yet unable to interpret them except in so far as they correspond to his own view of things, so correct interpretation is left to the reader who may be hardly better placed for the task. Repelled by Barclay's character and largely unprepared for or unequipped to take in the wider theological perspectives that Barclay's solipsism denies him, we are in danger of being baffled, confused and disappointed.[1]

If one major problem lies in the unreliable narrator, whose account of events requires adjustment or reinterpretation, another lies in the continuous shifting between literal and symbolic levels, between familiar stereotypes and their subversion, between dream and reality — and often the symbolic level, the subverted stereotype, the dream, seem to be of greater importance. An outline of the main events can reveal some of their underlying implications, but taken as a whole the book has a tendency to elude consistent critical interpretations, and this may well be exactly what Golding intended. After all, it is centrally concerned with a critic's clumsy attempts to pin down a writer on the printed pages of his projected biography. This attempt is so energetically and effectively foiled that the critic is finally forced to silence his subject, to reduce him to the status of an object by shooting him. Faced with such a theme it would be peculiarly arrogant for anyone to believe that it might all be summed up neatly, that one might pluck out the heart of Golding's mystery.

The story has a circular movement, ending where it began, at Wilf Barclay's secluded English country house. The opening and closing pages provide a pattern of reversal that characterises the structure at every level. During the rest of the book, Barclay travels across Europe, driven on as if by demons or in flight from God—a flying Dutchman or a wandering Jew. He is pursued by his aspiring biographer Rick Tucker, an unwelcome reminder of what he has been and is, and beyond Tucker by his master, the mysterious Halliday. He returns from his voyage of discovery having been forced to acknowledge the existence of God, yet the God he finds is formed in his own image, encased in a rigid structure, its eyes burning; it shares his intolerance and regards him as its chosen comic victim. Barclay's existential sense of his own absurdity is thus delicately balanced against his sense of personal and predestined damnation. His discovery of something beyond himself which is an infinite repetition of his finite self may be compared to Sophy's—for both of them, it involves an inversion of Christian values, an "Evil be thou my good." Yet whereas Sophy actively promoted evil, Barclay mainly acquiesces in it. So intensely self-absorbed, solipsistic, so Berkeleian, perhaps, is his conception of the universe that the God he finds there may hunt him down, but having insisted upon existence, seems powerless to change him. His sins remain those of omission, deadlier because more trivial than those of commission. A further vision reveals God not as an extension of himself, but as total Otherness, a blessed state which Barclay terms "isness" or (more technically) *Istigkeit*; again its impact on him seems negligible.

Barclay is bankrupt not only morally, but artistically. He cannot change because he has become a hollow man, a man encased in the straitjacket of what Golding has called "literary mummification,"[2] and with little left inside his shell. But in a society that is more concerned with the superficies, with image rather than reality, a society whose sacred speakers have become scarcely more than so many gas-filled balloons, it is hard to retain individuality or integrity. In some sense Barclay is the product of the corruption of his times, the man of his moment. It is not merely that late twentieth-century society pays scant attention to the truths of revealed religion; far worse, it seems to have reversed Christian moral values, so that sin is considered more exciting, interesting and life-enhancing than the inhibitions and rejections that necessarily accompany virtue. As Sophy had done, this society has discovered the ultimate thrill of hyper-violence or outrage. Near the end of *The Paper Men*, the sophisti-cates of Barclay's London club jokingly propose two modern pieces of statuary to correspond to the club's Victorian statue of Psyche, an idealised and ethereal image of the soul. These new and more appropriate icons for our times will represent characteristic forms of outrage—an act of incest (to illustrate "mother-fucker" in bronze) and one of homosexual-ity (to illustrate "Johnny's penetration" in "white marble, for purity"). This is the society that has made itself a false religion from paper and print, complete with its own literary idols. As part of its ritual, certain writers are elected to the status of secular saints and canonised for their energetic pursuit of experience. The more they sin, the more actively they indulge in alcohol, women and vice, the closer they come to the ideal of the artist as martyr, suffering an artificial passion for the sake of their art. Within the terms of this absurd and alarming travesty of Christianity Barclay discovers that he bears the stigmata, sign of his true election as a paper saint; he will eventually die from the fifth wound of Christ, a wound inflicted by the bullet of his thwarted and vengeful biographer.

At one level, Barclay's stigmata reflect how suggestible he is, some-thing that his experience of being hypnotised had confirmed. This trait is obviously connected with his sensitivity as a writer, and if we are to accept Golding's suggestion, may even indicate a lost potential for genuine sainthood: great novelists, Golding believes, may be people who possess a special kind of awareness, a kind of sixth sense, "a tincture of that quality which exists in full power among the saints."[3] This must seem almost paradoxical, given the modern view of the novelist as a man sanctified by his sins. Yet, though from one point of view Barclay's stigmata seem purely ironic, from another, they may be a measure of his self-betrayal, of gifts thrown away, their pain the pain of a vocation disappointed or unfulfilled.

Barclay himself finally comes to regard his stigmata as the last and most theologically witty of a long series of practical jokes played on him by God or providence. He had thought of them as indicating some form of election, until the vicar had commented acidly, "You must be very proud of them. . . . After all there were three crosses." Yet these dismissive words bring Barclay not disappointment, but relief—"the peace and security of knowing myself a thief." From another, and very different point of view, perhaps all writers are in some sense thieves, the best among them those who steal down fire from heaven. The pains in his hands certainly seem linked with the guilt of being a writer: at one point he admits "my writing hand hurt like the devil." And if Barclay has received his stigmata, spiritually speaking, "for cowardice in the face of the enemy," a similar charge may be made on artistic grounds. His earliest novels had not merely been successful, but "There were things, mantic moments, certain-ties, if you like, whole episodes that had blazed, hurt, been suffered for." Yet these had all been wasted on his readers. The critics, eagerly engaged in dissecting books into so many separate pieces, or disintegrating their sources, failed to recognise these moments, and now Barclay is content to write with less effort and more economy: "I did not need to invent, to dive, suffer, endure that obscurely necessary anguish in the pursuit of the—unreadable." He finds that books may be made by manipulating reality, fantasising around what he knows or desires. Indeed, he has little alternative, since by this stage he has irreversibly withdrawn from any involvement in or engagement with the world around him. Barclay's main moral defect thus becomes his main artistic defect, and since he is the ostensible author of *The Paper Men*, the reader is faced with the problem that Golding's success in presenting the withdrawn and self-absorbed world of his hero, in recreating this mimetically from within, risks undermining the book's appeal.

Golding has never, perhaps, fully allowed for the extent to which readers identify, or try to identify, with a novel's main character. He was understandably disappointed when they sympathised too readily with the depraved Pincher Martin in his struggle against the inevitable, and when they felt limited by Oliver's narrow outlook in *The Pyramid*. Yet both novels evinced their author's total commitment, his power to identify himself wholly with his own creations, to imitate their way of seeing and experiencing so completely that, in so doing, he created a further set of artistic problems for himself. In *The Paper Men* problems of this kind are well to the fore, and certainly contributed to the book's cool reception. The portrait of Barclay, in one sense a triumph in its accurate depiction of an egoism subordinating all experience to itself, is, in another sense, only too accurate, only too successful. An artist of self-effacing integrity has brilliantly reproduced a bad artist writing a bad book in bad faith—for Barclay's primary motive in writing his account is to anticipate and so frustrate his would-be biographer. Negative capability here proves something of a liability.

Barclay, then, is a false saint as he is a failed artist, a Judas to all that he most values, but the book tacitly recognises the gap between achievement and public acclaim, a gap which may disturb the best as well as the worst of writers. T. S. Eliot, assessing the gifts reserved for age that "set a crown upon your lifetime's effort" recognised that "fools' approval stings and honour stains." Literary canonisation is achieved, among other things, in terms of literary prizes. It cannot be entirely an accident that Golding published *The Paper Men* fresh from the triumph of the Booker prize awarded to *Rites of Passage* (Barclay discourses to Tucker on rites of passage at one point), and only a few months after he received the Nobel prize for literature, late in 1983. His latest novel might indeed be read as a passionate repudiation of a system that wants to elevate writers to a kind of priesthood, to find in their flawed gospels and the oracles of their interviews keys to the universe, or instructions for us all to live by. If so, it is a rejection of success in the very mode by which he has achieved it, a refusal of complacency, of his status as a fossilised "great" novelist, comparable to similar refusals by other major modern writers who have felt alarmed at finding themselves idolised, and elevated to institutional status. Yet however reluctant Golding is to participate, the juggernaut of adulation grinds on, its attendant academics fight for such latter-day relics as corrected manuscripts or page-proofs, rejected fragments, diaries, letters, any evidence that will advance the hagiographer's detailed record of a writer's follies and failings — the sins that guarantee his martyrdom genuine, that safely proclaim him a saint in the canons of literature.

As befits a paper man, Barclay has carefully hoarded everything he has ever written;[4] he has left the fullest evidence of himself in endless fragments of paper, sticky not merely with butter or marmalade from the dustbin, but also with the guilt or shame of the sordid events they record. The accumulating words pile up not only in his printed works, but in boxes in his house (from time to time his wife sends telegrams asking him to take them away), within the bound covers of his journal and, after he has lost this, "in telephone books or on walls or the windows of cars or lavatory paper." He has also left love letters, including the obscene ones he wrote to the only woman who refused him, letters that a bent lawyer failed to retrieve. But the incriminating documents stacked up against him are by no means all his own work, though the theme of the artist's pride and self-betrayal seems as important here as it had been in *The Spire.* There are other love letters written to him, like the fragments of Lucinda's which, salvaged from the dustbin, cost him his marriage. There is the unpublished manuscript once submitted to him from which he pinched the only promising idea. There are also photographs, obscene ones taken by the lubricious Lucinda with her instant camera, as well as the snap taken by Tucker which Barclay later rediscovers hanging in the Swiss hotel bar. Inside the camera that Tucker always carries with him is a tape recorder, so that their conversations are all on record. These, with much other material, have reverted to the possession of Halliday, the mysterious American billionaire, banker and ardent collector of all the relics and records of *literati* — a spiritual accountant as sinister and elusive as the purser in *Rites of Passage.* Like all gods, Halliday has his benevolent aspect. He has endowed the University of Astrakhan with "the ecumenical temple, the skijump and the snow machine and the courts for real tennis," but he is also keen in pursuit of his prey, and as Barclay realises how much of his essence Halliday already possesses, he begins to feel that resistance is vain, becoming almost reconciled to the persecution of this ubiquitous deity. Indeed, Halliday becomes scarcely separable from the infernal God who has pursued Barclay to an unavoidable confrontation, and the bleak recognition of where he is:

> "Why, this is Hell, nor am I out of it."
> "I. am. sin."

Yet though Barclay echoes the words of Marlowe's Mephistopheles, his role in the fable is rather that of Faustus, and it is Halliday's agent Rick Tucker who has been cast as Mephistopheles. This young academic with his pretended professorship and dubious credentials hopes to assure his own future by becoming "the Barclay man." He "badgers" or "dogs" Barclay — indeed he is initially taken for a badger as he rifles through the dustbin for cast-off relics. Tucker then tempts Barclay's vanity, urging him to sign a contract, an updated version of the traditional pact that will confer sole rights over Barclay's literary soul, giving unlimited access to his manuscripts and permission to write his official biography. In return Barclay is offered immortality as a plaster saint with an established niche in "the great Pageant of English Literature." Barclay shies away from this peculiar version of immortality for a number of reasons, not least among them a natural and understandable resentment at such blatant prying into his private life. But he feels other and deeper anxieties: to yield to Tucker's demand would be to have his actions called to account, to be summoned to a premature judgement which he cannot yet face. He is only too conscious of how sordid and contemptible his past would appear, and guiltily fears that Tucker might be able to unearth its buried secrets — such as having killed an Indian in a hit-and-run accident in South America — as if he were the all-seeing eye of God. He knows too that just as he is no longer prepared to pay the price necessary to create a work of art, so he cannot pretend to measure up to the level of excess required to give him the appropriate romantic stature. His wife Elizabeth perceptively taunts him with wanting to act the genius, to play the great man, while at the same time remaining a popular writer: "That's what you always wanted, Wilf . . . the sacré monster outside the accepted rules, a national treasure, the point about you being words that the world would not willingly let die. . . ." Yet Barclay lacks conviction even in this. He has neither the artist's passion nor his self-surrender. Everyone assumes that he is enacting this self-squandering role — "boozing, wenching, living it up" — when in fact he passes most of his time in absorbed self-contemplation. If Barclay is Faust, he is a Faust who refuses to sell a soul spotted with petty and largely incidental sins; who refuses Helen, perhaps from the fear of self-commitment; and who systematically tempts, frustrates and defeats his tempter. Tucker is the devil who makes an ass of himself and finally finds himself outwitted by the superior cunning of his victim.

Tucker is also the book's second "paper man," the aspiring Boswell to Barclay's Johnson. As Barclay depends for his living on the success of his novels, Tucker depends on Barclay's co-operation, and is thus his parasite; each is determined to survive at the expense of the other. The book is structured as a complex duel between them, with Tucker as the hairy Esau and Barclay the smooth Jacob, stealing a march on his brother, and perhaps even depriving him of his blessing, his peace of mind or his luck as well. Certainly by the end of the book Tucker has lost all these things, and also forfeited Mary Lou; he dangles with good luck charms which he hopes, possibly believes, will reverse this downward spiral. At first Barclay seemed to be pursued, even hunted down by the American, but as something altogether more powerful than Tucker forces itself into Barclay's field of awareness, so he changes; turning on his tormentor, he seems intent on destroying him, perhaps because he is the only human being left over whom he has any power. For Tucker worships at Barclay's shrine even though he is obscurely gratified by his idol's feet of clay. Johnny's suggestion that Barclay needs a chum, perhaps a dog, determines Barclay that Tucker must play out the part that his doggedness and uncritical admiration cut him out for; and he will die like the dog he is. Now their roles are reversed: Tucker also experiences paranoia, believing that he sees his master, waving the commission, in places Barclay has never in fact visited—just as Barclay had apparently imagined Tucker dogging his footsteps across Europe. As if Tucker were now Faust, time is running out for him, for the implacable Halliday has allowed him seven years in which to pull off the deal.

The contrast between the book's opening and closing scenes is designed to reveal the extent of their role-reversal. In the first scene Barclay discovers Tucker rifling his dustbin and accidentally shoots him with his airgun. Broad farce follows as he pulls Tucker's robe off to look for the wound he has inflicted: at the same time his own pyjama trousers fall down. Then his wife appears and unluckily picks up a fragment of an old love letter that has adhered to Tucker during his researches in the dustbin. The book ends with further undignified struggles between Barclay and Tucker: they fight at the Random Club where the air is filled with yet more detritus of the paper world: "menus, wine lists, order books, bits of manuscript flew up into the air and seemed to float like snow." Barclay makes a final effort to write his autobiography and destroy all the accumulated relics of his paper lifetime on a massive bonfire, while Tucker, his sanity finally snapped, prepares to shoot him.

In his depiction of Tucker, Golding has allowed himself to vent a certain amount of spleen against American academe of the kind Philip Larkin's sharp little poem "Posterity" had voiced; here the poet is reduced to a research topic allotted to a reluctant Jewish student, Jake Balokowski. Curiously, "Jake" also seems to have been the original name given to Rick Tucker—the rather carelessly prepared text refers to him as Jake three times. According to established comic tradition, American universities have absurd names (like Astrakhan) and absurd self-advertising clothes that go with them (Tucker's jumper proclaims "Ole Ashchan"). Even the youngest members of the faculty may be styled "professor," and their students take unlikely combinations of subjects for their degree: Mary Lou, Tucker's wife, majors in flower-arranging and bibliography. In addition to this mild xenophobia, *The Paper Men* satirises the whole Eng. Lit. industry, wastefully devoted to discussions of ludicrous or insignificant aspects of literature: Tucker reads a paper on Barclay's relative clauses at a conference. He would sell himself or his wife for so many scraps of paper—"letters from MacNeice, Charley Snow, Pamela, oh a whole chest full of goodies! Variant readings. The original MS of *All We Like Sheep* which differs so radically from the published version." Golding must often have been importuned for such "goodies" himself.

After Tucker's first disastrous encounter with Barclay at his English country house, they meet again, by Tucker's design, in Switzerland. Tucker is now married to the delectably beautiful, utterly naive Mary Lou. At one level she is a stereotype of the young American wife familiar from television situation comedy, her conversation alternately clumsy with periphrases, or simply absurd: "He said no one else was doing you as of this moment in time." Or, replying to Rick's query

> "Was there any sun, hon?"
> "Sun, hon?"
> In our room, this afternoon, hon?"
> "Why none, hon, I guess not."

At quite another level, she is Mephistopheles' succubus, brought to tempt the sensual Barclay to sign the pact, his Helen of Troy. Her peculiarly transparent beauty makes Barclay think of Helen, and it is as Helen that he writes of her in his journal and puts her in his next novel: "Perhaps she didn't exist at all but was a phantom of absolute beauty like the false Helen." Tucker appears to offer her to Barclay, but, when he touches her, her flesh is as cold and unresponsive as marble and he feels no desire to renew the contact. Rick explains more than once that Mary Lou is "not physical," which might encourage the supposition that she is really metaphysical, and thus a phantom, although her vomiting on the floor of the bar seems physical enough. After her failure to seduce Barclay she disappears from the novel, going back to Halliday—a progress which Barclay sees as further evidence of Halliday's greed and of Tucker's extensive debts to his master; after all Mary Lou is eminently covetable. But she carries a further suggestion of a stupidity and transparency that is in no way sinister, but rather purely innocent. Such a possibility contradicts her demonic phantom role, and perhaps also Barclay's view that she is merely an element in another malicious cosmic trick against him. Although this suggestion of untouched innocence remains entirely unverifiable, it leaves her as one of the book's several mysteries.

If the temptation to fall hopelessly in love with Mary Lou seemed to Barclay yet another version of "the clown's trousers falling down," the next episode affords him a more obvious pratfall, though it takes a second visit to the spot before he recognises this. The hotel in the Alps where he encounters the Tuckers disturbs him because he suffers from acrophobia, an irrational fear of heights, a weakness that has both a literal and a symbolic aspect. Though Barclay would like to be great, he is not prepared to pay the price, to risk the climb, and his lack of courage or self-reliance contrasts sharply with Jocelin's fearless ascent of his spire. Barclay and Rick take a walk along a mountain path shrouded in mist; as rocks tumble down close by them, Barclay leans against a rail which gives way beneath him, so that he slithers down, apparently over an infinite drop. Desperately clinging to the vertical rock face, he is gradually pulled to safety by Tucker, who hangs on to his collar, and subsequently carries him back to the hotel. Fainting with terror and furious at being rescued by the American, and thus finding himself in his debt, he resentfully mutters "It seems I owe you my life." His words unconsciously echo those of Jocelin to the dumb mason who saved him when the earth crept and the builders were seized with panic, and before that, the words of Caesar to Phanocles's near-silent sister, after she had removed the brass butterfly from the missile in "Envoy Extraordinary." Their melodramatic quality suggests that they might be some kind of private joke, deriving perhaps from one of the feebler plays Golding acted in at the outset of his career. Here their use is unconsciously ironic, since it only *seems* as if Barclay owes Tucker his life. When, some years later, he returns to the scene in bright sunlight, he realises that he was suspended only a few feet above a green meadow, a fact which Tucker must have known since he had already walked up that path on the previous day. Instead he had seized the opportunity to play the noble rescuer. For Barclay, the episode is yet another cosmic joke, this time in the form of a landscape: "Who was it, I thought, had set about designing something theologically witty?"

The episode exposes Barclay's extreme terror, not merely of heights, but also of death. Tucker here figures as deceiver, and the phrase which Barclay irrationally associates with him, "silence and old night" with its echoes of Milton's "Chaos and old Night," evokes the underworld and seems to reinforce his diabolic overtones. But, like Mary Lou, Rick also reveals features that are less consistent with his role either as Mephistopheles or as a satire on American academe. As Tucker draws Barclay's attention to the two voices of the mountain stream, his own talents as a listener become apparent. To listen properly is an activity that demands a self-effacing attention to the world outside the self, an ability that a man like Barclay entirely lacks, although he immediately recognises its literary potential; others, like Oliver in *The Pyramid*, who possess the ability fail to make proper use of it. Tucker, like Oliver, has a naturally good ear, the ear that made him start out by studying phonetics — it is a humanising touch. Worldly considerations have deflected him, it seems, from the one subject he really cares about. In Barclay's eyes, Tucker never fully achieves human stature, never really seems to be a man, capable of frustration, humiliation, even retaliation. But this is only a further instance of Barclay's limited powers of observation. Tucker, like the stream, also possesses a deeper, more mysterious life, whose true note cannot always be discerned beneath the high, over-anxious, sycophantic babble.

In flight from Tucker, Halliday and appeals from his wife, Barclay travels round the world, coming to rest on a Greek island. Here, as he contemplates the submarine world through snorkel and mask, he is interrupted by Johnny, an old friend from his London literary days. This encounter, occurring roughly at the centre of the book, is an important turning-point in several ways: the first half had been mainly concerned with Tucker's pursuit of Barclay, and had taken place in the everyday world; the second half is concerned with Barclay's flight not from Tucker but from God, and it constantly passes beyond the bounds of the familiar. If the first half had recorded Barclay's experiences fairly directly, experience itself now becomes confusing, evasive, hallucinatory.

The presence of Johnny, a shrewd commentator beneath his high camp mannerisms, helps the reader to recognise how far Barclay has come from any kind of normality. He is now only too evidently the victim of dislocating habits of body and mind, of drink and paranoia, as Johnny tries to warn him: "See a priest or a shrink. If not, at least keep away from doctors acting in tandem. Otherwise they'll have you inside before you can say 'dipso-schizo.' " Earlier, in trying to identify what has happened to Barclay, Johnny hits on an image so apt that it remains to haunt and terrify him: "You . . . have spent your life inventing a skeleton on the outside. Like crabs and lobsters. That's terrible, you see, because the worms get inside and . . . they have the place to themselves. So my advice . . . is to get rid of the armour, the exoskeleton, the carapace, before it's too late."

Barclay under his lobster shell, tormented by memories like worms eating into his flesh, isolated on his island, recalls *Pincher Martin*, the novel that most obviously anticipates *The Paper Men*. Both books make use of a dreamlike or phantasmagoric narrative mode, and in both an isolated hero, clenched upon his own sinfulness and self-regard, vainly attempts to escape from a ubiquitous God. Pincher also recognised his own nature in the hard-shelled lobster; by the end he is reduced to two rigid claws, locked one upon the other, rejecting whatever lay beyond that unbearable and inescapable grip. Pincher is also haunted by the worms of memory, and in particular by the story of how the Chinese prepare a certain fish, depositing it in a tin box to be consumed by maggots, which then proceed to eat one another until only the largest and fattest cannibal-maggot is left. The story links worms not only to painful memories, to the theme of the ruthless destruction of the weaker by the stronger, but also to the barely suppressed horror of death and the decomposing body. Pincher imagines he hears the sound of the spade knocking on the tin box that contains the maggots and is also a coffin. For both Pincher and Barclay, the lobster shell signifies a determination to isolate and protect themselves from any threat to their precious egos, but Barclay's intrusive worms show up the uselessness, and worse, the positive dangers of this brittle shield. For while it cannot effectively keep the worms of memory and terror *out*, it tends instead to keep them *in*.

Both Pincher and Barclay relive some of the more degrading episodes of their past in memory, as flashbacks: each had unsuccessfully attempted to bully or blackmail a girl he desperately desired into compliance; each had made those around him serve his own ends. But for Pincher there is no time left in which to learn the lessons memory might teach. Not for him Sammy's bitter regret, Jocelin's voluntary submission to suffering and the angel's flail or Matty's deliberate atonement, each in their different way prompted by a reconsideration of the past. Pincher can only discover from his past what he unchangeably *is*; he is in a state of being, not becoming, since he is already dead when the novel begins. Barclay, although still alive and tormented by memories, also seems to have passed beyond the point of change. It seems that he cannot learn from events any more than he can rewrite the book himself (whose composition is, in fact, dramatically interrupted by death), or reconstruct his image of the universe. He is fixed in a state of being in which even encounters with the divine seem unable to alter his nature or direction. The process of reviewing the past is potentially of great moral importance, since though we cannot alter what we have done, it may be possible to change our present selves. Memory is therefore central to the whole process of becoming something other, perhaps something better, and without the possibility of change there is little basis for optimism, either for the individual or for the race. Golding himself seems characteristically uncertain whether he regards man as a series of consecutive present moments, a sequence of "nows," or as the outcome of what he has performed:[5] "I think that in a sense there is nothing but the nowness of how a man feels. One side of me thinks that, and the other side of me — with thousands of years behind it — thinks that you are the sum of your good or your evil. If you have sufficient nonconformist or pagan background, you're stuck with what you are. . . ." Barclay seems to be a figure who is only too patently set in the mould of what he has been.

Yet despite being past change, perhaps even paradoxically because of it, both Pincher and Barclay come under the hammer of God. From Golding's first novel, mysterious voices, the voice of the Lord of the Flies, the instructions from above or beyond, ignored or rejected at one's peril, have insistently made themselves heard, and the extensive dislocation of the narrative, both in *Pincher Martin* and *The Paper Men*, could be regarded largely as the result of the pressure of the numinous upon the action. Elsewhere individuals — Sammy, Jocelin, Matty — are confronted with the supernatural within a more conventional narrative framework, within a world more obviously governed by everyday expectations or Aristotelean probabilities. Within such a world, a reductive view of their reactions — that they are under extreme pressure and have grown "a little crazy" — is allowed for. Such a view would miss other possibilities offered by the novels as a whole, but remains a way of licensing their testaments within texts written for a predominantly sceptical reading public. But in

Pincher Martin and *The Paper Men* the confrontation with the supernatural breaks up the surface reality more comprehensively, emphasising the limits of probability and throwing the narrative open to larger and less finite possibilities. To some extent such confrontations are more easily integrated into looser genres—forms such as science fiction or the ghost story; they are better adapted to the greater freedoms accorded to poetry than to the technique of verisimilitude traditionally associated with the novel. It is within this technique that Golding has mainly worked, but at times—notably in these two novels—he seems deliberately to stretch it very thin or (to change the metaphor entirely) to work against its natural grain.

Pincher Martin had offered two slightly different explanations for the surreal nature of its action; the first, proposed by Pincher himself, is that alone on a rock in the Atlantic he is going slowly mad. The second, implied by the book as a whole, is that Pincher was never alone on the rock at all, but that the whole week-long ordeal was part of a struggle not to die and surrender the self that was all he had ever cared for. The action thus takes place after his death, or in the few minutes between his hitting the water and drowning. *The Paper Men* too can be read along the lines Johnny suggests, as the testament of a dipso-schizo; yet the overall effect of both these books is to confront an inescapable reality beyond man, a reality whose power is fundamentally bound up with the terror of death, the failure to love and the rejection of everything but the monstrous and furious ego. Pincher, despite all the incontrovertible evidence—"Now there is no hope. There is nothing"—refuses to the last to recognise the place he has come to and so acknowledge defeat, but Barclay can afford to be more of a realist. Before he finally escapes from Johnny, he admits that he knows only too well where he is going:

"I'm old. I'm going faster and faster—"
"Where?"
I think I must have shouted
"Where we're all going, you bloody fool."

In the next chapter, Barclay comes face to face with the master of that dark realm, just as Pincher had faced its black lightning.

Barclay's encounter with the God he has been fleeing from takes place on yet another island. It is Lípari, off the coast of Sicily, one of a volcanic chain, whose soil seems to consist of "powdered pumice with knives of black glass sticking up through it." Beneath a "plume of black smoke like you'd get from a megaton," the earth shakes, in pointed counterpoint to Barclay's own shakes, themselves the symptoms of incipient "delirium trimmings." Entering the cathedral, he is confronted by a solid silver statue, striding forward with flaming red eyes, a figure that may be Christ or "Pluto, the god of the Underworld, Hades . . . I knew in one destroying instant that all my adult life I had believed in God and this knowledge was a vision of God." Screaming, unable to control any of his bodily functions, he falls to the ground with a fit or a stroke, and wakes to discover himself in hospital. The infernal ephiphany in the cathedral shows him that he was not merely on the road to Hell, but that he had reached it—indeed had always been there, that he "had been created by that ghastly intolerance in its own image . . . I saw I was one of the, or perhaps the only predestinate damned." He has discovered divine justice without mercy, and in this extremity ordinary English fails him; he finds himself speaking another language that seems to be his native tongue, a language in which "sunrise" comes out as "liquor," "end" as "sin," and sin is no longer what Barclay does, but what he is. The riddle of predestination (mulled over by Marlowe's Faustus at the beginning of the play) locks itself into its familiar vicious circle, so that Barclay either cannot change because he believes himself predestined to Hell—or, because he is so predestined, cannot change. The problem is as insoluble as the question of the relationship between the individual and his theology: has the intolerance created Barclay in its own image, as he supposes, or has he projected on to the figure of Christ his own attributes? And is it possible to decide whether the power that manifests itself in the cathedral is one of good or evil? In his essay "Belief and Creativity," Golding notes "God works in a mysterious way," adding "and so, it seems, does the devil—or since that word is unfashionable I had better be democratic and call him the leader of the opposition. Sometimes the two seem to work hand in hand."[6] Barclay warns Tucker that he cannot serve both him and Halliday—"it's like serving God or Mammon. Guess which is which."

Once Barclay has finally discovered where and what he is, he is filled with an acute sense of his own intolerance and lack of compassion, as well as with a bitter cynicism about the nature of freedom, a theme that has always been of the utmost importance for Golding. Just as his vision showed him only inescapable evil, so freedom confers only the right to damn oneself: "People should be warned against it. Freedom should carry a government health warning like cancer sticks." Up till now, Barclay's life has been characterised by his acquiescence to temptation rather than any very active pursuit of evil. Now he determines to commit a crime, and actively to further the evil of which he feels himself to be a part, or to treat another human being—in this case, Tucker—as he believes the intolerance has treated him. Ever since Johnny's advice Barclay has been conscious that in some sense Tucker is his dog, and further that if he really had a dog he would only want to kill it, partly because to do so would be to free himself from the threat implicit in its devotion, but also because to "kill something deliberately, a dog perhaps" is a special kind of rite of passage, an active step toward commitment to the intolerance and to evil. Like Sophy when she dismissed shop-lifting as too commonplace, Barclay nevertheless rejects mere murder as "childish stuff and unworthy of us both, unworthy of image and original. What was needed was something philosophically, or rather theologically *witty*." Using the permission for his biography as a bait, he sets out to torment and humiliate Tucker, making him lap up wine from a saucer on the floor and insisting that if he write the biography it must also reveal the role he played in offering Mary Lou first to Barclay and then to Halliday, as mortgage for his continuing academic career. The novelist relishes this assertion of power over his victim (Tucker cannot even hit him with the saucer), watching with sadistic excitement as his victim approaches breaking point; yet even as he does so, his chest tightens as if a steel string were cutting into it, and he shudders and yells with uncontrollable fear at what he has become.

In the same essay, "Belief and Creativity," Golding admits to guessing that "we are in hell," while insisting that there must be other and different universes that interpenetrate our own. He continues[7]: "To be in a world which is a hell, to be *of* that world and neither to believe in nor guess at anything *but* that world is not merely hell but the only possible damnation; the act of a man damning himself." This would be an exact enough description of Barclay's spiritual condition if the novel were to end at this point, but now comes an experience that nothing else in the book so far has prepared us for, and though it seems too late to change Barclay fundamentally, it can alter his direction as well as the implications of the novel as a whole. It does so by exposing the inadequacy of his theology since he is given a glimpse of mercy that is entirely uncovenanted, extended to the hardened sinner in the midst of his pursuit of evil, and thus casting doubt upon the "predestinate damnation" which Barclay assumed and which his failure to change had seemed to confirm.

Returning to Rome and still searching for evidence of Halliday, his great antagonist, Barclay discovers that whatever existence Halliday may have cannot be reduced to mere print on paper: the page in *Who's Who in America* that should have contained his entry "was bare, bare, just blank white paper." And as he makes this discovery he sees God, or Halliday (whose name etymologically means "Holy Day") standing on a church roof. Then follows a vision of transcendent beauty and unity of being. Its harmony of vision and sound recall Sammy's revelation on being released from his cell, and this experience too involves a symbolic liberation. The Spanish Steps become a curved instrument on which beautiful beings dance, "and the movement was music." He passes through a door to a dark, calm sea — "there were creatures in the sea that sang. For the singing and the song I have no words at all." If Hell's language is one of clumsy translations that acknowledge only the immediacy of evil, Heaven lies beyond the scope of earthly language altogether; the paper man's natural medium here reaches its terminus, and can only gesture beyond itself to silence, to the blank page, to something that cannot begin to be captured in print, something that exists beyond the human limitations of text altogether: "since singing starts just where words leave off, where are you?

Face to face with the indescribable, inexplicable, the isness, which was where you came in."

Barclay's vision, as he later tries to explain to Liz, has the effect of reversing his whole direction: "the boil had burst, the pain and the strain had gone." Instead of being clenched against death, instead of fighting back against the inevitable as Pincher had done, he discovers assent. Suddenly, and apparently for the first time in his life, he is filled with a sense of irradiating happiness: "the dream turned me round and I knew that the way I was going, towards death, was the way everybody goes, that it was — healthy, right and *consonant*." Yet it is with the bitterest of ironies that he tries to communicate the consolation of his vision to the dying Liz, tormented by a terror of death and a horror of life that his words seem to mock at rather than to assuage. Is it another of the book's "theologically witty" jokes that she who needed, and perhaps deserved some consolation could not find it? The comfort he offers her is as inappropriate as a sticking plaster for a severed artery. Barclay has been "turned round," the intolerance has withdrawn, and a dawning interest in other people has been kindled in him at last, yet no deeper change is evident. His dying wife, to whom he believed himself so profoundly connected, he views dispassionately, indeed callously. Without compunction, he abandons her and goes up to town to prosecute his plans for Tucker's gradual destruction. It is already apparent (Liz has told him this in so many words) that Tucker is mad; the paper men, it seems, are bent on destroying one another. In London, at his club, Barclay warns Tucker that he plans to pre-empt his proposed biography by writing it himself. A fight in the club restaurant ensues. Barclay returns, intending to carry out his promise, only to find that his wife has died, and to learn that the stigmata he now seems to suffer from (perhaps as punishment for writing, or for sneering at that of Padre Pio) might more appropriately be associated with the crucified thieves than with the Saviour. At this point, Barclay summarises what he believes to be the main pattern of the book's events so far, rather as Talbot had done near the end of *Rites of Passage* (see above, page 129): "Putting aside repetitions, verbals, slang, omissions, it's a fair record of the various times the clown's trousers fell down." Barclay still regards himself as the victim of a providence whose harsh and pitiless laughter is really only another version of his own cold and mocking treatment of others. His transcendent vision has apparently born no fruit, and his stigmata are only the blackest joke of them all: "I do think the best bit of the lot, the real, theologically witty bit of his clowning, was surely the stigmata awarded for cowardice in the face of the enemy! But St Francis and all the other suggestible creatures didn't just get it in the hands and feet, they got the wound in the side which finished off Christ or at least certified him dead. I'm missing that one; and there's hardly time or occasions for a custard pie to provide it. For I intend to disappear again. . . ." Barclay intends to set out on his wanderings once more. His constant travel throughout the book seems to have been a substitute, or perhaps a compensation for his failure to progress inwardly. He makes a point of never staying anywhere long enough to allow him to discover where (sometimes literally as well as symbolically) he is or what he is. Realisations of this kind have, instead, come upon him as sudden, almost forcible revelations. As for the fatal fifth wound, which he believes that there is scarcely the time or occasion left for, the presence of Tucker in the garden, flitting from tree to tree, gun in hand, guarantees its imminence. And perhaps this is the final cosmic joke, the one that exists outside Barclay's consciousness, encouraging the view that the book as a whole ratifies his interpretation. Certainly the last scene involves an ironic reversal of the first, and not merely because this time it is Tucker who shoots Barclay in retaliation for invading what he (symbolically) regards as *his* territory. In a wider sense Barclay has succeeded in turning the tables on Tucker, retaining a grip on his own life and instead destroying, if not Tucker's soul, then at least his sanity. But Barclay has miscalculated, has underestimated his victim's spirit; the worm finally turns and turns on him; the dog bites the hand that fails to feed, the foot that has spurned. When Tucker is finally convinced that Barclay no longer intends to surrender the rights to his life, he can find no alternative but (quite literally) to take the life he believes Barclay owes him. If Barclay has become one kind of thief, Tucker becomes another. This is not so much a cosmic joke as a great reckoning, a settling of overdue debts.

But Golding is too cunning to round off the book neatly with the black theological joke that his hero in one sense did not expect and yet in another sense did. At the very last Barclay makes one last effort to free himself of the "paperweight of a whole life," assembling it — as poor Bounce had done — into an enormous funeral pyre of everything that he had been. Setting fire to it will not only be a symbolic act of self-purgation, it will be the very last rite of passage of all, the rite of passage that carries its subject across the boundaries of life itself. Freed of the stacked-up acts of a lifetime, he will, like Lear, "unburden'd crawl toward death." With no one left to mourn his departure, he intends to perform the final disappearing trick. And it seems to be the very act of preparation for this final rite that brings a softening of the sinner's heart, a relenting that one thought would never come: suddenly the autobiography is no longer to be used to thwart Tucker, but will be handed over to him as a (literally) uncovenanted mercy, a mercy such as Barclay himself received in the form of the blessed vision and such as he still hopes for in the form of eternal annihilation of the self in death. And suddenly the hopeful possibilities that his way of life had repeatedly denied are asserted — not merely happiness, which he had already found, but the change that had continued to elude him: "I am happy, quietly happy. How can I be happy? . . . Either I have broken away from the intolerance which is impossible, or it has let me go, which is also impossible. Who could I change? But I have changed . . . who knows?" It is precisely at this moment, when the influence of the vision finally seems to have become active, even redemptive within him, that Tucker shoots Barclay. Is there some further and subtler cosmic joke to be read into this that realigns the book with divine comedy rather than with hellish farce? Does Tucker's revenge save his victim, as Hamlet had feared that he might save Claudius by killing him when he was at prayer? The parable of the vineyard holds out a hope of salvation even to those who repent at the eleventh hour, with the promise that "the last shall be first." It would be the ultimate repudiation of the Faust pattern if the Mephisophelean Tucker were finally to prove the agent of salvation rather than damnation, if he should not seize but release the man who had once passionately wished "for there *not* to be a miracle." Barclay's final and, for him, exceptional "Who knows?" echoes Jocelin's "God knows where God may be." In *The Paper Men* Golding has spun an elaborate fugue out of some of the most ancient and unresolvable theological problems. It was scarcely to be expected that he should find easy answers to some of the most difficult questions man has asked himself throughout recorded history. At the end of the essay "Belief and Creativity," Golding warned his audience that if they had "detected contradictions and some screaming fallacies in what I have said . . . I am unrepentant . . . I claim the privilege of the storyteller; which is to be mystifying, inconsistent, impenetrable."[8] And then, as Barclay had planned to do, Golding performed the Indian rope-trick by disappearing into his own text.

Notes

1. A characteristically sympathetic account of the book was given by Frank Kermode in *The London Review of Books* (1 March 1984, vol. 6, no. 4), pp. 15–6, to which I am indebted.

2. "Belief and Creativity," MT p. 185.

3. "Rough Magic," MT, p. 144. In "My First Book" (MT, p. 152) Golding described his own experience of being hypnotised as a young man.

4. A habit he shares with his creator: "I keep everything I have scribbled on; there's masses and masses of it" Golding told Victoria Glendinning in an interview for *The Sunday Times*, 19 October 1980, p. 39.

5. Interview with John Haffenden, in *Quarto*, p. 10.

6. MT, p. 198.

7. MT, p. 201.

8. MT, p. 202.

"*Furor Scribendi*": Writing about Writing in the Later Novels of William Golding

John S. Whitley*

"Can it be that I have evaded the demon opium only to fall victim to the *furor scribendi?*"

Edmund Talbot in *Rites of Passage*

Many of William Golding's non-fiction writings are about literature. This comes as no surprise, particularly when it is remembered that he achieved cult status remarkably quickly (a casebook on *Lord of the Flies* appeared in the United States only eight years after the original American publication) and so his audiences expected (perhaps demanded) that he persistently give clues as to the genesis and development of his work. His fictions also, and increasingly, show an interest, not simply in the artistic vision, but in the ways in which such a vision might be translated into reality, particularly written reality, and they do this by playing off one kind of writing against another, one kind of writer against another. A reviewer of the new festschrift for Golding suggests, with more than a little justification, that Golding is one of the finest contemporary romanciers[1] but it could also be argued that, in his concern for writing about writing, he is not altogether worlds removed from the concerns of the writers of metafiction; those who, according to Patricia Waugh, reflect "a more general cultural interest in the problem of how human beings reflect, construct and mediate their experience of the world";[2] of how "the observer always changes the observed."[3]

From the outset, Golding's novels have been carefully patterned, particularly because the first three novels all referred back to and sometimes overturned the ethos of earlier works: *The Coral Island* for *Lord of the Flies*; *The Grisly Folk* for *The Inheritors*; and *Robinson Crusoe* for *Pincher Martin*. The reversal of literary expectations involved in these "debts" itself establishes a pattern for understanding existence, a pattern further fostered by the typology of the fable which allows characters, however brilliantly drawn, to signify certain approaches to existence: Simon, Jack, and Piggy in *Lord of the Flies*; Lok and Tuami in *The Inheritors*; Nat and Mary in *Pincher Martin*. Such is the power of Golding's writing that we are never in danger of dismissing these works as diagrammatic, but this method of character depiction means that the ideological framework of the fable, what John Peter has called the "anterior thesis,"[4] is rarely in doubt. Third, the "gimmick"[5] endings of each of the first three novels are clearly techniques for placing that

---

*This essay was written specifically for this volume and is published here for the first time by permission of the author.

ideological framework in a more complete perspective. In *Lord of the Flies*, the officer from the "trim cruiser"[6] is a useless, unknowing god from a machine of war, a complement to the impotent beast from the air. In *The Inheritors*, Tuami and his fellows, in order to provide a fabulistic contrast to the innocence of the prehumans, would have to be a less innocent development and therefore closer to the fallen humans who people Golding's other works. In *Pincher Martin*, the revelation that the central protagonist died on the opening page of the novel does not merely serve, like the ending of Ambrose Bierce's "An Occurrence at Owl Creek Bridge," to provide the sting in a well-made tale, but to point to the unchanging nature of Pincher's massive self-absorption, to signify that he has always been spiritually "dead." In each case the "gimmick," though it shocks the reader, does not complicate or reverse his or her response to the rest of the novel, it clarifies that response.

Don Crompton was right to say that with his fourth novel, *Free Fall*, Golding "had dealt directly and for the first time with normal human relationships in a contemporary setting, and though the larger themes were still present, the narrower context had encouraged his readers and critics to expect a conventionality they did not find."[7] The crucial difference between *Free Fall* and the previous three novels surely resides in the first-person narration, which Golding was to use in three of the next five novels. Wayne C. Booth remarks that "In fiction, as soon as we encounter an 'I,' we are conscious of an experiencing mind whose views of the experience will come between us and the event."[8] In his use of such narration Golding allows, for the first time, for the possibility of change and development in his characters. It used frequently to be said that Hawthorne was an allegorist. Henry James held this, however sympathetically, as a point against his predecessor: "Hawthorne, in his metaphysical moods, is nothing if not allegorical, and allegory, to my sense, is quite one of the lighter exercises of the imagination."[9] A more recent, and truer, sense of Hawthorne's work would divide it between a predominantly allegorical mode, such as "The Maypole of Merrymount" and a darker, subtler treatment of the allegorizing intelligence in, say, "Roger Malvin's Burial" where Reuben Bourne creates a pattern out of his past experiences, a warped and melodramatic pattern which leads to the death of his son, or "The Ministers Black Veil" where Hawthorne's real interest lies not in what Hooper's black veil *means* but on how members of his parish set about attributing meaning to it. In his only extended use of first-person narrative, *The Blithedale Romance*, Hawthorne again shows considerable interest in the ways in which Coverdale's imagination seeks to make Hollingworth, Zenobia, and Priscilla "indices"[10] of his own particular problems.

Similarly, in *Free Fall*, Golding moves from creating a pattern to writing about the ways in which a narrator/artist seeks to find or create a pattern in experience. With this novel Golding uses, also for the first time, a bildungsroman structure, a structure which often searches out a diagram of development, such as the Oedipal obsessions of Paul Morel in Lawrence's *Sons and Lovers*, leading him to establish relationships with Miriam and Clara which elucidate different aspects of his relationship with his mother. The bildungsroman, however, more often than not has a narrator (and this holds good for the kunstlerroman, too) who is not *conscious* of searching for and articulating the pattern which governs such a formula. Sammy early displays an awareness at least of the more popular manifestations of the formula: "Perhaps he sounds like the hero of one of those books which kept turning up in the twenties. Those heroes were bad at games, unhappy and misunderstood at school—tragic, in fact, until they reached eighteen or nineteen and published a stunning book of poems or took to interior decoration."[11]

The very first paragraph of the novel shows Sammy establishing himself as an artist, not merely through the emphasis on the power of vision (". . . where books . . . have burst with a white hosanna. . . .") but through deliberate links with poetic tradition (". . . I have felt the flake of fire fall . . ."). Having established his credentials, as it were, Sammy at once asks the crucial question: "When did I lose my freedom?" (5) and decides that to answer it he must become a story-teller, the teller of a story which "presents itself" and, therefore, perhaps, comes complete with a structure: "Then why do I write this down? Is it a pattern I am looking for?" (6). He is suspicious of the possibility of such a structure: "But then I remember that all patterns have broken one after another, that life is random and evil unpunished" (25), but still feels that a pattern might be there. He admits, however, that in this search he will have to act the part of a writer properly: "Perhaps if I write my story as it appears to me, I shall be able to go back and select" (7). He also senses that, like Golding, he is a writer in search of the numinous, that interface, impossible to articulate, between a person and the sum of things outside his self: "To communicate is our passion and our despair (8) . . . I speak your hidden language which is not the language of other men" (13). In his essay "Rough Magic," Golding describes succinctly what Sammy is after: "The thing without which the run-of-the-mill novelist with a whole international reputation can pass his life amid respect and admiration—that better thing is a passionate insight."[12]

Sammy's twin roles of writer and painter come together at times in interesting ways. The numinous is almost literal and pictorial in his endeavours to define the object in the middle of his cell floor: "But the shape of the thing on the floor was communicated to me through one enslaved finger that would not let go, that rendered the outline phosphorescent in my head, a strange, wandering haphazard shape with here a tail drawn out in shiny thinness and there the cold, wet bulk of a body" (182). The visual impression of typing out a story seems to suggest the kinds of firm closure associated with a fabular structure. The typewriter keys become "rivets." Ma is "as complete and final as a full-stop" (10). The story, despite Sammy's doubts, might be a "straight line" (46). The characters could arrange themselves into a "triangle" (47): one remembers the spire and the pyramid. When Sammy decides "That must be the end of a section" (78), we promptly meet the end of a chapter. In a novel which uses Miss Pringle and Nick Shales as signpost characters like Piggy, Simon, and others in the first three novels, Halde makes an authorial underlining of this device: "And between the poles of belief, I mean the belief in material things and the belief in a world made and supported by a supreme being, you oscillate jerkily from day to day, from hour to hour" (144). This may remind the reader uncomfortably of those authorial interjections ("The two boys faced each other. There was the brilliant world of hunting, tactics, fierce exhilaration, skill; and there was the world of longing and baffled common-sense." [89]) which are apt to jar in *Lord of the Flies*. Yet surely an advance has been made by recognizing that all narrators may wish to create a fabular structure but are often forced, by an awareness of the complexity of existence and the language used to describe that existence, to abandon such a wish. At the end of chapter 8 Sammy re-reads his story and finds that he still does not understand why he is frightened of the dark. In the darkness of his cell he tries in his head to construct a "diagram" (168) of his surroundings but fails, rather, as he later suggests, like the narrator of Edgar Allan Poe's "The Pit and the Pendulum," because both are removed from the known definitions of space and time. In the later stages of the novel he comes to see the truth of T.S. Eliot's proposition that:

> Words strain,
> Crack and sometimes break, under the burden,
> Under the tension, slip, slide, perish,
> Decay with imprecision, will not stay in place,
> Will not stay still[13]

and has to admit that "language is clumsier in my hands than paint" (184), forcing him close to absurdity: ". . . let me be exact where exactitude is impossible . . ." (221).

These realizations, it could be said, force Sammy away from the search for pattern towards two recognitions essential to a novelist (rather than a fabulist). The first is his equivalent of Golding's need for the "passionate insight": "Standing between the understood huts, among jewels and music, I was visited by a flake of fire, miraculous and pentecostal; and fire transmuted me, once and forever" (188). The other truth which lies at the end of Sammy's quest is that the justification for telling a tale rests not in the demonstration of a pattern in which characters act as significations for various philosophical positions but in a celebration of the multi-faceted nature of the human character and its capacity for change. In an interview given in 1958, just before *Free Fall* was published, Golding said "This time I want to show the patternless of life before we impose our patterns on it."[14] In "Rough Magic" Golding elaborates on this idea: ". . . the novelist's characters must be seen to undergo a change. He or she must change in a way that is credible and before the very eyes of our spirit."[15] In *Free Fall* Sammy comes to see that Miss Pringle and Nick (and, by extension, himself) are more complicated than any "straight line" or "triangle" could show. What is important is "the relationship of individual man to individual man" (189). "People are the walls of our room, not philosophies" (226).

Although neither of the next two novels, *The Spire* and *The Pyramid*, have central protagonists who are writers or even artists, their concerns follow from those shown in *Free Fall*. Jocelin, the central figure of *The Spire*, is certainly a kind of artist, a man with a commitment to a vision and to the reproducing of that vision in reality. To him, the spire is a "diagram" of his dream and everything is to be sacrificed to the maintenance of that pattern. Away from humanity, removed from its confusions, the artist can feel free to contemplate ideal structures and see essential unities, as Jocelin feels able to do from the heights of the spire: "Up here we are free of all the confusion . . . The rivers glittered towards the tower: and you could see that all those places which had been separate to feel and only joined by an act of reason, were indeed part of a whole."[16]

From this vantage point tiresome individual quirks can be obliterated and people reduced to ciphers. Again, the fabulist can be usefully linked to the allegorist. In his sketch "Sights From A Steeple," Hawthorne explains how, sitting on the top floor of the Old South Church, the romancer can acquire a tremendous sense of prescience and, hence, of power: "The full of hope, the happy, the miserable, and the desperate, dwell together within the circle of my glance."[17] However, at the end of the day he has to climb down from that Olympian height and mingle once again with the crowd outside, whose inconsistency and complexity provide the significant matter of his work. Similarly, Jocelin must learn to take full account of what lies at the bottom of his dream building: "I dread to go down there, he thought. Here is my place. But it must be done, since no man can live his life with eagles" (109–10). He must confront the pit of muck and slime and the equivalent sensuality of his own nature.

The Spire could, then, be said to be about the necessities of novel-writing and thus an ironic reflection on the method of Golding's first three novels. To Jocelin, the dumb man is only like a good dog; the Dean's failure to "see" Pangall helps to perpetuate the mob's treatment of the cripple as an object; his conscious blindness to Goody's womanhood causes him to arrange her marriage to an impotent man who denies that womanhood, and Jocelin's ability to "look through" (98) Rachel blinds him to any truths she may be able to tell him about Roger (rather like Emma Woodhouse's treatment of Miss Bates).[18] Thus Golding's central protagonist illustrates not only the triumph of the visionary pattern-maker (for his dream *is* a great one) but also his limitations, his willingness to deny complexity in order to vindicate that pattern. This inclines the reader to remember early criticisms of Golding the fabulist's inability to come close to his characters, of his treating them too coldly and clinically, a criticism inherent in Margaret Walters's view that "Golding has somehow to assert a universal significance in characters and events that remain irredeemably trivial."[19] In the end Jocelin, like Hawthorne, moves from diagram, from overt signification, to symbol. Just as the meaning of the scarlet letter is *The Scarlet Letter*, so the spire, allied indivisibly to the apple tree, encompasses all the human truths of the novel. This could hardly be said of the figure of the pyramid, in the novel of that name. Here the use of a teenage narrator, while it allows Golding to paint an authentic portrait of adolescence, does not lead to major recognitions. There is no governing symbol and, as Don Crompton pointed out, the novel "does not draw on sustaining myths, as several of his other books do."[20]

Darkness Visible was Golding's first novel for twelve years and a work he has declined to discuss. It is a novel which begins with a mystery. During its memorable opening pages a small child, hideously burned, walks out of the horror of the Blitz. How could he have survived? Why was he there? Who is he? One of the firemen might have had the answer: "The bookseller was saying nothing and seemed to be staring at nothing. There was a memory flickering on the edge of his mind and he could not get it further in where it could be examined. . . ."[21] But the bookseller *might* be Sim Goodchild, in which case he is no more likely to have the answer than any other character in the novel. Sim is one of several major characters in the book all searching for a pattern in human life. For Toni Stanhope, neglected by a father who has retreated from life to the patterns created by chess problems, the answer lies in terrorism. For her sister, Sophy, it lies in the importance of her power in an entropic world, a power created by her total self-absorption. For Sim, the answers lie in literary tradition; for his friend Edwin, in some form of mystical experience. Both Edwin and Sim dimly feel that some answers may lie in the figure of Matty, the burned boy now became a strange adult, and are particularly interested to learn, at the end of the novel, that Matty, now dead, had been keeping a journal: "Somehow and for no reason that he could find, Sim felt heartened by the idea of Matty's journal — happy almost, for the moment" (261).

One reason for Matty's journal is, perhaps, to establish some sense of his own importance, even identity. People wish to avoid him and cannot remember his name. Constantly rebuffed, he ceases, early in his life, trying to confide in anyone. He has difficulty in speaking, so that words seem to emerge from his mouth like golfballs. It is small wonder, then, that having endured a kind of descent into the Underworld in Australia, he should feel that the only way of translating his sense that "there were things moving about under the surface" (55) is to begin a journal. Like Golding, Matty is a religious man and seeks to describe experiences which approach the numinous. For if Sophy believes that the world is atrophying and is thus driven into herself, Matty believes that everything is building to some great revelation and is driven to recognize supernatural visitations. How far he creates these visitations in his imagination is one of the questions the book does not answer (although, as with all of Golding's fiction, a purely psychological analysis would not provide the answers). At least, however, he "creates" his visitors by writing down an account of their appearances, even if "Remembering changes it" (86). If they are so awesome as to make him tremble in fear, they are also *his* and they persistently emphasize his importance: "I think perhaps it is something to do with my feeling that I am at the centre of an important thing and have been always" (87). In his essay "Intimate Relations," Golding feels that "the more we look, the more collecting and possession seem deeply rooted in a journal."[22]

The spirits do not hurt, deceive, or spurn Matty by speaking to him, but seem to allow him to read their words in greatly speeded-up process. They justify his desire to be silent and obedient and act as potential instruments of a vengeance which might be personal: "They showed: We are pleased with your obedience to Mr. Pierce though he is a bad lot. He will be paid out for it" (100). So Matty, like Jocelin and Golding himself, has to find ways in his journal (written at least for himself to understand) of linking the numinous with a grimly comic worldliness. The above quotation suggests how that is accomplished stylistically; Matty continues this juxtaposition of the Biblical and the contemporary by creating himself as the main character in a narrative formula not unlike the Christmas story: "And when you bore the awful number through the streets a spirit that is black with a touch of purple like the pansies Mr. Pierce planted under the rowan was cast down and defeated and the child was born sound in wind and limb" (101). Lonely, ugly, inarticulate, Matty writes himself into the center of a narrative by "creating" guardian angels who demand what he wants and who act as validators of his identity and justificators of his world-view. In the entry for 5/2/67, thinking of the grand purpose for which he has been "called," he ponders: "Can it be that what I am for is something to do with children I ask myself" (100), and on the next page, in the entry for 20/4/67, we find: "Then I said, hardly knowing what I did, Who am I? What am I? What am I for? Is it to do with children? Then they showed: It is a child" (101). Both Matty and Sophy create versions of existence with themselves in the center; Matty's is a world of light and Sophy's of darkness but this fact should not blind us to their similarities. The title of the novel comes from Milton's description of Hell in book one of *Paradise Lost*, and in a way the world of the novel is hellish — a modern, confused world signally lacking in love. Matty, Sophy, and Toni all begin in neglect and loneliness; no functioning families are present; Sim's daughter lives abroad and his son is a permanent mental patient; Edwin is an effeminate man living with a rather masculine wife;

Pedigree's notions of beauty have turned him into a pederast. Furthermore, the picture of English society, fuller and more contemporary than in any other Golding novel, resembles Graham Greene's earlier work in its relentless display of grotesquerie. Yet there is a kind of triumph for light. Golding's move back to omniscient narration is needed because the characters involved are isolates lacking the normal links in love, so that a knowing narrator is needed to create plot links in coincidence and irony. The method is a little like that used in *Bleak House* where the knowing, relatively pessimistic omniscient narration is balanced by the first-person narration of Esther, all sweetness and light. Here the omniscient narration is balanced by the wonder and awe of Matty's first-person account. If Matty becomes a sacrificial victim, he also fulfils the direction of his narrative by saving the boy. He remains the center of his story to the end. Sophy, by contrast, ends up an appalled dupe, pushed into insignificance by the exploits of her terrorist twin sister.

The second and briefer section given to Matty's journal shows his very human response to Sophy, but also suggests an advance on his earlier enlightenment through its use of a vision not unlike Simon's in *Lord of the Flies*: "What good is not directly breathed into the world by the holy spirit must come down by and through the nature of men. I saw them, small, wizened, some of them with faces like mine, some crippled, some broken. Behind each was a spirit like the rising of the sun" (238). This is a marvellous passage. Just as Simon sees that the pig's head evil is part of the boys on the island, an irremovable aspect of human nature, so Matty sees that the "holy spirit" is part of the human spirit, even among the maimed of the world, like himself. At this point the self-justifying cause of the visitations becomes inextricably intertwined with something larger, beyond the mere will of man, an effective counter to the destructive powers of the Stanhope twins. The angels' statement that "you are to be a burnt offering" (238), though it describes what Matty has been/has wished to be, could be seen as having the status of a genuine prophecy, and the final entry in the journal describing the sight of the godhead/special angel ("He was dressed all in white and with the circle of the sun round his head" [239]) has a truly magical status, a moment in art when, as Golding remarks elsewhere: "We may stare through a rectangle of canvas into a magically perfect world and get a touch of paradise."[23]

Any critical response to this densely rich and complex book must be necessarily tentative but two final points need to be made. If *Free Fall* and *The Spire* represent, in different ways, a reaction against the restrictions of the fable, so *Darkness Visible*, after such a long gestation period, represents a move from Golding's "marvellous, almost Victorian mastery of romantic narrative"[24] towards a modernist fiction, from the idea of a "truth" vested in however complex a symbol, to a recognition of the impossibility of one single illumination and the acknowledgement of a multiplicity of views. In the chapter "The Doubloon" the modernist nature of *Moby-Dick* becomes startlingly apparent when the "mad" cabin-boy Pip reacts to the Ecuadorian gold coin by declining the verb "to look." In Golding's novel various characters try to reach the "truth" about human experience. Even after his terrible humiliation, Edwin Bell still believes in the possibility of such a single interpretation: "I shall track down and cross examine everybody who had anything to do with the whole ghastly business and I shall find out the truth (258): Sim rounds on him for this: "No-one will *ever* know what happened. There's too much of it, too many people, a sprawling series of events that break apart under their own weight" (258), but still feels elated at the prospect of reading Matty's journal. Perhaps Sim's statement has validity. It is possible to argue that you always have a multiplicity of viewpoints for any event, but this does not require assent to the proposition that all have equal validity. At the end of "Billy Budd" there is more human truth in the view of the sailors' ballad than in the official version of what happened on Vere's ship. Matty may have more to offer in his interpretation of the human condition than other characters in the novel. Less soiled by the corruption of language ("Think of the mess, the ruckus, the tumultuous, ridiculous, savage complications that language has made for us and we have made for language . . ."[199]), he gains by being the one character to write it down and so engender an act of creation rather than, as in Sophy's case, destruction. He is the writer as both maker and prophet.

Darkness Visible was followed, a year later, by *Rites of Passage*, a much more accessible work. As in five of Golding's previous works (including *The Scorpion God*), the confusions of present society are avoided by setting the novel in the remote past, in this instance the early nineteenth century, and by setting the action in an enclosed space, a ship travelling from England to Australia (related to the island in *Lord of the Flies* which is "roughly boat-shaped" [31] and to the medieval cathedral in *The Spire* which is several times likened to a ship with Jocelin as its captain). Golding uses an epistolary narrative, a device which allows the reader to share the most intimate thoughts of the narrators. Talbot keeps a journal of his voyage but, unlike Matty's, the journal is not entirely private. He is writing it for the edification and amusement of his godfather, an unnamed but highly influential English nobleman, and he seems aware of his own, and Golding's, literary progenitors, referring on the first page to Goldsmith, Fielding, Richardson, and Smollett and, somewhat later, remarking that: "My entries are becoming short as some of Mr. Sterne's chapters!"[25]

So much scribbling goes on in this novel that it could have been called *Writes of Passage* (a "passage" after all, is a portion of writing). Talbot is writing a journal; so is Colley. Captain Anderson is keeping his log and billets-doux are flying around between Zenobia and her various admirers. The physical act of writing is persistently mentioned ("So by eleven o'clock at night—*six bells* according to the book—behold me seated at my table-flap with this journal open before me." [18]) and the written passages take on active force as Talbot blackmails Anderson with the presence of the journal and Anderson makes counter-entries in his log in order to provide some "official" evidence of the events. Critics such as John Carey[26] and Don Crompton[27] have already made the point that the central opposition of the novel lies in the comparison between the journals of Talbot and Colley. Talbot is an eighteenth-century Enlightenment man whose view of life accords with that of John Locke: "If we can find out how far the understanding can extend its view; how far it has faculties to attain certainty; and in what cases it can only judge and guess, we may learn to content ourselves with what is attainable by us in this state. . . . Our business here is not to know all things, but those which concern our conduct."[28] Against Talbot's socially-bound view we can place Colley's Romantic imagination: "Once more and with that same terrifying instantaneity came flashes of lightning in the mist that were awful in their fury. I fled to my cabin with such a sense of our peril from these warring elements, such a return of my sense of our suspension over this liquid profundity that I could scarce get my hands together in prayer" (194). His most obvious literary mentor is, of course, Coleridge; but, in his sense of the power and sublimity of forces beyond the dictates of self, he can remind us of Wordsworth too:

> When I ran behind that craggy steep, till then,
> The bound of the horizon, a huge cliff,
> As if with voluntary power instinct,
> Uprear'd its head, I struck and struck again,
> And, growing still in stature, the huge cliff,
> Rose up between me and the stars, and still,
> With measured motion, like a living thing,
> Strode after me.[29]

and the novel records Talbot's journey from the Enlightenment to some appreciation of the Romantic perspective. Also, Colley is a man of God in seemingly godless surroundings and, as such, offers a search for the numinous not unlike Matty's in the grim contemporary world of *Darkness Visible*.

But if the contrast between the two journals is central to an understanding of *Rites of Passage*, there is no equality of importance between the two characters. This is Talbot's story. As he narrates what happens to Colley he tells the reader about his own development and he does so in terms related to writing, invention, creativity. His journal has a story to tell but there is so much material that selection becomes vitally necessary: "I find that writing is like drinking. A man must learn to control it" (29). A major attempt at control comes through Talbot's use of the idea of a theater. Beginning with the theatrical posturings of Zenobia at the service, he is intrigued by the comic idea of the lady and Colley in the guises of

Beatrice and Benedict and he half engages to carry out the "farce" of bringing them together. Stopping himself short, he becomes half-seriously moralistic: "here was I, who considered myself an honourable and responsible man, contemplating an action which was not merely criminal but despicable. . . . *Plato was right!*" (102–03). The reference to Plato might possibly remind us of the amateur theatricals at Mansfield Park (which was being written during the time at which Golding says this voyage took place) and the moral dangers of getting people to pretend they are other than they are. Zenobia's makeup and arch mannerisms are intended to disguise the fact that she is an ageing tart. Plato seems indeed appropriate to the mind of a spectator watching a ship of fools. But is Talbot merely a spectator? Immediately after the reference to Plato he discusses the possibility of a deus ex machina and then produces a very revealing paragraph: "Or may I stay with the Greeks? It is a play. Is it a farce or a tragedy? Does not a tragedy depend on the dignity of the protagonist? Must he not be great to fall greatly? A farce then, for the man appears now a sort of Punchinello. His fall is in social terms. Death does not come into it. He will not put out his eyes or be pursued by the Furies — he has committed no crime, broken no law — unless our egregious tyrant has a few in reserve for the unwary" (104).

Either of the terms, "farce" or "tragedy," presuppose a set of "rules" governing the action of the drama. Colley will not, according to Talbot, fit into any scheme of tragedy because he is not high-born, lacks dignity, and so might fit more easily into the realms of farce since his fall would be "social" (he would make a fool of himself but the class structure of the ship, a concept dear to Talbot, would remain unchanged). He would commit no crime and suffer no major punishment, such as death. He would be the scapegoat of the comic world and unlike those earlier Golding scapegoats, Simon and Pangall, would only have to suffer minor humiliation (in the saturnalia attendant on crossing the Equator) to ensure the bonding of society into closer harmony. Talbot knows his drama and seeks good-humoredly to establish some pattern based on the rules of dramaturgy. But the passage is full of hideously ironic foreshadowing. Colley's relatively humble social status causes a lack of confidence which leads him to make mistakes. He commits (to his notion) a grievous crime and suffers death in consequence. The pattern will not hold: the reality of human folly and viciousness spills over the tidy lines of the "rules." Talbot's literary bent is indicative of his blindness.

Yet Talbot does show a capacity to learn and this capacity is often specifically related to literary activity. Like Sammy Mountjoy, he can re-read what he has written and learn from his mistakes, both of expression and point of view. He keeps recognizing that the journal seeks frustratingly to set a frame round human action, action which is too swift and mercurial to remain within that frame: "Yet even while I was busy leading up to the events, the further events of his fall raced past me" (119). He soon admits that disappointment repeatedly occurs if you expect the tidiness of dramatic illusion to be a true reflector of the messiness of real life: "I was never made so aware of the distance between the disorder of real life in its multifarious action, partial exhibition, irritating conceal-ments and the stage simulacra that I had once taken as a fair representa-tion of it!" (110).

Talbot sees himself as a spectator of a play unfolding before him but this is scarcely half the story. He also seeks, within his journal, to create a drama in which the characters behave as he thinks they should behave because he believes he knows them. In intention, though not in personality or act, Talbot resembles Iago, wishing to make the world conform to his private ethic. He is a kind of fabulist because he feels that he has a superior knowledge of the ways of the world and wishes to have that knowledge confirmed. He is, nonetheless, a young man of good heart, and the journal is a record of a tentative but definite learning process ("But I am learning, am I not?" [149]). He has the honesty to admit that he cuts a rather pathetic Iago-figure: "I sat before this journal, upbraiding myself for my folly in my attempt to play the politician and manipulator of his fellow man! I had to own up that my knowledge of the springs of human action was still in the egg" (146). As in *Free Fall*, the learning process is a natural one in opposition to an artificially-imposed "created" pattern which seeks to place a pre-ordained grid of meaning over experience, as one might argue that a fable does. Captain Anderson points to a constantly objective recording of events on the ship: "You might as well think a ship is ballasted with paper. We record almost everything somewhere or another, from the midshipman's logs right up to the ship's log kept by myself" (167), and Talbot admits that, in contrast, he has to "select." His selection is an attempt to impose a meaningful pattern on experience but it ends, when he re-reads it, as a record of the recorder. Like Ishmael in *Moby Dick*, Marlow in *Heart of Darkness* and Nick Carraway in *The Great Gatsby*, he tells someone else's story in order to tell his own. There are manifold ironies in his view that his journal "has become as deadly as a loaded gun" (184).

Talbot's journal is interrupted by his reading of Colley's account but since he includes that account in his narrative to his godfather it becomes a part of that narrative and hence a further illumination of Talbot's shallowness and arrogance as a writer. Talbot learns from Colley's journal just as Sim and Edwin hope to learn from Matty's; Golding brilliantly measures that learning process by making Talbot's final words concerning "all that is monstrous under the sun and moon" (278) a deliberate echo of Colley's terrifying vision of the sun and moon in the sky at the same time: "Here plainly to be seen were the very scales of God" (233).[30] Colley *is* what Talbot earlier merely created him to be in dramatic terms, a "Good Man," and, though his naivete leads him into absurd errors of judgment, his sense of wonder and his dedication to something larger than himself makes him more open and sympathetic to experience than Talbot; hence his example teaches Talbot how to see and write more clearly and honestly.

After the end of Colley's journal Talbot's "education" hurries towards its awful graduation. He realizes that his journal has turned into "Colley's drama" (264) but now the image is less theatrical than personal. There was about Colley's life on board ship an inexorable chain of events leading to a catastrophe but that can only be understood by someone looking deeply into the situation and seeing it whole, as Talbot finally does: "I do not know how to write this. The chain would seem too thin, the links individually too weak — yet something within me insists they *are* links and all joined, so that I now understand what happened to pitiable, clownish Colley" (276). Talbot now sees that "Life is a formless business. . . . Literature is much amiss in forcing a form on it" (265), and he is right in that the proximity of death and birth on board ship is a "natural" order against the restrictive order of the journal. Talbot does grow, despite making mistakes to the end, to a point where he is able to discern what really happened to Colley. Now he will write a letter to Miss Colley which will be "lies from beginning to end" (277). Like Marlow, in *Heart of Darkness*, he finds that the truth is hard, can drive people "a little crazy" (278) and hence should be kept from members of a "normal" society. His particular "kind of sea-story" (277) is to be wrapped in sailcloth, like Colley, until its readers (including his godfather) are readier to recognize what it has to say.

Following the *"furor scribendi"* (45) which goes on throughout *Rites of Passage* it is hardly surprising that Golding's next (and latest) novel, *The Paper Men*, should have as its central character someone who writes for a living. Wilfred Barclay is a successful novelist who is writing an autobiography (the novel itself) in order to spite a parasitic American academic, Rick L. Tucker, who is literally prepared to burrow in Wilf's dustbin for scraps of letters. Barclay mistakes him initially for a badger and he assuredly "badgers" the novelist incessantly throughout the book. On one level the novel is an act of literary vengeance. At the beginning of "Belief and Creativity," first given as a lecture in Hamburg in 1980, Golding complains: "For a quarter of a century now the person you see before you has undergone a process of literary mummification. He is not entirely a human being: he is a set book,"[31] and the burden of his essay "A Moving Target," first delivered as a lecture in Rouen in 1976, is that a living, developing novelist cannot be pinned down and fossilized like a butterfly by the assiduity of thesis writers: "But years first of reading theses on me and then more years of not reading theses on me have made me more elusive than a professor."[32] Thus *The Paper Men* is full of defensive gestures. His first experience of Tucker is at a conference where the American gives a paper on Barclay's use of relative clauses. Critics understand the wholeness of works of literature only by tearing them to pieces: "The question to be asked when reading one book is, what other books does it come from."[33] He considers putting Tucker in one of his books which he will call *The Paper Men* (at this point the novel begins to sound like Flann O'Brien's *At Swim-Two-Birds*) and finally decides he will accomplish this by forcing Tucker to give an account of his (Tucker's) odious behaviour in the biography of Barclay he intends to write.

Added to these almost metafictional convolutions is a constant concern with the terminology and physical acts of writing (though, disappointingly, too little about the vision involved from a writer whose intensity of vision is unparalleled in contemporary writing—but then Barclay is not Golding). While writing novels with typewriters, Wilf keeps a journal in longhand. The different methods of writing seem to indicate the greater intimacy and privacy of the journal, its greater potential for self-understanding: "I decided I'd use my journal to get things straightened out and understand what the score is" (159). Various authors are mentioned, such as Ibsen and Ambrose Bierce, both of whom have been mentioned as influences on Golding, and there is even a jokey reference to Golding's own recent work: "This lecture. It's about rites of passage. You know about them, Rick, I'm talking to myself" (146). Quotations are used and the reader asked to note that they are being used. Of greater importance is the relationship between literary terminology and the idea of "pattern." At the beginning of chapter two, Wilf makes a hopeful comment: "If I had been sufficiently aware, I might have seen in its appearance from the dustbin the corner of a pattern that was to prove itself universal" (17). He speaks of his "personal nemesis" which is "the spirit of farce" (11) and the opening confrontation with Tucker as "a peripeteia to end all peripeteias" (13). Almost immediately afterwards, he realizes that "Fact" contains a "farcical improbability" beyond "all the contrivances of paper, manipulations of plot, delineations of character, denouements and resolutions . . ." (14). Like Sammy Mountjoy and Talbot, Wilf feels a great need to *select* material in order to emphasise such a pattern: "No more invention, only selection—I must actually study a living person" (79).

Yet running through this commentary on the act of writing is the kind of revelation occurring to Sammy, Matty, and Talbot, the virtual impossibility of writing the truth; the inevitability, given the willed or unwilled search for pattern, of distortion, partiality, and lack of total comprehension. The paper used by the paper men is early likened to flypaper; the writer is trapped by his medium. Although Wilf states that his interest in churches is not religious he recognizes that its value lies in a direct apprehension of stained glass without having anything "written down" (26). When he has his "leedle estrook," an excessively religious experience in a church, he emerges with a natural language "which wasn't even English *but my native tongue*" (126), a language which he cannot write down. Like Matty and Talbot, he discovers that writing changes that which is written about (". . . and I see now that I've written it down that it wasn't that at all" [27]) and, as in *Rites of Passage*, this leads him, like the creators and characters of metafiction, to consider the proposition that the writer is a liar, to point to "the prisoner's habit of scrawling lies on paper into a shape that the weak-minded have taken as guide, comforter and friend, allegedly, often to their cost. I would remind you, m'lud, that the principal witness for the prosecution, the man Plato, is a foreigner" (47). Increasingly, he moves toward a recognition that the essential truths of existence cannot be defined and enclosed by words and may even only fully reside in silence: "I think that there was a dark, calm sea beyond it, since I have nothing to speak with but with metaphor. Also there were creatures in the sea that sang. For the singing and the song I have no words at all" (161).

As in *Rites of Passage*, Golding seems to oppose some sort of natural form to an artificially-induced one. A quarter of the way through the novel, Wilf has a strong insight: "I was seeing a process. It was not an intellectual concept, it was felt as well as seen, feared as well as grasped. It was simple, trite. It was universal" (55). This is, now, not a universal pattern, but a universal "process" and the word is repeated two pages later: "Oh God, oh god, oh god, the process, link by link, we don't know what will come from this seed, what ghastly foliage and flowers, yet come it does, presenting us with more and more seeds, millions, until the whole of *now*, the universal Now, is nothing but irremediable result" (57). "Pattern" is indicated by literary terminology, "process" by natural imagery. Of course, there are obvious ironies in writing about the difference between writing naturally and writing artificially, for all writing involves the use of artificial conventions, but Golding, through his later novels, nonetheless wishes to make such a distinction, to suggest, through his writers/narrators, that the imposed pattern (perhaps of the fable) is hardly to be preferred to the art of seeing natural processes at work: "Also, my mind noted and put away in some drawer to be taken out later that there was a lengthy piece of prose to be written on listening to natural sound-listening without comment or presupposition" (83).

I will continue to use examples from Golding's latest novel to try and sum up the points I have been making, while hoping that, if I have fallen into the trap of creating a pattern for his works, it has, at least, been seen as a developing process and not some diagram I have imposed upon the multivalence of the apple tree. It would be absurdly pretentious to overestimate the links between Golding and the creators of metafiction. Certainly he could never agree that truth is merely a fictional abstraction and that the only effort creative literature can make is to point to the artificiality of all attempts to engage with the truth of one's perceptions. Ronald Sukenick's view that "God was an omniscient author, but he died; no-one knows the plot"[34] would surely be contemptuously dismissed by someone who can write, within the last few years "On any of us the moment may strike, the awareness of something not argued over but directly apprehended, perception that the sun makes music as of old."[35]

For William Golding, it must repeatedly be asserted, is a religious writer for whom, according to Samuel Hynes "The problems which are central to his novels are the eternal questions of the religious man: the nature of good and evil, guilt and responsibility, the meaning of death, and free will."[36] In novel after novel moments of religious insight have been put before the reader with remarkable fullness: Simon and the pig's head; Sammy in his "cell"; Jocelin's view of the apple tree; Oliver at Bounce's grave; Matty and his white angel; Wilf and the moment when "Fright entered the very marrow of my bones" (123). Yet Golding seems to have come increasingly to see that his early diagrammatic structures were not the most valuable method by which to reach that insight or place it. This has led not simply to changes in the kinds of fiction he has written but, as it were, a description of those changes worked out by reference to acts of writing/creativity on the part of the central protagonists. Acts of writing in the novels become images not merely of Golding's art but of more general human creativity. Feeling that the intelligibility of the world cannot be dismissed according to the tenets of the writers of metafiction, he nevertheless seems to feel uneasy, despite his gift for romantic narrative, with the notion of much nineteenth-century fiction that writing can image a coherent, decipherable universe. Insight is difficult and tenuous, words are slippery and treacherous; there are more often "truths" than TRUTH. He seems close to Melville in this kind of self-reflexiveness.

So, in *The Paper Men*, there are constant reminders to the reader that writing, with all its qualifications, is taking place and that the only possible form of closure is death. A long distance has now been travelled from the "gimmick" endings of the early novels. By drawing such attention to writing, the narcissism of the writer is underlined and this is particularly true of the use of journal writing. Wilfred's search for the God-figure, Halliday, results in a blank sheet perhaps because, as Julia Briggs suggests, in seeing God Wilf sees himself.[37] The writer, like Pincher Martin, remains locked in the pattern of his own self-absorption. But just as Matty countered Sophy, so Wilf does move, like Talbot, towards some sort of recognition of the world outside him before he dies: ". . . where was the big, warm-hearted and final Barclay Book that had floated before me every now and then since the dream? We were about as warm-hearted as scorpions" (174). Perhaps here resides an important clue to the rejection of patterning: it is too reductive of the human experience and hence does not allow for that wide empathy so necessary for the novelist. In "Belief and Creativity" Golding mercilessly hammers the figures he sees as the great reductionists, Marx, Darwin, and Freud, for reducing human beings in much the same way as the totemistic figures in Macy's Thanksgiving Parade: "Down the main street of our communal awareness they come. They dwarf the human beings, dwarf the buildings."[38] By writing about people writing about writing Golding is able, at least fitfully, to show some development toward a recognition of the variety of human experience and the need to love that variety. "If thou be among people make for thyself love, the beginning and end of the heart."[39]

Notes

1. Julian Symons, "Golding's Way," *Guardian* 26 September 1986.

2. Patricia Waugh, *Metafiction* (London: Methuen, 1984), 2.

3. Ibid., 3.

4. John Peter, "The Fables of William Golding," in *William Golding's Lord of the Flies: A Source Book* (New York: The Odyssey Press, 1963), 22. This article was originally published in *Kenyon Review* 19 (Autumn 1957): 577–92.

5. The term was originally used by Golding himself. See James Gindin, *Postwar British Fiction* (Berkeley and Los Angeles: 1962) and John S. Whitley, *Golding: Lord of the Flies* (London: Edward Arnold, 1970).

6. William Golding, *Lord of the Flies* (London: Faber and Faber, 1954), 223; hereafter cited in the text.

7. Don Crompton, *A View from the Spire* (Oxford: Basil Blackwell, 1986), 9.

8. Wayne C. Booth, *The Rhetoric of Fiction* (Chicago: University of Chicago Press, 1968), 151–52.

9. Henry James, *Hawthorne* (London: Macmillan, 1967), 70.

10. Nathaniel Hawthorne, *The Blithedale Romance* (Columbus: Ohio State University Press, 1964), 69.

11. William Golding, *Free Fall* (London: Faber and Faber, 1959), 48; hereafter cited in the text.

12. William Golding, *A Moving Target* (London: Faber and Faber, 1982), 143.

13. T.S. Eliot, "Burnt Norton", *Four Quartets* (London: Faber and Faber, 1959), 19.

14. Quoted in Samuel Hynes, *William Golding* (New York: Columbia University Press, 1964), 35.

15. Golding, *A Moving Target*, 132.

16. William Golding, *The Spire* (London: Faber and Faber, 1964), 104–05; hereafter cited in the text.

17. Nathaniel Hawthorne, "Sights From A Steeple," *Twice-Told Tales* (Columbus: Ohio University Press, 1974), 196.

18. Golding, *A Moving Target*, 136.

19. Margaret Walters, "Two Fabulists: Golding and Camus," in *William Golding's Lord of the Flies: A Source Book*, 102. This article was originally published in *Melbourne Critical Review*, 4 (1961): 18–29.

20. Crompton, *A View from the Spire*, 70.

21. William Golding, *Darkness Visible* (London: Faber and Faber, 1979), 15; hereafter cited in the text.

22. Golding, *A Moving Target*, 123.

23. Ibid., 190.

24. Julian Symons, "Golding's Way" *Guardian*, 26 September 1986.

25. William Golding, *Rites of Passage* (London: Faber and Faber, 1980), 72; hereafter cited in the text.

26. John Carey, *The Sunday Times*, 19 October 1980, 42.

27. Crompton, *A View from the Spire*, 127–56.

28. John Locke, *An Essay Concerning Human Understanding*, ed. Peter H. Nidditch (Oxford: Clarendon Press, 1975), 45–6.

29. William Wordsworth, *The Prelude*, Book 1 (Oxford: The Clarendon Press, 1959), 24.

30. I am grateful to my colleague, Stephen Medcalf, for making this point to me.

31. Golding, *A Moving Target*, 185.

32. Ibid., 170.

33. William Golding, *The Paper Men* (London: Faber and Faber, 1984), 25; hereafter cited in the text.

34. Ronald Sukenick, "The Death of the Novel," quoted in Larry McCaffery *The Metafictional Muse* (Pittsburgh: University of Pittsburgh Press, 1982), 13.

35. Golding, *A Moving Target*, 190.

36. Samuel Hynes, "Novels of a Religious Man," in *William Golding's Lord of the Flies: A Source Book*, 70. This article was originally published in *Commonweal* 71 (18 March 1960): 673–75.

37. Crompton, *A View from the Spire*, 177. Julia Briggs, who wrote the chapter on *The Paper Men*, edited and completed this book after Don Crompton's death.

38. Golding, *A Moving Target*, 188.

39. A quotation from *The Instructions of Ptah-Hotep*, used by Golding as an epigraph for *The Pyramid* (London: Faber and Faber, 1967).

INDEX